W9-BJN-722

THE PROBLEMS OF PEACE

THE PROBLEMS OF PEACE

LECTURES DELIVERED AT
THE GENEVA INSTITUTE OF
INTERNATIONAL RELATIONS .
at the *Palais des Nations*
August 1926

*together with Appendices
containing summary of
discussions*

FIRST SERIES

Essay Index Reprint Series

BOOKS FOR LIBRARIES PRESS
FREEPORT, NEW YORK

First Published 1927
Reprinted 1970

STANDARD BOOK NUMBER:

8369-1468-6

LIBRARY OF CONGRESS CATALOG CARD NUMBER:

73-105015

INTRODUCTION

THIS volume is the first of what it is hoped will be a series of annual publications to record the proceedings of the Geneva Institute of International Relations, and is, therefore, a milestone in the history of the Institute.

The Institute began, soon after the establishment of the League at Geneva, as a Summer School of the British League of Nations Union, which met for one week at Geneva to study the constitution and working of the League on the spot, through lectures and personal contacts with League officials. After some years the American Non-Partisan Association and one or two other organizations in America combined with the British society to convert the Summer School into an Institute. At the same time, the programme was widened so as to strike a balance between those who wished to discuss international problems at large and those who were interested primarily in the structure and activities of the League.

The biggest and most successful meeting, with four hundred participants and another two hundred refused admission owing to lack of space, was held in the summer of 1926. The nature of the subjects dealt with is apparent from the contents of this book. They form a series of lectures intended to give a picture of the organization, growth, and working of the League, together with a discussion of the main international factors and problems in the world to-day, such as the foreign policy of the United States and of the Soviet

Union, the question of sovereignty, public opinion in relation to war and peace. The lecturers were drawn partly from the Secretariat but to an increasing extent from outside, the broad object being to secure the leading authorities on the subjects discussed. In addition to the lectures, there were several so-called 'group discussions' on e. g. the subject of national minorities, mandates, the health work of the League, the opium traffic, &c. The chief value of these discussions, however, was that they gave an opportunity for full and free discussion with the Heads of the Sections concerned in the Secretariat on how the League's work in these matters is conducted, and the discussions were, therefore, regarded as private.

The membership of the Institute has hitherto been chiefly American and British, and the standard of knowledge and ability in both groups has varied widely. The American group in 1926 contained a contingent of fifty professors of international relations, from different universities all over the United States. Recruiting is done in Great Britain through the League of Nations Union and in America by the American Committee of the Institute. The meetings of the Institute are for one week (in 1927 the second week in August), and hitherto have been held on the premises of the League Secretariat itself.

For next year it is hoped, since the Institute is now in the happy position of having more applicants than accommodation, to raise the standards by some selective process which would ensure the attendance only of men and women who already know the elementary facts about the League and international organization generally and are ready for a more ' advanced course ' on the task of organizing peace, to which most of civilized mankind finds itself officially committed since the war. For the same purpose the programme for next year will be made stiffer, and there will be greater opportunity for discussion. On the other hand, to take care of those who want simply a grounding in the constitution and working of the League, a Summer School will be held at Geneva during the previous week (i. e. 1–7 August). At the same time, a big effort will be made to attract to the Institute not only British and American but English-speaking men and women of other nationalities, so as to make it truly international and thereby heighten its interest and value to the participants.

This first volume of the proceedings of the Institute is to be regarded rather in the light of an experiment, and criticisms and suggestions, which should be addressed to the Committee of the Institute, Geneva, would be welcomed. The lectures have been left as they were delivered since it would not have been possible to remove the personal and colloquial tone of a lecture without re-writing the whole thing, and in so doing, losing much of the sense and savour of the original. A few slight alterations have been made in order to eliminate all purely ' local ' references that would have no meaning to those who did not attend the Institute.

The greatest liberty has been taken with Professor Zimmern's lecture, half of which was on 'The Development of the International Mind' and the other half on the work of the Committee and Institute for Intellectual Co-operation. I have taken the liberty of putting the first half of this lecture as an introduction to the whole series and embodying the other as a separate chapter among those dealing with the organization and working of the League. I take this opportunity to thank Professor Zimmern for giving the Institute so generously of his wit and wisdom, and beg him to take this in lieu of an apology for making two lectures grow where only one was delivered.

Wherever questions and answers at the end of a lecture have brought out any points of importance, they have been summarized and put as an appendix corresponding to the chapter in question.

THE EDITOR.

CONTENTS

SECTION II

THE LEAGUE IN ACTION [1]

[1] The programme of the Institute contained discussions under the direction of the heads of the sections concerned on the question of national minorities, the operation of the mandates system, opium traffic, and the work of the Social Section, and international public health work, but these were not reported for the reasons stated in the Introduction.

Contents

Contents

SECTION I

NATURE AND STRUCTURE OF THE LEAGUE AND LABOUR ORGANIZATION

CHAPTER I

THE DEVELOPMENT OF THE INTERNATIONAL MIND

Mr. ALFRED ZIMMERN :

I MUST begin my treatment of the subject which has been assigned to me, namely, the development of ' the international mind ', by confessing that I am not very much in love with that phrase, and I am not sure I have ever met any one with an international mind. I am not sure that I have ever read a book by any one with an international mind. Plato had a Greek mind ; Dante an Italian mind ; Shakespeare an English mind. You may think me a little pedantic in seeking to define more closely what I mean by such terms, but the term ' international ' implies something in between ; it implies a relationship between two things and the mind that has stuck in between is serving no useful purpose. There are such persons ; you may find them at Monte Carlo, for example. They are in a sense international but they are not always equipped with minds. I would rather re-word my subject and put it in this way : the development of the international attitude in the national mind. I think probably all of us here are very conscious of being representatives of our countries and sharing in the traditions and habits of thought of those countries. In addition to that, however, we want to develop an attitude which will enable us to understand the peoples of other countries and the large-scale problems of the modern world. By an international attitude I mean a power of reaching out across one's own country to the people whose roots are in a different soil. The development of that attitude is necessary because the world we live in has grown so much larger and more complicated, because there are so many more problems we need to understand. A generation or two ago we could comfortably live in our own English or American house without bothering ourselves about the problems which arose in Germany, France, or other parts of the world. To-day that is impossible, so that this problem of reaching out, this development of an international attitude, is urgently necessary. The problem is that of stretching our own minds to reach across the gulf; it is not a problem of changing the texture or quality of those minds.

What then is the international attitude that we ought to develop? First of all, what is it not? It is not a matter of mere information. An international fact is no better than any other fact. We do not develop an international attitude by filling our minds with information drawn from a field outside our own country. Such information may be useful to us or it may be useless, but it does not of necessity give us the quality of mind that we need. In fact, for persons who are beginning the study of international relations I should say a good knowledge of history, geography, and economics is much more useful than a wide assortment of facts even though they include the activity of the League of Nations itself. History, geography, and economics if well taught are a wonderful discipline in stretching the mind. No one can study economics without being forced to let his mind play over the whole field of the world's economic activities. The same is true of geography ; and, therefore, a sound training in those subjects is, I consider, essential to the study of international relations. Any one who has tried to teach League of Nations problems to secondary or university students who have little knowledge of geography or who have been badly taught and crammed in history will know what a hopeless task it is.

Secondly, the international attitude is not a question of opinions. It is not a question of having what are called advanced opinions. Any fool can have advanced opinions. You will all remember the personage in Bernard Shaw's *Man and Superman*, the old gentleman who is brought into contact with an ardent young man and who rebukes him by saying, ' My dear young fellow, I was advanced before ever you were born.' Hard and fast opinions, whether advanced or reactionary, are no use to us in our problem, and that is why it sometimes happens, by a curious paradox, that persons who call themselves pacifists are a menace to the cause of peace, because although they may be pacifists in intention they have not a pacifist attitude.

What is this attitude ? To have the international attitude is to live in a room with windows open on a wide prospect over the world. A mind with that international attitude is an open mind rather than a closed mind. A man possessing such a mind is sympathetic to new ideas ; he is curious ; he is alert ; he is active-minded ; he is what I think you call over the water a ' live wire ' intellectually. For him the task of getting into touch with new conditions is itself an adventure, something he enjoys. His internationalism starts as an

adventure and later becomes a habit. In my experience—
and I have seen a good deal of it in this building and elsewhere—the development of that attitude is exactly like
learning to swim. Once you have adapted yourself to meeting foreign minds, minds which work in a way unfamiliar to
you, and once you have acquired the technique you never
lose it. One of the reasons why this building has done such
magnificent work is because nothing is ever lost, because you
start to-morrow where you leave off to-day and because the
people of this building have acquired a discipline which
makes their work easier from day to day and makes the people
who come in from distant countries to do business with them
immediately feel at home and feel that their needs are
understood.

Coupled with that open-mindedness there is another
quality required—the habit of intellectual integrity, of
applying one's reason to all and not only to selected problems. Those of you who have studied the writings of
psychologists know that they call attention to the fact that
the human mind has a tendency to forget things which are
disagreeable. A servant girl when she drops a plate does not
say that she has dropped it, but that ' it dropped '. The
phenomenon itself is too disagreeable for her to remember
how it occurred.

One of the first duties of a true internationalist is to shirk
no problems, but to stretch his mind to the point when it
hurts. He must stretch it to cover and deal with problems
which are difficult to deal with. It is when it hurts that we
are touching questions that are most worth thinking about.
They may not always be questions which are most worth
acting upon, because such questions can with difficulty be
taken up by the League or by the individual Governments ;

but they are questions we must always think about, realizing that if there are enough people honestly thinking about them, sooner or later the bitterness, the passion, the disagreeableness, will be cleared out and they will become suitable subjects for action.

There is an increasing body of persons in all countries for whom that kind of thinking, that kind of use of the mind, has become not merely a habit but a need. There are people who feel that their lives are incomplete unless their minds are able to reach out to problems in other countries and encounter them with joy and with a sense of adventure. It is to that body of persons, internationally thinking persons, persons with the international attitude, that the League of Nations is such an immense advantage.

I am talking now of the League of Nations not as a political organization, not as an organization which this or that country has or has not joined, but as an element in the international life of the world. In that sense of the word the League of Nations is not simply an organization but a focus and centre for thought. It provides a centre for thinking on international questions.

If you think yourself back to the period before the war you will realize at once how the existence of an international centre such as we have here—an international political centre —has made an enormous difference to the international intellectual life of the world and to all persons engaged in politics and in thinking about politics.

I think you will realize that in the period before the war people were unconsciously looking for a League of Nations. They were unconsciously hampered by the absence of such a centre as we have here. Take, for instance, the minds in a pre-war generation that had conspicuously the international attitude and that loved large visions and wide horizons, and were perpetually reaching out to something new—take, for example, Cecil Rhodes and Theodore Roosevelt. How different the intellectual life and practical projects of those men would have been, how differently they would have envisaged the whole progress of the world, if there had been a League of Nations during their lifetime.

The League of Nations has come into existence almost too late, because so much could have been achieved in the hundred years before the war when international economic organization, the organization set on foot by the industrial revolution, the private organization of trade and industry, was making such enormous advances in its international quality.

The League of Nations is a very difficult thing to define from the point of view that I am describing. A friend of mine in the Secretariat finally hit on this one : The League of Nations represents the maximum of co-operation between governments at any given moment. That is a very neat definition because it makes the League expand and contract according to the psychological conditions and political possibilities at any given moment.

Geneva provides a centre for co-operation of minds. You cannot think of international planning to-day without thinking in terms of the League of Nations. All roads in the political range of thought lead intellectually to Geneva. By that I do not mean to say that Geneva is going to become a centre of all policies ; I do not think it will. I am a good deal less ambitious than some of my friends in that respect. I think that for a long time to come, and perhaps always, it will be very difficult to co-ordinate international policies from this place, but I think this place will henceforward supply the conditions for the thinking out of such policies and the stimulus which will lead to their being thought out. That is an immense international service.

Let me make my meaning clear by means of a metaphor. Before the foundation of the League the world of international politics might be compared to a chessboard—that is a familiar analogy. People like Bismarck played that game of chess excellently, but it was a chessboard without the most important piece. The coming of the League of Nations has put a queen on that board, and the movements of that queen now dominate the whole board and the whole game, although there are certain movements the queen, by the rules of the game, is unable to perform.

It may be asked why it is necessary to analyse the international attitude since it is to be displayed in the course of the lectures you will hear this week. I have analysed it in order to draw your attention to the fact that you are here to study not only what the lecturers say but how they say it. Mazzini, who was the first man who thought constructively about these problems, used to say that the nations were like an orchestra, each with its own special instrument to play. The League of Nations shows that orchestra in working, and in the course of this week you are going to hear not the whole orchestra but a number of instruments playing separately. To-morrow you will hear not only about disarmament but about Spain, although Spain will never be mentioned. On the following days you will hear something about France, Italy, Norway, the United States, and so on. That is to say if you are interested in the mind of the speaker and not only in the message he gives you, you will get this additional knowledge. If you are thus interested you will be able to compare what I would call the stretched variety of the national mind with the shrivelled variety you sometimes find in your own countries.

Speaking before an audience composed of Britons and Americans I think it is perhaps legitimate, before I sit down, briefly to consider the bearings of what I have been saying upon our own special British and American ways of thinking. It is very seldom that I have an opportunity nowadays of talking to an audience composed of my own countrymen and Americans, and where no members of other nationalities are present. I want to take this opportunity, therefore, to say a few words to you in your national capacities from the point of view of international intellectual co-operation.

Both British and American people are eminently international in their attitude of mind. They bring to this common task wonderful qualities and wonderful possibilities. Both possess fine traditions and both suffer from certain fairly obvious limitations. I think it is worth while trying to consider both the qualities and the limitations.

I will take Britain first. Britain is the great school of politics, the greatest fund of political experience in the world. I would single out three qualities in that British tradition : (1) What we call public spirit, or to put it in another way, the fact that Englishmen and Englishwomen enjoy sitting on committees (laughter). They go to committee meetings with zest because they feel that to sit on a committee is a duty which has become for them almost a pleasant duty. (2) The quality of what we call common sense, which is really an extraordinary fine judgement in public issues and a power of diagnosing the situation by seeing the important and the unimportant factors in it and realizing what should be done as a result of that diagnosis. That common sense and judgement is really based, although we do not always know it, on a very intimate sense of the permanent factors involved in a situation, and the permanent factors in the national life. Take the general strike. The general strike brought out the English attachment to institutions, the English sense of humour, and so on, which every one who knew England knew existed, but which foreign observers did not know was there. (3) The education of the will. Our wills are attuned to action and enjoy action. When the moment for action comes the Englishman is much happier than he was when it was his duty to think and to plan. There is the curious paradox that when an emergency, say a general strike or a war, occurs he feels that it is up to him to be English, and acts with extraordinary efficiency—with much greater efficiency than the people of most other countries.

With those great assets what are our liabilities? What are the limitations these qualities bring with them to the new field of work in which we are engaged in the post-war world?

(1) In the first place, public spirit. Our public spirit is used to working on national committees or, at least, on imperial committees, and sometimes only on committees with people of our own class and social standing. That last difficulty has diminished greatly of late years. It was much greater in my youth than it is now. We are not yet accustomed, however, to applying our public spirit in the international sphere. We are not quite accustomed to working on equal terms with those strange animals we call foreigners. We still feel a certain embarrassment in meeting foreigners, similar to that which a generation ago an English gentleman felt when brought into contact with a working man. (2) The common sense on which we so much rely is not so sure as it was before the war because we are moving in a world the permanent features of which are unfamiliar to us.

That is a fact which has made a very great difference in English public life. If you talk to us about free trade and protection we know all the ins and outs of the game, but if you talk about guaranteeing the security of parts of Europe and undertaking responsibilities in connexion with people of whom we have little or no knowledge and of whom we are prepared to believe what any one may tell us—or rather prepared to doubt whatever any one may tell us, because we are told so many different stories—it is another matter, and since we are not fond of making up our minds until we feel we have grasped the whole situation involved, our judgement falters; we become slow and we irritate people who are accustomed to our ordinary swift and decisive method of action. There is a further difficulty. We are accustomed in our judgements to the world moving at a certain pace, and a rather slow pace, the sort of pace at which British constitutional institutions grew up. Since the war the world has been developing rapidly and the rhythm is different. Things move faster. We are not yet accustomed to the altered speed. If you study post-war history you will find that time after time a situation has changed and an opportunity has been lost because British public opinion did not have time to size up a situation. It wanted a little longer. It wanted a little longer to think the matter out, and before it had finished, the difficulty it was thinking about had disappeared and something else had taken its place. (3) Our will power for action is inhibited because our judgement does not give a sure signal for action. We do not know how to act because we do not understand the situation, and that has given to our policy an appearance of slowness and even obstructiveness which has caused a great deal of irritation. These are phenomena of a period of transition. I believe we shall meet these difficulties, but we must be conscious of them and of what the Continent feels about them if we are to overcome them. The only remedy I can suggest is more stretching and more effort to co-operate.

Now I should like to say a few words about the United States. The United States has three strong points :

(1) A large framework. It has that wonderful American sense of space, that wide-ranging mind which can move from New York to San Francisco with much less difficulty than the English mind can move from London to Paris. The English mind can move in time in centuries ; the American mind in space in hundreds and thousands of miles.

(2) Another great contribution of the American mind is the habit of large scale organization; large scale organization very similar in scope to such an organization as we have here.

(3) There is also the habit of living in the future rather than the present—that forward-looking habit which results in a student who goes to college being labelled with a label four years ahead of the date when he enters.

What are the difficulties Americans have to face in the new international framework ? (1) In the first place there is the difficulty of fitting one large frame into another. It is much easier to fit the Swiss Federation into the international world or the League than it is to fit the American Federation. There is a certain similarity of size between the new international world and the world of North America. (2) This is a much more serious difficulty. The American large-scale organization is an economic rather than a political organization, built up by pioneer adventurers for purposes of trade and the development of that vast country. We have at present the great difficulty of applying pioneer economic methods to governmental institutions and political problems.

The debts question, which many of you in visiting Europe must have found somewhat disagreeable, is nothing more than this : the confrontation of political standards with economic standards. The two sides to the controversy are unable to meet because they are thinking in different terms. When the American mind has learnt to politicize itself and its large-scale institutions and habits and to see these problems as political problems they will be three-quarters solved, because the two parties will then understand one another. (3) Lastly, the Americans are forward-looking. But to what are they looking forward? To a future conceived in their own terms. They want others to walk in step with them to that same future. They are not very much accustomed to looking into the other man's future and seeing what his projects are. The only remedy is international co-operation, a stretching of the mind and the habit of working together.

One last word. We British and Americans have different intellectual traditions but we have one common weakness. It is what James Russell Lowell called a certain condescension towards foreigners, particularly towards those who are non-Nordic and more particularly towards those who are not of the white race. Dr. Nitobé is the only person in the room who does not belong to this wonderful white or white-pink race of which we are all so proud. (Laughter.) In touching on the subject of the race I am doing what I said we ought to do ; I am touching on something which hurts and which is very disagreeable and which people wish to avoid. I purposely touch upon it because, from the intellectual though not the political point of view, it is a subject we must not avoid. We shall have a war about it in the political arena unless we face it frankly in the intellectual arena. I touch on it because of a scene I remember in this room when the so-called Japanese amendment to the Geneva Protocol was discussed two years ago. I happened to come into the room in the course of that discussion after an absence of several hours and I came into an atmosphere which reminded me of the British House of Commons on 4 August 1914. The air was tense ; as a French journalist put it, the shadow of the goddess of war had appeared on the wall. All sorts of subconscious instincts had arisen from the bottom of people's consciousness and were crowding to the top. That tone was not found amongst the delegates ; it was entirely amongst the audience and almost entirely amongst the Anglo-Saxon audience. As we went out of the room an excited young American lady said to me : ' It is fine meeting the English. The British Empire and the United States stand together on this issue.' I said to her : ' My dear young lady, out of seven subjects of King George V only one has a white face.' She was very angry with me ; but really the British Empire is not a white Empire, neither is the United States wholly a white community. One of the great dangers at present is that British-American collaboration may fortify us in certain common prejudices so that we may come to form a kind of psychological block consisting of people with common affections and repulsions standing against the races of the world. That would be a disaster against which I can see you are forewarned and forearmed by the reception you have already given to our dear friend Dr. Nitobé. (Applause.) If we are to stand together and to work together, as I believe we will and must, let us work together so that each one of us, like Shakespeare's Puck, may learn how to stretch a girdle of thought and of sympathy round the entire world. (Renewed applause.)

The CHAIRMAN :

I can see that in spite of the way all of you have enjoyed Mr. Zimmern's address, many of you have been wanting to reply to him on numerous points. His general description of the international attitude was not accepted everywhere in the hall. I think I detected on the faces of some of the English people a disagreement with the analysis of English character, and I am sure I detected on the faces of some of the American members unwillingness to accept the diagnosis of the American mind. Dr. Maxwell Garnett has been bold enough in the past to have a controversy with Mr. Zimmern and I think I should confide to him the task of moving a vote of thanks to Mr. Zimmern. Dr. Maxwell Garnett is the Secretary-General of the British League of Nations Union and it is largely due to his skill that we are confronted this evening with the prospect of such an excellent programme during the forthcoming week.

Dr. MAXWELL GARNETT :

Among the many brilliant things which Mr. Zimmern said to us was this, that the League of Nations represents the maximum of co-operation of Governments at any given moment. We want our Geneva Institute to represent the maximum of intellectual co-operation between all its members at all possible moments. I am quite sure we have been co-operating intellectually with Mr. Zimmern during his fascinating discourse this evening and are going to co-operate intellectually to-morrow and throughout the week, but I do not think we can do so much longer to-night. Many of us were sitting eight in a compartment in a second-class railway carriage throughout last night and we have had a long day to-day. I do not think we ought to break up, however, without thanking very heartily those who have entertained us so delightfully this evening.

First of all we want to thank Dr. Nitobé, and through him the Secretariat of the League of Nations. It is to many of us a great delight to come back here year after year and to feel that for one week in August we are closely one with the Secretariat of the League of Nations. The essence of the matter seems to me this. In the beginning when men were forming States they did it largely in order that they might be able to pursue their own lives peacefully and effectively without too much interruption of the kind that is bound to occur where you have not a stable government and the suppression of the use of force for private ends. In the modern world people also want to pursue their lives usefully and effectively, but their interests are now world-wide and no community realizes that so well as the English-speaking ones. Something has to keep the peace of the world to-day and many of us look for this to the League of Nations. If it is true, as I think it is, that many of our statesmen realize clearly it is no use making any proposal to their parliaments because they think such a measure is in the interests of their own nation unless it is clearly also in the interests of the world as a whole, we have made a great step forward. If it is not in the interests of the world at large, the world will say so in the Assembly of the League of Nations, and if they did that in the long run the measure in question would be against the interests of the country which proposed it. Statesmen want to put the world first in their proposals but they cannot do it if people will not go with them. So long as people have narrow minds statesmen cannot have a wide states-manship.

We want during this week to get hold of wider ideals so that we in turn may hope to widen the minds of our fellow countrymen. Therein we see the real co-operation between our Institute and the Secretariat which is carrying on the work of the League of Nations all through the year and particularly do we see the link with the work Dr. Nitobé has been doing so wonderfully. The very last bit of work the League has seen through has been the meeting of a Committee to consider how we can in future arrange that intellectual co-operation shall appeal to the youth of the world as the normal method of conducting world affairs. That was being discussed here three weeks ago, and by the very Committee on Intellectual Co-operation that Dr. Nitobé and Mr. Zimmern have been concerned with.

We have also to thank Mr. Zimmern most heartily for his wonderful address. Not only was it brilliant and intellectually co-operative, but it was tactful. I notice Mr. Zimmern said the world had grown very much larger. I remember once telling a Pittsburg audience last November that the world was getting very much smaller. My host took me aside afterwards and said, ' You must not say that again. People in America don't like to think that anything they are dealing with is getting smaller.' (Laughter.)

I am going to deal later with my controversy with Mr. Zimmern on the subject of the international mind, so that I will not trouble you with the subject this evening, but I may venture this here. I quite agree we must have national minds, but it does seem to me that the international mind is really only an extension of the national mind. We do not think of a man who is a good Lancashireman or Cornishman as being in consequence a bad Englishman, and I do not see for a moment why a man who is a strong nationalist should be for that reason a bad internationalist ; but he must go on, he must not stop at the nation.

The CHAIRMAN :

It is our practice to devote a large part of our time during the session to general discussions, but with your permission we will dispense with the discussion this evening because the hour is somewhat advanced.

We are very grateful indeed to Dr. Nitobé, Mr. Zimmern, and Dr. Maxwell Garnett for this opening programme, and we are pleased also to see a number of distinguished people on our platform.

I declare the meeting closed.

CHAPTER II

THE LEAGUE OF NATIONS AS AN HISTORICAL FACT

Professor W. E. RAPPARD :

BEFORE analysing the League of Nations in its manifold activities, in its achievements and in its failures, in its prescribed tasks and in its applied methods, it may be well to consider it synthetically, as a great historical phenomenon.

That it is an historical phenomenon of the first magnitude, comparable in importance with, say, the establishment of national States in Europe at the close of the Middle Ages, or the spread of parliamentary government in the nineteenth century, no one can deny. Whether we ask its friends or its foes, whether we question the statesmen of Europe or large bodies of the governed throughout the whole world, whether we consult the political historian or the student of international law, the reply will be the same : for good or for evil, the League of Nations, as an ideal and as an institution, has in the course of the last decade become a factor of prime significance in human affairs. It has everywhere become a subject of political controversy, in the countries which have joined it hardly less than in those which remain aloof. It has everywhere influenced the politics of parties and the policies of governments. It has settled some international disputes which might, without its intervention, have remained unsettled, and it has given rise to other international disputes which would, without its creation, never have arisen. Like motor-cars, wireless telephony, aviation, prohibition, fluctuating exchanges, Russian bolshevism, Italian fascism,

American opulence and European impecuniosity, but more far-reaching in its consequences than at least some of these, the League of Nations faces the student of contemporary affairs as a fact which may be hailed as a triumph and a blessing, deprecated as a nuisance or a curse, ridiculed as a sham or a fad, but which cannot be ignored.

I shall not, on this occasion, seek as a moralist to estimate its value for mankind, but merely as an historian to understand it and to locate it in the general scheme of human institutions and events. For that purpose I propose to examine it, first, as it was intended to be by its founders; second, as it actually is, or at least would appear to be to an independent witness; and finally, as it seems likely to develop according to human probabilities.

I. *The League of Nations as it was meant to be.*

It is customary to say that the League of Nations was born of the world war or that it is a child of public opinion. Both statements are as true as they are incomplete. The war itself—that is, guns, submarines, poisoned gases, and other technical devices in the hands of soldiers and sailors—wrought nothing but destruction.

Public opinion, that uncrowned and anonymous royalty, may imperiously impose or decisively oppose any change. It can act, however, only through the instrumentality of its ministers, the individual poets, artists, scientists, and statesmen of the world.

Of the countless spokesmen of public opinion during the war none was more eloquent nor more effective than Woodrow Wilson. Many others in high places had before him advocated the creation of a league of nations, and not a few had given the subject more constant and more penetrating thought. No one as influential, however, had been as insistent in the matter and no one as insistent, as influential. Posterity will therefore doubtless vindicate the judgement of my fellow citizens of Geneva who dedicated the memorial tablet to Woodrow Wilson : ' Fondateur de la Société des Nations.'

The future biographer of the present incumbent of the American presidency may suffer from certain perplexities quite unknown to the historian of the Wilsonian age. There is no difficulty whatever about ascertaining what, according to Wilson's hopes and expectations, the League of Nations was in the main intended to be and to do. His public utterances and his now published written statements on the subject are numerous, and we have every reason to believe that they were as explicit as the nature of his thought—or should we say of his vision ?—permitted.

Before the war Wilson warmly welcomed the ' many happy manifestations . . . of a growing cordiality and sense of community of interest among the nations ', and ' their willingness to bind themselves by solemn treaty to the processes of peace, the processes of frankness and fair concession '.[1] He firmly believed in international co-operation, arbitration, and publicity, and actively promoted their progress. His famous Peace Proposal of the Spring of 1913, which gave rise to what is known in Europe as the Bryan treaties, contained no provisions for international sanctions of any kind, nor even for arbitration in the narrowly technical sense of the term. It was based solely on the idea that the peaceful settlement of all disputes between the signatory powers might be secured by means of impartial investigation, aided by the pacifying influence of public opinion.

[1] First annual message to Congress delivered on 2 December 1913.

Shortly afterwards President Wilson went a step further in the direction of international or at least of Pan-American solidarity. The draft treaty discussed in Washington from 1914 to 1916 with representatives of the Latin American world provided that ' the high contracting parties to this solemn covenant and agreement, hereby join one another in a common and mutual guarantee of territorial integrity and of political independence under republican forms of government '.[1] Although the guarantee thus suggested was not expressly defined it, of course, implied the possible use of force. This was the less surprising as the United States never disclaimed it as a legitimate method—unilateral, it is true—of upholding the traditional Monroe doctrine.

If I recall these early manifestations of Wilson's international philosophy it is because they have a direct bearing upon his later policies. What he set about to accomplish for the whole world from 1917 onward was, as he once told me in private conversation, nothing else than what he had unsuccessfully attempted to do for the American continent in the preceding years. That is why for him the essential function of the League of Nations was to maintain peace by a mutual guarantee of territorial integrity and political independence. That is why also article 10 of the Covenant, in which this guarantee is formulated and prescribed, remained to the end the most vital feature of the whole document in the eyes of Wilson, who was its real author.

Interesting as it would be both from the psychological and ·from a political standpoint this is not the place to trace the evolution of Wilson's conception of the League of Nations, from his first statements made before the League to enforce

[1] J. B. Moore, *The Principles of American diplomacy*, New York, 1918, p. 406 and seq.

peace at Washington on 27 May 1916, through his various war notes, messages, and speeches, up to his final approval of the Covenant in 1919. The general outline of his views on the subject may be very briefly summarized as follows :

The world war must end in a lasting peace. It must give rise to ' some definite concert of powers which will make it virtually impossible that any such catastrophe should ever overwhelm us again '. Peace, in order to be secure, must be guaranteed by more than ' mere agreements '. ' It will be absolutely necessary ', Wilson declared in his address to the United States Senate, as early as 22 January 1917, ' that a force be created as a guarantor of the permanency of the settlement so much greater than the force of any nation now engaged or any alliance hitherto formed or projected, that no nation, no probable combination of nations could face or withstand it. If the peace presently to be made is to endure, it must be a peace made secure by the organized major forces of mankind.'

But only a just peace ' is worth guaranteeing ' by a league of nations. What is a just peace ? It is one that ' plays no favourites and knows no standard, but the equal rights of the several peoples concerned ', ' no matter whose interest is crossed '. A just peace is one by which the issues of the war are settled ' definitely and once for all and with a full unequivocal acceptance of the principle that the interest of the weakest is as sacred as the interest of the strongest '.[1] Furthermore, a just peace is one that respects ' national aspirations ' and ' self-determination ', that ' imperative principle of action which statesmen will henceforth ignore at their peril '.[2] A just peace also is one that cannot give rise

---

[1] Fourth Liberty loan address of 27 September 1918.
[2] Address to Congress of 11 February 1918.

to undeserved hardship and thereby to just resentment. Therefore it should provide for ' the removal, so far as possible, of all economic barriers and the establishment of an equality of trade conditions '.[1]

If such a peace is publicly made and collectively guaranteed 'by a League of Nations formed under covenants that will be efficacious ', nothing should prevent national armaments from being ' reduced to the lowest point consistent with domestic safety ', and, indeed, such a reduction should be an essential part of the peace settlement itself.

Such were the main elements of the peace programme which Wilson brought to Paris in December 1918. Its importance was all the greater as it had in principle been agreed to by all the belligerents as the basis upon which the final settlement was to be made. It should be noted that although quite naturally and even necessarily vague it was none the less sufficiently defined to show that in Wilson's mind the League was not primarily conceived of as an organ of conciliation or arbitration and not at all as a medium of peaceful co-operation. It was essentially the instrumentality through which a just peace should be permanently guaranteed by the concerted will and power of its member states.

Before ascertaining in how far the Covenant conformed to this programme let us briefly consider the views and expectations of a few of those statesmen who share with President Wilson the honour and the responsibility of the paternity of the League of Nations.

Ever since 1914 the idea of some international organization for the prevention of future wars had been freely discussed in Great Britain and advocated in Parliament with peculiar force by Mr. Asquith as Prime Minister and Sir Edward

[1] Fourteen Points Speech of 8 January 1918.

Grey as Foreign Secretary. As both of these liberal ministers resigned in 1916, and as they took no personal part in
the peace settlement, their views can have had but an indirect influence on the framing of the Covenant.

The British statesman who from 1916 onward was most
active in favour of the establishment of a league was undoubtedly Lord Robert Cecil. As a member of Mr. Lloyd
George's Coalition Ministry he succeeded in obtaining the
appointment of a Committee to prepare the draft Covenant
and closely followed its labours. In 1919 he represented
the British Government on the League of Nations Commission. Shortly before the Armistice he prepared a speech
on World Opinion and the League of Nations, which he
delivered before the University of Birmingham on 12 November 1918.[1]

When we compare the conception of the League outlined
in this speech with that of President Wilson we cannot fail
to note several very appreciable differences.

For both statesmen, of course, the League was destined to
prevent war, and both held that it should be established by
the Peace Conference. Both hoped that it might promote
disarmament, although Cecil's views were rather pessimistic
on this point, and both insisted on the pacifying virtues of
open diplomacy and public opinion. But, whereas, for the
American president, the League was essentially to guarantee,
if necessary, by military force, a just territorial settlement
based on the principle of self-determination, for the British
blockade minister, it was to forestall conflicts between nations
by compelling them to resort to a peaceful procedure of conference, discussion, and delay in restraint of war. Whereas

[1] Lord Robert Cecil, *World opinion and the League of Nations*. League
of Nations Union, London, 1918.

Wilson had deliberately disregarded the technical proposals of the American League to enforce peace and displayed an utter lack of interest in what he rather contemptuously called ' its faith in machinery ', Cecil showed a corresponding distrust of simple formula and of ' any ambitious scheme ' which inevitably made ' a large invasion of national sovereignty '. He was very sceptical about the possibility of submitting vital international questions to the judgement of courts of law and ' confessed to the gravest doubts ' as to the practicability of enforcing the decrees of such courts by any ' form of international force '. On the other hand, he firmly believed in the efficacy of economic pressure as a means of coercing a country bent on aggression in violation of its pacific agreements.

Lord Robert Cecil's main conception of a league of nations, neither too indifferent to the susceptibilities of national sovereignty to be acceptable, nor too mindful of them to be effective, is well summed up in the following lines :

' The most important step we can now take is to devise machinery which in case of international dispute will, at the least, delay the outbreak of war and secure full and open discussion of the causes of the quarrel. For that purpose . . . all that would be necessary would be a treaty binding the signatories never to wage war themselves or permit others to wage war till a formal conference of nations had been held to inquire into and, if possible, decide upon the dispute. It is probably true, at least in theory, that decisions would be difficult to obtain, for the decisions of such a conference, like all other international proceedings, would have to be unanimous to be binding. But since the important thing is to secure delay and open discussion—that is to say time to enable public opinion to act and information to instruct it, this is not a serious objection to the proposal. Indeed, from one point of view, it is an advantage, since it avoids any interference with national sovereignty except the interposition of a delay in seeking redress by force of arms. That is the essential thing, and to secure it, the treaty would require each of the signatories to use their whole force, economical as well as military, against any nation that forced on war before a conference had been held. To that extent, and to that extent only, international coercion would be necessary.'

Besides advocating such limited measures to prevent the outbreak of war, Lord Robert Cecil, in his speech also briefly alluded to various forms of international co-operation such as the revision of obsolete treaties, control of backward races and certain social activities, which the League of Nations should promote to remove the causes of war. Thus, Lord Robert Cecil added to the Wilsonian conception of a league to guarantee peace, which he at bottom did not share himself, the idea of a league to prevent war by international conference and co-operation.

The third author of the Covenant whose name must be mentioned here, in view of the importance of his contribution, is General Smuts. His great influence was due to his personal qualities more still than to his official position. Endowed both with an acute legal mind and a vivid political imagination—a very rare combination—this former Boer soldier was Lieutenant-General in the British forces and a member of the Government of the Union of South Africa. Having gained the confident friendship of several of his leading British colleagues at the Peace Conference, as well as that of President Wilson, he became the second British representative on the League of Nations Commission.

Just before the opening of the peace negotiations at Paris he published a remarkable booklet [1] in which he expounded

---

[1] General Smuts, *The League of Nations, A practical suggestion*, London, 1918.

a conception of the League, as novel as it was ambitious. ' My reflections ', he wrote in his foreword, ' have convinced me that the ordinary conception of the League of Nations is not a fruitful one nor is it the right one, and that a radical transformation of it is necessary. If the League is ever to be a success, it will have to occupy a much greater position and perform many other functions besides those ordinarily assigned to it. Peace and war are resultants of many complex forces, and those forces will have to be gripped at an earlier stage of their growth if peace is to be effectively maintained.'

Besides the immediate prevention of war and the promo-tion of international co-operation, notably in the economic field, the League, according to Smuts, was to assume great burdens of government. The war had overthrown the four great empires of Europe, Germany, Austria-Hungary, Russia, and Turkey. It had set free many peoples to whom self-determination had been promised. Not all of these peoples were as yet capable of ruling themselves, but the pledges given by the allies, as well as wise foresight, forbade the annexation of their territories. Surely then, Smuts remarked, ' the only statesmanlike course is to make the League of Nations the reversionary, in the broadest sense, of these empires. In this *débâcle* of the old Europe, the League of Nations is no longer an outsider or stranger, but the natural master of the house.' [1]

The European estate to which the League was to be the heir should be administered either directly by its new master, or on his behalf, by certain so-called mandatory States. ' It is not improbable ' Smuts added,[2] ' that the supervision of the European States will impose the heaviest task of all on the League of Nations, at any rate for this generation. But

[1] Smuts, *ibid.*, p. 11.　　　　　　　　[2] *Ibid.*, p. 26.

it will have to be performed efficiently, as there is little
doubt that the old historic feuds surviving among the European nationalities may easily become a fruitful source of
war danger. If the League is ever to be a reality, it will have
to succeed in this great task. And it will succeed if it takes
itself seriously and looks upon itself not as a merely nominal,
but as a real live active heir to the former Empires and is
determined to discharge the duties of the great beneficent
position which has devolved upon it as supreme guardian of
the peace interests of humanity.' As to the functions of the
League as a maintainer of peace Smuts closely followed the
views of Cecil. He displayed, however, a greater faith in
arbitration, which he wished to see rendered compulsory
in all juridical disputes, and he was more insistent than
his imperial colleague on the obligations of national disarmament.

The Covenant, as it was finally signed, contains little that
is not at least foreshadowed in the utterances of the three
statesmen to whom allusion has just been made. It is in
fact essentially and almost exclusively the product of British-
American political experience and practical idealism.

Even within the limited space at our disposal we must,
however, recall at least the name of Léon Bourgeois, the
leading French exponent of the League of Nations. Although unlike Wilson, Cecil, and Smuts, the venerable French
statesman had devoted a large part of his life to the elabora-
tion and propagation of the doctrines of international organization, and had in 1910 already published a book under the
title of *Pour la Société des Nations*, his effective influence at
the Peace Conference was very slight. The country he represented having borne the brunt of the war, was, in 1919, more
interested in matters of security, territorial readjustments,

and economic reparations than in the establishment of a League of Nations. Besides, its Prime Minister, the ' Tiger ' Clemenceau, was notoriously sceptical about the possibilities of establishing peace on a permanent basis, and openly hostile to any schemes which might tend to deprive France of the spoils of her hard-won victory and of the advantages of her momentary military superiority. Furthermore, even Bourgeois himself, whose political philosophy was far less cynical than that of his chief, shared with the great majority of his countrymen what we may call the punitive, as opposed to the Wilsonian impartial conception of peace.

At the end of 1916 he had declared that the League could only be founded after the establishment of a victorious peace.[1] After Wilson's Mount Vernon address of 4 July 1918 he gave out an interview advocating the immediate foundation of the League among the allied powers.[2] Both views, contradictory as they were, pointed in the same direction, a direction totally different from that envisaged by Wilson, Cecil, and Smuts. The League, according to the French conception, was either to serve as a weapon to hasten on the day of victory or as a protective instrument to safeguard its fruits. On the eve of the Armistice Léon Bourgeois presided over a gathering at which the French League of Nations Union was founded. In his presidential address he declared : ' Voici que l'heure des libérations, des réparations, des restitutions a sonné. Et voici également que vient l'heure des châtiments.' [3]

---

[1] Léon Bourgeois, *Le Pacte de la Société des Nations*, Paris, 1919, 2ème mille, p. 13.   [2] *Ibid.*, p. 52.
[3] Association française pour la Société des Nations, *Discours prononcé à l'Assemblée générale constitutive du 10 novembre 1918*, par M. Léon Bourgeois, Paris, 1918, p. 4.

While warning his audience against the frailty of territorial guarantees he went on to say : ' We do not deny that such guarantees are necessary. Justice itself demands the punishment of the culprit.' [1]

The League, as he saw it, was to be founded by the Allies alone. Those neutrals, whose policy had been deemed acceptable during the war, were then to be admitted. As for Germany her day might come later, when she could give evidence of sincere penitence. ' The League of Nations ', he declared,[2] ' tends towards universality, but, in order to attain its very purpose, it can include only free peoples who have proved faithful to their given word, who have observed all the obligations to which their past faults may have committed them, who, in a word, offer all the necessary actual and legal guarantees.'

Among such peoples an international institution should be set up by ' a contract of mutual assurance against the risk of war '.[3] This institution, in whose favour no signatory State should absolutely abandon its sovereignty, was however to be endowed with the authority of laying down the law in case of disputes and of enforcing its decisions by means of diplomatic, economic, and military sanctions. For that purpose an international force was to be organized ' which would be able to overcome all opposition, unjustified and henceforth criminal, on the part of any covenant-breaking State '.[4]

The neutral powers although they cannot, in any true sense, be considered as co-authors of the Covenant, were offered an opportunity of presenting their views about it

---

[1] Association française pour la Société des Nations, *Discours prononcé à l'Assemblée générale constitutive du 10 novembre 1918*, par M. Léon Bourgeois, Paris, 1918, p. 7.   [2] *Ibid.*, p. 18.
[3] *Ibid.*, p. 22.   [4] *Ibid.*, p. 14.

before its final adoption. They were unanimous in favour of immediate universality, and with one accord insisted on the necessity of developing, in a spirit of absolute impartiality, the conciliatory and judicial functions of the League. The reticence on the subject of sanctions, which they also displayed, sprang from their obvious misgivings about the possibility of enforcing League decisions on recalcitrant nations, in the present state of international solidarity.

Such, very succinctly summarized, were the main wishes, hopes, and expectations, of those chiefly concerned with the foundation of the League of Nations at the beginning of 1919. After prolonged discussions and many mutual concessions these various views were embodied in the Covenant. In perusing its twenty-six articles it is not difficult to discover the various sources of its inspiration. As a whole the Covenant may be regarded as the charter of the League of Nations, such as it was intended to be by those who created it.

II. *The League of Nations as it actually is.*

Turning now to the League as it actually is, after six and a half years of legal existence, let us see what has become of the various conceptions from which it sprang.

The Wilsonian idea of a League for a mutual guarantee of the territorial integrity and political independence of its members is expressed in article 10 of the Covenant. What, in political reality, survives of it to-day?

Although the provisions of this article have never been clearly violated since the birth of the League, they have been the object of so much hostile comment, not only in the United States but also at the various Assemblies of the League, that faith in its efficacy has been very severely

shaken.   As I have shown elsewhere,[1] the value attached to
article 10 by the different nations of the League stands in
direct ratio to the protection they expect from it, and in
inverse ratio to the undesirable obligations which it may
impose upon them.   Whereas for a State in the position of
Poland article 10 is ' one of the corner-stones on which the
whole organization of the League rests ', it is looked upon
as an unmitigated evil in countries situated as Canada.

It must be said that the Wilsonian conception of the
League and article 10, which is its most faithful expression,
have not been given a fair chance in the contemporary world.
A mutual guarantee of territorial integrity is conceivable as
an effective safeguard against war only under two conditions,
neither of which are fulfilled to-day.

The first of these conditions, which Wilson himself repeatedly stressed, is that the frontiers to be guaranteed be
just frontiers, and that they be universally or at least generally
recognized as such.   Although the Peace treaties of 1919 are
sometimes criticized with undue severity and with insufficient regard for the difficulties under which they were negotiated, it is still not easy to understand how Wilson, on his
return from Paris, could expect the world to share the
enthusiasm with which, in his last speeches, he professed to
consider them.   It is certainly impossible to reconcile not a
few of their more important provisions with the principle of
impartiality towards great and small States, victors and vanquished, and with the doctrine of self-determination, which
he had done so much to establish in the eyes of the present
generation as being the essence of international justice.

The other condition under which alone a mutual guarantee

[1] W. E. Rappard, *International Relations as viewed from Geneva*, New
Haven, 1925, p. 129 and seq., and 171 and seq.

of territorial integrity could prove effective and workable is that a practicable method be adopted for the peaceful modification of frontiers according to changing national, racial, and demographic conditions. In Wilson's third draft of the Covenant, a method was suggested by means of which the dangerously rigid principle of guaranteed territorial integrity might have been rendered somewhat more flexible. But that suggestion was not embodied in the Covenant. All that remains of it are the provisions of article 19 relating to the reconsideration of treaties, which can hardly be considered as sufficient for the purpose.

Lord Robert Cecil's proposals with respect of the pacific settlement of international disputes, the procedure of delay and discussion in restraint of war, and economic and military sanctions were adopted almost without change and have been embodied in articles 15 and 16 of the Covenant. Although they also have never been violated, except perhaps in the case of Corfu, it would be rash to maintain that they were really and completely in force to-day. The emollient interpretation which several clauses of these articles have received, notably at the hands of the Assembly of 1921, appreciably weaken the protection which they might have afforded. In consequence, efforts have been continuously made to reinforce their provisions. But these efforts, which led to the draft treaty of mutual guarantee in 1923, to the famous Protocol in 1924, and indirectly even to the Locarno agreements in 1925, have not yet been crowned with success.

Here also various unfavourable conditions have impeded progress and indeed forced back the lines of defence against war which had been established in the Covenant. The most unfortunate of these conditions has undoubtedly been the lack of universality of the League. It is quite obvious that as long as several of the largest and most powerful States of the world hold aloof, the economic blockade, as a weapon in the hands of the League, can deter no would-be aggressor from his evil designs nor therefore reassure his threatened victims. Lord Robert Cecil had in consequence very consistently urged in his Birmingham address that membership in the League should not only not be withheld from the defeated States, but should, in fact, be imposed upon them.

On the other hand, the League as a medium of international conference, conciliation, and co-operation has more than fulfilled the expectations of those who, before its birth, shared Lord Robert Cecil's hopes on this score. As we shall see, it is in the fields of uncontentious or only semi-contentious action that the progress of the League has been most rapid and its contribution to peace most striking.

The modifications undergone by the main proposals of General Smuts offer a curious example of the uncertain destiny of ideas when thrown into the melting-pot of international legislation. The South African statesman had devised his scheme of government by mandate as a method by which the League might assure the administration of those of the inhabitants of the former empires of Europe who were not yet able to stand by themselves. He had expressly excluded from its scope the ' barbarian ' natives of the former German colonies who, he had declared, should be dealt with in accordance with the fifth of President Wilson's fourteen points.

When Wilson learned of the mandate idea, he was so much struck by its possibilities that, in the Supplementary Agreements which he added to his second draft, circulated on 10 January 1919, he provided for its application, not only to the ' peoples and territories which formerly belonged to Austria-Hungary and to Turkey ', but also to ' the colonies formerly under the dominion of the German Empire'. In the Hurst-Miller draft of the Covenant, the system was restricted to ' territories which formerly belonged to the German Empire and to Turkey '. In the text finally adopted by the Peace Conference, the words ' colonies and ' were placed before ' territories '.[1] Thus the scheme was applied to peoples for whom it had not been intended by its originator and not applied to those for whom it had been primarily devised.

If on this special point therefore the intentions of General Smuts were thwarted, on the other hand his main conception of the relations between the League and the peace settlement proved true, more so perhaps even than was realized when the Covenant was finally drafted. Barring article 22, which deals with the former German colonies and the former Arab provinces of Turkey, the Covenant itself contains no mention of territorial problems arising out of the peace settlement. By other international agreements, however—peace treaties, minority treaties, decisions of the Supreme Council—the League has been saddled with many important and irksome duties, quite foreign to its main purposes, as first defined by Wilson and Cecil.

The influence of Léon Bourgeois on the drafting of the Covenant was, as we have remarked above, very slight. His

---

[1] It is curious to note in this connexion that General Bliss, who obviously had great misgivings about the plan, wrote to President Wilson in his memorandum of 14 January 1919 : ' It would seem desirable to avoid phraseology that would give colour to the idea that the proposed League of Nations has for one of its principal objects the control of situations growing out of the present war. . . . The sole object of the proposition of General Smuts is to bring the United States into line with Great Britain in exercising supervisory control over certain areas of the earth.' Cf. R. S. Baker, *Woodrow Wilson and World Settlement*, London, 1923, vol. iii, pp. 114–15.

position on the League of Nations Commission of the Peace Conference was unfortunate and paradoxical. On the one hand, whereas his American and British colleagues who led the debate in their language which he did not understand, had only been attracted by the idea of the League through the war, Bourgeois had for a score of years heartily supported it. Furthermore, he was since 1917 chairman of an official French Commission, which had worked out a draft much more liberal and democratic in its inspiration and much more drastic in its ambitious pacifism than was the British-American proposal on which the discussion was based. On the other hand, however, every one knew that his government was not fully behind him and his draft and that his chief, M. Clemenceau, believed in material security much more than in legal principles of international organization. Besides, Bourgeois himself, being imbued by what we have termed the punitive conception of the League settlement, was led to defend views which were at bottom inconsistent with the political philosophy underlying his draft.

The result of this ambiguous position was sterility. While only feebly arguing in favour of a more democratic and juridical form of the League organization, of the absolute prohibition of war and of compulsory arbitration, which were provided for under the French draft, but probably not prescribed by his official instructions, Bourgeois in fact insisted only on the exclusion of Germany, on the choice of Brussels instead of Geneva as seat of the League, and above all on the importance of military sanctions and the necessity of establishing an international general staff. He was fully successful only in limiting the membership of the League to allied and neutral powers, not a particularly constructive achievement nor a very happy one as subsequent developments have shown.

As for the influence of the neutrals, it was no more or even less effective. It may have tended somewhat to strengthen the hands of the friends of arbitration among the allied representatives and to improve the wording of the provisions of the Covenant dealing with the admission of new members.

Having thus very hastily sketched how the Covenant came to be drafted as it was in 1919, and how many of its clauses, deemed essential by their authors, have since proved inapplicable, let us see what the League actually is, as we have it before us to-day.

That it is not at all what the majority of its founders intended it to be needs no further demonstration. It does not effectively guarantee the territorial integrity and political independence of its members. It does not effectively expose any aggressor to the dangers of automatic economic and military sanctions. It has not as yet effectively promoted disarmament. It has not made arbitration compulsory nor established international relations on the foundations of justice, that is of impartiality as between great and small, victorious and defeated nations. Nor has the League succeeded to the sovereignty over territories of the former European empires. Having thus failed to realize the expectations of its founders in all these important respects, must it therefore be held to have actually failed in the realization of its ultimate aims? Nothing would seem less justified than such a pessimistic conclusion.

The League of Nations, as a whole, is but the response to the needs of a war-sick humanity whose various national elements have become more and more conscious of their essential interdependence. Gropingly they have set up an international institution for the discussion of their common interests, the chief of which is peace. This institution, like most other constitutional creations of history, has not developed along the lines of its fundamental charter, but has nevertheless tended by other, rather simpler processes towards its natural goal, the pacific organization of international relations.

If we seek to dissect its organism and to analyse its various activities, we will, I believe, discover that it is in reality composed of three leagues, different from one another not only in their immediate functions, but also in their membership, their structure, and even in their spirit. We may distinguish a league to execute the peace treaties, a league to promote international co-operation, and a league to outlaw war, as I termed it in America. Perhaps, in Geneva, it might be wiser to call the last institution a league to attempt to do away with war.

The League to execute the peace treaties is practically confined to the States represented on the Council. It deals with problems such as those of the mandated territories, minority populations, the Saar basin and Danzig, which are not, or at least did not, in 1919, appear to be susceptible of purely national solutions. No unbiassed observer could maintain that the Council had always treated these and similar questions in a spirit of complete judicial impartiality. Nor could he deny that the League's action, such as it has been, had on the whole inured to the benefit of the populations concerned, rather than the contrary. Doubtless it might have been wiser to deal more generously and more fairly with the vanquished of the great war in various questions of territorial adjustment. Doubtless also it might have been better for the League, as well as for the pacification of the world, if the Council had, in the years following the war, shown that it was ' playing no favourites ' in the execution of the peace treaties. But given the state of mind which prevailed at Paris in the spring of 1919 and which Wilson did so much to combat, but still not enough to counteract completely, it is certain that the League has tended to attenuate and not to aggravate its consequences.

Whereas the members of the League to execute the peace treaties are appreciably less numerous than the States which have adhered to the Covenant, the League to promote international co-operation in fact comprises the whole civilized world. When, for instance, as is more and more generally the case, the United States and Germany (before becoming a member) participate in the activities of this League in the fields of economics, finance, social legislation, public health, and public morals, their influence is potentially, if not always effectively, as considerable as that of the other great powers and certainly more so than that of the lesser signatories to the Covenant.

The development and the success of the League to promote international co-operation have been the great revelation of the last years. They do not seem to have been fully foreseen by the authors of the Covenant, except possibly by Lord Robert Cecil. The experience he had gained as blockade Minister in the management of interallied organizations would seem to have led him to realize more clearly than most of his colleagues that the world was fully ripe for voluntary international co-operation, but not yet for compulsory collective action. The fact that several of the most constructive minds in the Secretariat—Jean Monnet of France, Sir Arthur Salter of Great Britain, and Attolico of Italy—had been active in these organizations, was certainly not without influence on the evolution of the League towards the accomplishment of the so-called technical tasks. This evolution was due also to the difficulties encountered in the field of political organization for which the League had been primarily devised. It was due chiefly, however, to the demand for positive reconstruction which was felt throughout Europe and which, it is to-day more and more generally realized, cannot be accomplished on a purely national basis.

By establishing and maintaining personal contacts and continuous co-operation between the leading statesmen, government officials, bankers, and other experts of the principal nations, by developing new methods and traditions of work in common, and by setting new standards of international ethics, the League to promote international co-operation is perhaps to-day the most effective league to promote peace. Its procedure is not dramatic nor such that brings it into the headlines of newspapers. Although this may disappoint the journalists, for whom bad news is proverbially good news and good news invariably bad news, it should on the contrary reassure the rest of peace-loving mankind, for whom the best news is no news.

In spite of the great and varied successes of the League to promote international co-operation, and in spite of the many difficulties encountered by the League to prevent war, the latter purpose remains of course the chief aim of the institution as a whole. An analysis of the Covenant shows that its authors sought to combat international violence by means of five distinct weapons. Enumerated in the order of their apparent effectiveness up to date, these weapons are publicity, arbitration in the broadest acceptation of that elastic term, disarmament, sanctions, and the revision of treaties.

The greatest service the League of Nations has so far rendered the cause of peace, besides the habits of international co-operation it has fostered, is, to my mind, the very widespread interest it has created and stimulated the world over in foreign affairs. The Wilsonian formula concerning the pacifying virtues of ' open covenants openly arrived at ' has often been scoffed at. As many other famous oratorical phrases, if taken literally, it constitutes an easy mark for critical sarcasm. At bottom, however, it expresses a vital truth.

The secrecy which in the past has always surrounded diplomatic negotiations has often favoured intrigue and has invariably bred distrust. Diplomatic intrigue may of itself endanger peace, and international distrust invariably does. The sunlight of publicity alone can dissipate the fogs of suspicion and melt away icebergs of instinctive antagonism which to-day constitute the two gravest perils of international navigation. Now, may we not say without exaggeration, that in the history of the world there has never been a time when foreign affairs have been so widely and so intelligently discussed by the man in the street as the present ? The sun of Geneva is effectively breaking through the clouds of ignorance and indifference which darkened and narrowed the intellectual horizon of past generations.

This is due, not only nor even mainly to the publication of treaties which the Covenant has rendered compulsory. It is due to a high degree to the methods of public debate adopted by the Assembly and other League conferences, as well as to the growing measure of publicity which surrounds the deliberations of the Council. And it is due also to the establishment of a permanent laboratory of international politics in Geneva which, situated in a wall-less glass room, has attracted an increasing number of increasingly well-informed journalists and other students, who day by day follow the varied experiments which are there continuously carried on and report on them to their respective audiences. Doubtless much, very much remains to be done before the citizens of the world will be in a position and in a mood to judge of international affairs as the citizens of our most enlightened commonwealths judge of their own national affairs. But in this respect at least, humanity is on the march and its progress has been made easier and quicker through the efforts of the League.

As a weapon to combat war, arbitration is much more closely related to publicity than would appear at first glance. As we define it for our present purposes, arbitration is the procedure by means of which disputes are submitted to the judgement of an impartial authority. This authority must be impartial, in the sense that it cannot be a party to the dispute. It should also be impartial in the further sense that its decisions should be based solely on the merits of the case before it, and not on any special solidarity or sympathy with either of the litigants.[1] It will be noted that arbitration thus defined includes arbitration in the technical acceptation of the term, judicial settlement, and investigation and report by the Council under article 15 of the Covenant.

In all these cases, international arbitration by itself can do no more for peace than to propose a solution for a problem which might otherwise be solved by the sword. In order that war be avoided, it is necessary that the litigants

[1] That is why the policy of alliances and of mutually pledged ' diplomatic support ', which dominated European pre-war relations, is radically incompatible with a régime of general impartial arbitration. That is why that policy, so clearly expounded by Viscount Grey, for instance, in his *Twenty Five Years*, was always mercilessly condemned by President Wilson. That is why also, so long as that policy survives in international relations, the Council of the League cannot become a universally trusted arbiter in international disputes.

accept the proposed solution. This they may be obliged to do by the fear or by the effects of diplomatic, economic, or military sanctions. They are, however, far more likely to do so as a result of the pressure of domestic and foreign public opinion brought to bear on their respective governments in favour of the solution proposed by an impartial authority. That is why publicity, which alone can create an enlightened public opinion, is always a useful and may be a necessary auxiliary to arbitration as a means of peacefully settling international disputes.

Arbitration, as we have defined it, has been promoted by the League both directly and indirectly. Directly, it has rendered compulsory reference to the Council of all disputes arising between its members which cannot be settled by other means. Indirectly, it has encouraged and facilitated arbitration properly so-called and judicial settlement through the provisions of article 13 of the Covenant and the establishment, under article 14, of the Permanent Court of International Justice. Furthermore, it has given a great impetus to the movement in favour of arbitration by voluntary agreement under article 36 of the statute of the court, as well as by special bilateral treaties. The multiplication and the enlarged scope of such arbitration treaties as have been concluded in the course of the last years between a large number of European states are undoubtedly due to the influence of the League, as their authors will be the first to admit.

Although no statement implying a judgement as to what might have been under other circumstances can ever be fully and scientifically substantiated, I have no hesitation in declaring that international publicity and arbitration combined under the aegis of the League have in fact served to avoid war in the course of the last six years. It may suffice, not of course as a proof of my contention, but merely as an indication of what is in my mind when making it, to glance at the map and to allow one's eyes to rest for a moment on such danger-spots as the Aaland Islands, Upper Silesia, Corfu, Austria, Albania, Mossoul, and the Greco-Bulgarian frontier.

Compared to publicity and arbitration, the three other weapons which the Covenant has placed at the disposal of the League have so far proved practically useless. No more real progress seems to have been made in the field of disarmament than one would quite naturally have expected after a world war, even without the establishment of the League of Nations. No international sanctions, except that of public opinion have ever been applied or seriously considered even in the cases when a strict interpretation of article 16 would seem to have called for them. And no Assembly has yet advised the reconsideration of any treaty, although it would be rash to assert that there were to-day no inapplicable treaties or no ' international conditions whose continuance might endanger the peace of the world ', to quote the terms of article 19.

To ask why these weapons, forged in 1919, have never been used is to ask why the League as an international organization has fallen short of the hopes and ambitions of its founders or at least of the hopes and ambitions aroused in the public mind by the most optimistic among its founders. It is at the same time to consider the probable course of future developments. This we shall now proceed to do in a very brief conclusion.

III. *The League as it seems likely to develop.*

If we were to sum up in one phrase the results of our previous discussion, we might say that, in so far as the League has sought to serve and to promote voluntary international co-operation, it has been a great success, but that in so far as it has sought to exercise any coercive influence on world conditions, it has, except in the sphere of arbitration and publicity, almost completely failed. That is but to say that the League, far from being the dreaded super-State that its foes would like to be able to dissolve, has, as yet, made no appreciable inroads on the national sovereignty of its member States. The centre of gravity of political life is in no true sense in Geneva, but primarily in the capitals of the great powers of the world. Or, to speak the language of business, Geneva is a clearing-house, not an executive office, an international stock exchange, not the head-quarters of a world trust.

The legalistically-minded commentators of the Covenant and the impatient friends of peace may deplore it, but the fact remains. Judge it as we may, it should at least reassure those whose ardent devotion to the principle of national independence has so far prevented them from joining the ranks of the supporters of the League.

But what about the future? If, as we staunchly believe, the League, as it is, has served the interests of peace without encroaching upon the sphere of national sovereignty, is it not desirable that it should, and probable that it will, remain as it is? It is always rash to venture on the perilous paths of prophecy. Were I asked, however, my reply to both these questions would be in the negative.

The creation of the League at the beginning of the

twentieth century and on the morrow of the great war was not an accident. Setting in after the Napoleonic period over a hundred years ago, a movement towards increasing international organization is clearly observable ever since. Promoted and hastened by the development of the means of communication, stimulated by the economic needs arising out of the international division of labour, large scale production and world trade, as well as by the social and political needs which have resulted therefrom, this movement expressed itself in countless voluntary, semi-official and official international associations and unions.

The present League also is clearly the child of this vast co-operative movement. The world war, which is often looked upon as its parent, might perhaps more fitly be described as a midwife who merely assisted in its birth. Now, the underlying factors which produced this movement are to-day more actively at work than ever before. It is, therefore, not to overstep the bounds of scientific caution to believe that the League of Nations, viewed as the latest product of a long evolution tending towards the political organization of the world, will live and grow. It does not seem at all probable, but it is not absolutely inconceivable that it might die, in order that another institution, which could not be essentially different in function, might take its place. But some permanent international organization there must be to meet the increasing common needs—economic, social, and political—of a world composed of interdependent nations, which can thrive in peace and progress only through co-operation.

If there be any truth in this evolutionary conception, it is obvious that the League, as all living organisms, cannot remain as it is. It must either die, or grow and change.

In which ways may it be expected to develop? If the

law of causality prevails in the political sphere as elsewhere, one may confidently assert that the League of Nations will tend more and more perfectly to fulfil the purposes for which it was created.

Following the lines of least resistance, it will from the first not improbably continue to multiply its co-operative functions. In respect of these functions, it will soon become universal in membership, as international co-operation is useful for all nations and cannot be fully effective except with the help of all. One may remark that for this purpose it is quite immaterial whether the number of the States signatory to the Covenant increases or not.

Furthermore, one may expect co-operation gradually to extend to spheres which are as yet the exclusive domain of national sovereignty, such as the regulations governing the exploitation of natural resources, international trade, and international migration. The progress in this field may first be regional—something like a European customs union already appears to loom up on the distant horizon of political possibilities. But here also the movement can hardly fail to become universal in time—time counted not by years, but by generations or even by centuries. It is curious to note in this connexion that while the international regulation of trade and migration, which is as yet taboo in America, is beginning to be discussed in Europe, the position as regards the international regulation of the exploitation of natural resources is exactly the reverse.

While some such evolution is proceeding in the field of co-operation, perhaps under the threat of another war—let us hope that it will not be as the consequence of another war—one may expect the League to grapple more effectively with the problem of international security.

The peoples of the world are unanimous in demanding
security and they are becoming more and more restive under
the burden of national armaments, which the lack of security
alone obliges them to maintain. Here also it is normal to
expect that progress will first proceed along the lines of past
experience. Arbitration and publicity combined may, for
many States, increase the feeling of security and thereby promote a gradual reduction of national armaments.
But real and general international security can never be
achieved unless and until the League is endowed with what
President Wilson called ' the organized major force of
mankind '.

In closing his memorable address before the League to
enforce peace on 27 May 1916, that statesman, whose greatest
failing was perhaps a far-sightedness which caused him to see
the possibilities of the distant future more vividly than the
difficulties of the immediate present, declared :

' I came only to avow a creed and give expression to the confidence I feel that the world is even now upon the eve of a great
consummation, when some common force will be brought into
existence which shall safeguard right as the first and most fundamental interest of all peoples and all governments, when coercion
shall be summoned not to the service of political ambition or selfish
hostility, but to the service of a common order, a common justice,
and a common peace. God grant that the dawn of that day of frank
dealing and of settled peace, concord, and co-operation may be
near at hand.'

After six years of the existence of the League of Nations
which President Wilson, in spite, or rather on account of
his generous illusions, did more than any other man to found,
we may safely say that the dawn of that day has broken.
But it will be a day singularly long and arduous before the

world, delivered from the curse of war, will truly be able to hail the great consummation which he foretold.

That it will come is not merely an ardent hope, but a reasonable expectation. We believe in it, not only because something tells us that the poet did not err when he wrote :

> For right is right, since God is God,
> And right the day must win ;
> To doubt would be disloyalty,
> To falter would be sin.

We believe in it also because we wish to avoid that which for men of science is almost worse than disloyalty and sin, namely blunder and error. If civilization does not overcome war, war, with the progress of science, will overcome civilization. But suicide, individual or collective, although not an impossible accident, is not a likely contingency that it is rational to anticipate.

E

CHAPTER III

THE INTERNATIONAL LABOUR ORGANIZATION

I. *The Nature and Aims of the International Labour Organization.*

Mr. W. J. ELLISON (Member of the Staff of the International Labour Office):

I AM very sensible of the privilege of being allowed to talk to you to-day. I have no qualifications for so doing except that I happen to have been on the staff of the International Labour Office almost since its inception, and have thus had a grand opportunity of seeing the organization grow. I propose to give you a brief sketch of its machinery, and I hope you will afterwards ask me such questions as may arise in your minds with regard to it, in order that from such experience as I have had I may give you a few examples of the work that is being done.

I would like to make quite sure that you know what the International Labour Office is and what it is doing. One of the members of the staff was at his window the other day, when a guide came round with a motor-coach full of tourists, and the guide said: 'This is the International Labour Office. The gentlemen who work inside are there to fight strikes.' That is putting our case rather simply. I think you will want to know rather more of it than that.

I will therefore take you back to our Bible, which is Part XIII of the Treaty of Peace, and which states quite plainly two good reasons for the existence of the International Labour Organization. The first is that the world has reached a stage where labour is no longer to be considered as a commodity or article of commerce. That is a step towards the realization of the importance of man which it perhaps needed the Great War to bring out and put in the form of an international understanding. There was a time in the past when social economics were exceedingly simple. If you wanted a haunch of venison or a wife, you went outside and if you were strong enough knocked down the nearest man and took it! The world has gone far beyond that stage of social economics. It has reached the point where public opinion holds that the weakest must not go to the wall without some attempt to weight the balance so that his life is worth the living. That is the first point that arises out of Part XIII of the Treaty of Peace.

The second point is this. It is in this connexion that we link so closely on the work of the League itself: it is the realization that without social justice you cannot have peace. Let me state perfectly frankly that we are not a benevolent institution, a kind of glorified soup-kitchen. We are here for a practical purpose, which is to save the world from another upheaval. Just as the League aims at peace through political and diplomatic agreements, we are trying to achieve the same end by removing causes of discontent which must otherwise inevitably lead to war.

I must say a few words about the previous history of social progress without which this organization could not have been built up. I do not intend to give you a dissertation on Robert Owen or Daniel Le Grand; you can all read about them in any text-book. I must, however, mention the conference which took place at Berne in 1905, and which was the first international conference to deal, on an international basis, with labour questions. That conference arose out of the activities of a voluntary association—the International Association for Labour Legislation—which had begun to realize the injustices that arose through competition out of modern conditions of life. The Conference was faced with a very striking example, the manufacture of matches. It was found that the use of a poisonous kind of phosphorus in the preparation of matches made a slight—a very slight—difference to the price at which they could be manufactured and sold. While the element of competition existed unrestrained, no country would take the first step towards using the non-poisonous but slightly more expensive kind of phosphorus. The Conference met, therefore, with the practical purpose of arriving at an international understanding that the match-making industry should employ non-poisonous instead of poisonous phosphorus.

This first meeting was attended by technicians. In the following year, 1906, the diplomats of the different countries set their august signatures to the agreement; and in the years that followed, countries began very slowly to ratify that agreement, the importance of which lies in the fact that it constituted the first attempt to arrive at an international understanding on an industrial topic.

The experiment was sufficiently satisfactory for it to be repeated in 1913, when the night work of women and the work of children was discussed. Unfortunately, the war broke out; and the agreement arrived at by the technical experts in 1913 never became the basis of diplomatic agreement and consequently fell to the ground.

I will pass over the years of war and come now to the period when peace was being made. By that time labour in the different countries had assumed an importance which it had not previously attained. It began to voice the opinion : ' We have helped to win the war : we want a voice in the making of the peace.' Even before the termination of hostilities organized labour in Europe had formulated certain points which they wished included in the peace settlement. When the legislators arrived at Paris, therefore, they said to themselves : ' We must have a committee to discuss the labour side of these problems ', and that committee set to work under the chairmanship of the late Mr. Gompers of the American Federation of Labour, and produced Part XIII of the Treaty of Peace.

We come then to the International Labour Organization itself and what it is doing. I should like at once to say that the words ' International Labour Office ' have been a very frequent cause of misunderstanding. I know that in America many regard us only as gentlemen who wear red ties. I know that even in England—I say ' even in England ' because that country is much nearer than America ; I do not wish to discriminate between the British and American intelligence —there is much misunderstanding of our functions.

We are an industrial organization, and the representation from countries at our official meetings is one-quarter worker, one-quarter employer, and one-half government ; i. e. the workers have one-quarter of the votes cast, the employers another quarter, and governments the remaining half. That is the first point of importance to remember about our organization—that we adopted the principle that you cannot have agreements on labour questions without frank and free discussion between employers of labour and labour itself, the public also being represented as those who utilize the results of industrial production and pay the taxes.

How is this representation made effective ? Conferences are essential in order to collect and compare the views of the Member States, and at a given date each year provide an opportunity for corporate discussion. Provision was therefore made for an annual conference, and that conference has now met on nine occasions. This year we had a double shift and held two conferences, one immediately after the other ; and as we started in 1919 we have thus got ahead of the League. At these conferences you get two representatives of the Government, one representative of the workers, and one representative of the employers from each country which wishes to be represented. They have before them an agenda which has been very carefully selected by our Governing Body, and the main points of which have been previously circulated to all countries for their views.

I will say a word about the agenda when I come to deal with the Governing Body, but first I wish to give you a few points about the annual conference.

Although we have had nine conferences, and although we have discussed questions of fundamental and vital importance, we have not yet had a single break. We have had no sort of calamity. To-day that may not seem extraordinary. Our position has become stabilized. But when we started we were an entirely new experiment. No one knew at all how that experiment would work out. Not only were the governments to some extent suspicious of us, but the trade unions were suspicious of us. They had seen too many administrations which had put things on paper, but arrived at few practical results. The employers too were suspicious of us on financial grounds. We had, therefore, to show that there was no cause for these suspicions, that we were not a paper but a practical organization, and that we were not merely useful but necessary. The world has been passing through a very critical period. The fact that we have carried on through these years is such a proof that we are doing work which is worth the doing.

The Conference has adopted twenty-three draft conventions, twenty-seven draft recommendations, and a large number of resolutions. Let me say one word as to the importance of our resolutions. Draft conventions when ratified become international legal obligations. Draft recommendations lay down the general principles on which countries are recommended to base their social legislation. But in both instances some delay is unavoidable. Resolutions, on the other hand, can deal immediately with the problems of to-day. Let me give you an example. Last year, the miners were beginning to get into difficulties. The International Federation of Miners felt they should study the conditions of miners throughout the world, and Frank Hodges, who is their President, said : ' I quite agree that the only remedy is an international remedy, but the International Federation of Miners has not the staff or experience necessary for the investigation. But the International Labour Office at Geneva can do it.' The miners passed the suggestion on to one of the Workers' representatives at the International Labour Conference, and he put it in the form of a resolution which was carried by the Conference. The result is that to-day the Office is making an international study of conditions in mines throughout the world, and I hope that when we publish the figures we are painfully collecting they will constitute a real step towards the solution of that critical problem.

Let me give you another instance of the effect of our resolutions. We all know that America is working out its labour problems in a fashion entirely different from that which Europe has hitherto employed. Americans do not believe very much in trade unionism or in State interference ; they believe in getting employers and workers together, forming shop committees and letting industries solve their difficulties in joint consultation. We must know whether the world has evolved to the point where we must all imitate America ; and so at the last Conference a resolution was adopted inviting the International Labour Office to undertake a complete study of the question of management in industry ; we want first to see exactly what lessons America can teach us and then take advantage of them ourselves.

There is one other important point I wish to make with regard to our annual conferences, and that is the method by which the delegates are appointed. The two Government representatives are of course directly nominated by the Governments from their ministers, civil servants, or technical experts. As regards the representatives of the employers and workers the Treaty says that they must be nominated by their Government after consultation with the most representative organization of employers and workers in the country concerned. And this is not a mere form of words. Year after year we get complaints as to the credentials of employers' or workers' representatives on the grounds that they have not been properly nominated and do not really represent the opinion of the workers or employers of their country. Those of you who are sufficiently interested to read the debates which have taken place at the last three sessions of the Conference with regard to the Italian workers' representative will realize the importance attached to the question, and will incidentally get an excellent insight into Fascism. I emphasize this point in order to make it clear that the employers' and workers' representatives are not puppets or figureheads : they are men able to speak with authority on the various questions under discussion.

I must now say a word about the Governing Body. Just as the International Labour Conference roughly corresponds to the Assembly and the International Labour Office to the League Secretariat, so the Governing Body corresponds to the Council of the League. The general scheme of the Governing Body is the same as the Conference; i. e. there are representatives of the workers, of the employers, and of the governments. If you visit the room set apart for the Governing Body in our new building here, you will see that it is arranged to accommodate three groups—a large group in the middle for the governments, and smaller groups on each side for the workers and employers. There are twenty-four of these gentlemen—twelve from the governments, and six each from the employers and workers.

The Governing Body has to decide important points of policy for the Office, and gives instructions to the Director. In particular it decides the items to go on to the agenda of conferences. This involves a very real responsibility, for it has carefully to weigh the multitude of topics which might be discussed at the Conference, to limit the vast field of possible subjects of discussion and narrow it down to positive and practical issues; and it has to attempt to stem the enthusiasm of the Director and the members of his staff.

What do we all do in this Office? There are three main things. I have told you a little about the Conference. Now a conference of that kind does not work automatically, nor does it achieve success without a great deal of preparatory work and trouble. Let us take a subject like social insurance or—to particularize a little further—the subject of insurance against accident risks. That is a very real problem in the life of the worker. Just as in the case of matches a country which prohibited the use of white phosphorus put itself at a disadvantage in international competition with a country using the poisonous variety, so to-day a country which establishes a system of State insurance against workers' accidents puts itself at a disadvantage in comparison with countries which do not possess that particular type of social legislation. The element of competition runs right through the industrial field ; and so it was decided, two years ago, that the question of workers' compensation for accidents was ripe for international regulation.

What had the Office to do ? It had to find out exactly what the law on the subject was in every country. It had to go farther ; it had to discover what was the practice of every country, for law and practice are not always identical. It had to collate the results. The report and conclusions arrived at had to be put into French and English, the two official languages of the Office. With this basis a questionnaire had to be drafted and sent to the different countries asking them their opinions. Their replies had to be examined. All that meant a great deal of trouble.

Then there comes the Conference itself. It has to be staffed ; you have to have your interpreters and your secretaries and to provide for the necessary technical and legal advice. And when a draft convention has been adopted, you have to see what the various countries are doing— whether it is being pigeon-holed or whether legislation is being provided to give effect to it. All these duties, and others I have no time to enumerate, fall to one section of our Office—the Diplomatic Division—which is responsible for all official communications with governments and with the various employers' and workers' organizations, and for following the social and industrial legislation of countries of the world.

The Office has another large task, namely, that of information. One of our duties under the Treaty is to provide information on social subjects to those who ask for it. I will give you one or two instances of this. I have mentioned the 1925 Conference and the Convention for Compensation for Accidents. Two or three years ago South Africa decided to draw up a State law on compensation for accident risks. The Government of South Africa wrote to us and said : ' We want to draft this law, but we are not quite sure how to do it. Will you tell us what has been done in other countries and give us your advice ? ' The instance I have cited is that of a Dominion, but similar instances have occurred in the case of the new ex-war countries. Countries which have not social tradition or legislation constantly turn to this Office for information and advice, and where there does not exist an international convention or agreement on a given subject, draft legislation in consultation with us.

Let me take another example of the work of the Information Division. You all know that there has been trouble recently in connexion with the Civil Service in Great Britain, and questions asked as to the right of civil servants to strike when other workers strike. I was not surprised therefore when last Friday evening I found a request on my table from the Trade Union Congress of Great Britain saying ' Please send us as soon as you can regulations for countries in Europe on the right of Civil servants to syndicate and to strike '.

The fact that we get so many inquiries from governments, organizations, and individuals proves that people are beginning to realize that we exist, and that we exist for a purpose. America asked us forty-one questions last year, and they did not pay for the information ! Altogether we had 687 requests for information last year, and to answer them is not always an easy matter. It involves a close knowledge of working conditions in all countries and close relationship with workers and employers throughout the world. That is part of the work of the Information Division.

There is a third division—the Research Division. Mr. Phelan, who is to speak to you after tea, is responsible for the Diplomatic Division, and as he is to deal with results, will probably devote his attention more particularly to the diplomatic and conference side of our work. We have to have our draft conventions. We must have our shop window! We must show practical day-to-day results. But if I may venture a purely personal opinion, in the long run it will perhaps be our research work which will prove to have been of the greatest utility. Let me give you an example in regard to that gravest of all workers' problems—unemployment. We have had conventions and recommendations and resolutions dealing with unemployment, and Governments have been invited to send us all the statistics they possibly can on the subject. These are of great value. But how in the long run is this question of unemployment to be solved? Certainly not by scratching on the surface; you must go deep down into main causes. You have to apply to the problem the trained intellect of research workers, investigate trade fluctuations, the cost of living, economic barometers, cyclical changes, painfully dig through the mass of material representing the past experience at our disposal, and see if you cannot in the end arrive at the fundamental causes of unemployment. I am sure it is clear to all of you that if by research we can reach basic issues, we shall do an inestimable service to humanity. We have therefore groups of research workers dealing with unemployment, agricultural questions, hours of work, industrial health statistics, and so on. An examination of the catalogue of our publications will show you to some extent the range of their studies. That is the third division.

We have also a smaller section which translates, publishes, and sells and distributes the results of our inquiries; and we have a section dealing with office material, finance, salaries, staff, and so on.

One word about the staff. There are about 350 permanent members, among whom 33 nationalities are represented. When I say ' represented ' I do not mean that the officials of any given nation are here to represent that nation. When they arrive in this building they are meant to become international. I am not sure we all do become international in our private opinions, but I hope that in our official attitude we do get this atmosphere of Geneva which is so much talked of, and work from the international viewpoint. In addition there are a certain number of temporary officials to study the special questions that may be put to us from time to time and are not of a permanent character. For instance, the Office has recently been invited to make a study of conditions in the East, and so one or two persons with particular knowledge of the East have been appointed temporarily to help us.

In addition we have special commissions set up to give the Office the value of their practical experience. We cannot attempt to deal with emigration, unemployment, agriculture, industrial health, disablement questions, and so on, without the valuable assistance of the world's experts on these subjects. The Organization picks the brains of these wise men at very little expense by nominating them to correspondence committees. When we have a difficult problem to solve we write to them and say : ' Tell us what you think about this '; and we utilize the information and advice they are kind enough to give us.

Finally, I should like to suggest that after all you are the people who make our Organization go. It is entirely dependent on public opinion. If at any given moment the public opinion of the world set against the International Labour Organization, the Organization would cease to exist. We are not allowed as an office to do propaganda. Our business —as is very clearly emphasized by the employers every time they come here—is to keep our noses close to the grindstone and do the work they tell us to do without talking about it. But even churches have their chimes, and to influence public opinion some one must go out and tell the world that after all something is being done. As I say, we—the staff—cannot do that, but I cannot think of any more effective manner for an Institute such as yours to show its power and influence than by helping the Organization in this all-important direction.

II. *Current Progress of International Labour Legislation*

MR. E. J. PHELAN :

THE previous speaker has told you something of the origin of the International Labour Organization and of its machinery. We have now to examine the results which it has achieved, to weigh them, and to attempt to form a judgement of their value.

You are aware that the essential object of the International Labour Conference is the preparation of international conventions or treaties which by providing for equal or equivalent progress in a given social field will enable that progress to take place unhampered by unfair international competition. These conventions aim at securing that there shall be at all events a certain minimum of social protection removed from the field of action of unrestrained competition, that there shall be certain minimum standards which must be respected whatever other changes economic circumstances or variations in bargaining power as between employers and workers may produce.

The Conference, as you know, cannot impose these standards. It can only prepare them and submit them to the sovereign decision of the Member States who then decide whether by ratifying them they will enter into a solemn international contract to observe them. That decision to ratify or not to ratify, remember, is taken long after the Conference itself—any time during the eighteen months which follow. It is taken in complete independence, remote from any pressure in the Conference or from that so-called ' atmosphere of Geneva ' which is sometimes accused of leading cautious and practical statesmen into imprudent and unpractical follies which they would never have looked on with favour had they remained securely at home. Ratifications then are the result of cold national reflection and not of any transient international enthusiasm. They have to find their place among the multitude of pressing affairs which any Government or legislature has to deal with in its normal work ; they may be put aside for any urgent domestic reason ; they may be refused because of internal political changes ; like all other national questions they are at the mercy of political chance and circumstance. If national decisions to ratify labour conventions are taken, it must therefore be that they are felt by the States to have a considerable importance. They must correspond to something real and urgent. The number of them obtained is therefore a first and a severe test of the work of the International Labour Organization. If the Conference should be led to the formulation of idealistic conventions there is little chance that they would survive this kind of State referendum.

Let us examine, therefore, the number of ratifications which has been obtained.

The International Labour Conference has adopted in the course of its nine sessions twenty-four conventions. I do not propose to describe their content. It would be impossible in the time at my disposal to discuss exactly what progress has been made with the solution of each of the problems with which these conventions deal. We can only apply a general test. If these conventions constitute a serious and practical contribution to the solution of the problems concerned we should expect to find the Governments adhering to them. If they represent unpractical idealism or mere empty formula their success will be likely to have ended with

the Conference which adopted them. That is the general
test which I propose to apply for the moment. As to how
far it is a complete test will be discussed later.

There are fifty-six Members of the International Labour
Organization and twenty-four conventions. If you multiply
56 by 24 you get a figure in the region of 1,300. Hence if
all the conventions had been ratified by all the Members of
the Organization we should have a little more than 1,300
ratifications. The figure to-day is 206. At a first glance
this might be read, and sometimes is by critics of the Organization, as only a 15 per cent. success. A moment's reflection,
however, will show that to work out the proportion in that
way is unsound.

First of all, our conventions are of different ages, and,
since ratification is often a slow process, time is an element
of importance. For example, we held two Conferences this
year, the second of which closed only about six weeks ago.
It would be quite impossible for any State to have ratified
any of the three conventions adopted at those Conferences.
Again, last year the Conference adopted a certain convention
which gave rise to a request for an Advisory opinion from
the International Court of Justice. Doubts were expressed
as to whether a certain clause in that convention was within
the competence of the Organization, and machinery was put
in operation to consult the Court which is the body desig-
nated to decide any such question. It will be easily understood that while a question of that kind is *sub judice* the
process of ratification is in practice suspended, and so that
convention has only begun to run its chances of ratification
since the decision of the Court—which was favourable to the
competence of the Organization—was given a few days ago.

But if all the conventions are not to be counted alike for

F

the purposes of our calculation neither are all the Members of the Organization. Not all of them have been Members since the Organization began, and those who were admitted to membership later have had a large number of conventions presented for their consideration all at once instead of having received them in the more digestible form of annual instalments. It is difficult to determine any factor which could be allowed in such cases and I do not propose to attempt to do so. There is, however, another discrimination which can be arithmetically made with some precision. There are States in respect of which certain conventions have, what I may call, no immediate expectation of ratification. For example, there have been two maritime Conferences, that is, conferences which have dealt exclusively with problems of conditions of labour at sea. It would be absurd to expect that the conventions adopted by those Conferences would be ratified by non-maritime countries which have no maritime interests, or even by countries with a coast line which have little or no merchant shipping.

Again, many of the conventions set a minimum international standard for countries which are highly industrialized or on the road to becoming so. It is not reasonable to expect those conventions to be ratified by States which are just starting out on their industrial career. We have no hope, for example, at all events in the immediate future, of seeing the Eight Hours Convention or the Unemployment Convention ratified by a country like Ethiopia.

Lastly, there is the constitutional difficulty which exists in certain Federal States whose labour legislation is within the competence of the units within the Federation and where accordingly the Federal authority cannot enter into international engagements in respect of labour matters.

If taking account of these considerations we were to calculate the number of ratifications for which a reasonable expectation might be held to exist we get the figure of approximately 600. We have therefore up to the present moment [1] secured 206 ratifications out of a possible 600. To estimate the value of that proportion we require something with which to compare it. I think it will be found to compare very favourably with the rate of ratification of any other general international treaty or convention. But a better test will no doubt be to compare it with the ratification of the earlier Labour conventions, that is, of those which were negotiated prior to the creation of the International Labour Organization. As you know, an international convention prohibiting the use of white phosphorus in the manufacture of matches was signed at Berne in 1906. In 1912 that convention was effectively binding on only six States. Seven more ratifications had been obtained by 1914, but a delay of five years had to elapse in each case before the State concerned was bound to observe the provisions of the convention.

If, therefore, you look at the figure of 13 ratifications in eight years (more than half of which only became effective several years later) of one very simple convention dealing with one very definite form of industrial poisoning, and affecting in the countries concerned only one industry, and that an industry of by no means first-rate importance, and if you compare that result with the 206 ratifications in a period of six years of 24 conventions, some of which have a general application to all industry, the conclusion is not unfavourable to the International Labour Organization.

In making the above comparison I have counted only

[1] August, 1926.

ratifications actually registered with the League. But there are a series of steps leading up to registration which mark definite stages in the process. When a Government has gone to its parliament and recommended ratification and parliament has approved, ratification may then be regarded as certain, although no international obligation is created until the formalities of communication and registration have been completed. There are some thirty cases of this kind at the present moment, where only purely formal action remains to be taken. One might, therefore, give the figure of 230 as representing the number of cases in which an international obligation has been or certainly will be assumed. Or one might go a step still farther back in the process. An additional number of 153 ratifications have been recommended by Governments to their parliaments. We do not yet know what the parliaments will decide, but from past experience there is good reason to expect that where a Government enjoying the confidence of its parliament recommends ratification, ratification is approved. It may therefore be said that at the present moment 383 ratifications have been registered or are in sight. More no doubt will be forthcoming, but these may be regarded with a very considerable degree of certainty as achieved.

That the whole 600 will be achieved is unlikely. Of the 217 which remain some will probably not be obtained. But that does not by any means imply that in those cases the conventions will have been productive of no positive result. The above analysis takes us as far as one can go on a strictly statistical basis. In the case of a given country and a given convention, ratification is the maximum result which can be obtained. There is of course the question of application, but once ratification has been achieved the constitution of the Organization provides a whole system for annual reports and mutual supervision which undoubtedly guarantees effective application. We have at the moment, however, to consider the nature of the positive results where ratification is unlikely or is probably certain not to take place. In many of these cases States have modified their legislation in the sense of a convention, but not so as to correspond completely with all the provisions of the convention. For example, a convention may apply to all industrial establishments. A State may apply by legislation the terms of the convention to all its industrial establishments employing more than three workers. It may not wish to go farther because its system of factory inspection may not cover small establishments and therefore it has at its disposal no means of supervision and enforcement as regards such establishments. It will have adopted legislation giving the protection of the convention to the great majority of its workers, but because that legislation is not a complete fulfilment of the convention it will be unable to enter into a contract to observe its terms—that is, it will be unable to ratify, at all events until such time as it can also incur the expense involved in extending its system of factory inspection. No ratification can be counted, but nevertheless a substantial increase in social protection may have been achieved.

Again, the mere existence of a convention adhered to by a number of other States may suffice to set up an international standard from which it becomes impossible to recede, even though it may not have been completely attained. The respect of a certain minimum standard, which, as I pointed out at the beginning, it is the object of the conventions to secure, may thus in fact be secured although no legal international obligation to that effect may have been formally entered on. And lastly the standard set by the conventions tends to become something to be definitely and progressively arrived at.

Time will not allow a discussion of the somewhat similar results which might be credited to work of the Organization through the medium of the recommendations adopted by the Conference. I leave them out of account because they do not result in definite international obligations. They serve as guides to the Members in their industrial legislation and undoubtedly they are an instrument of progress. But, since States may apply them in the degree they will and relax them as they please, it is impossible to make any simple calculation as to the degree to which they are effective. All that can be said in the present brief survey is that they have given rise in many cases to the introduction of legislative and administrative measures in many countries which have increased social protection.

Taking, however, only the conventions, the number of ratifications registered or in sight, and the standards tended to or maintained where ratification has not been forthcoming or is of still distant expectation, it may be said with confidence that the results of six years working of the Organization are positive, and that it has in a very large measure reason to be satisfied with the results of its first six years and confident of achievement in the future.

No estimate of the progress of the Organization would, however, be complete if it were confined to the mere arithmetical calculation of the number of ratifications registered or laws promulgated. I am inclined to think that there are other results not statistically measurable, not even always susceptible of tabulation, country by country, which are perhaps even more important. They were not seen clearly, if at all, by the authors of the Organization's constitution. They are not mentioned in the preamble. They are by-products of which we have only become aware through actual experience, and yet possibly in the long run they may prove to be the foundations on which the Organization really rests. They are indirect results, but it may be that if they had been absent, or if they should fail to continue, the more definite and more limited direct results might never be achieved.

It is possible to indicate some of them, though it is difficult as yet to estimate their full results or even to describe them accurately.

In the first place, the existence of the Organization has led to an improved degree of organization among workers and employers both internationally and nationally.

The preparation by the Conference of an international convention involves not only an attempt to discover a kind of average of existing tendencies in social legislation but also the more fundamental task of reconciling or finding a compromise acceptable to interests which are or believe themselves to be in opposition to one another. For the successful accomplishment of that task it is essential that those interests should be vocal. Their points of view should be formulated authentically, and this is only possible in the degree in which they are organized. If a reconciliation or a compromise is to be of value it can only be made between bodies highly organized. Durable results from negotiation with a mob or with a series of fractions are impossible.

It was at the Washington Conference in 1919 that the first International Federation of Industrial Employers was formed, and thus was brought into existence an international organization in which employers throughout the world could discuss and formulate a common policy in industrial matters.

On the workers' side no single international federation has been brought into being for the reason that rival international federations already existed. But in the workers' group of the Conference, which has a definite organic existence during the sessions, the rival federations of Amsterdam and of the Christian Unions, together with the representatives of certain national movements not affiliated to either, work together and in fact produce an *ad hoc* organization of over thirty million workers.

The results of the stimulus to national organization are perhaps even more important. It will be remembered that it is the most representative national organization of employers or workers which has the right to nominate employers' or workers' delegate from the country concerned. The appointment is made by the Government in view of the diplomatic character of the Conference, but the agreement of the most representative organization must be secured, which means that in fact such organization possesses the right of appointment. Here again where rival organizations exist there is a definite tendency towards collaboration ; elements of unity are stressed and elements of difference tend to be submerged. Agreements are reached as to a rotation as regards the appointment of the delegate and as to a share in the appointment of the technical advisers who accompany him. What may be the result over a longer period it is impossible to forecast, but already the bringing to the surface of points of agreement in policy and aims between rival organizations cannot but help to simplify many national industrial problems.

It is, however, in a special class of countries that the

indirect effects on organization have been of the greatest importance and of peculiar value. In certain countries like Japan and India, countries with very large populations and with considerable material riches, a rapid industrial evolution is taking place. People do not, I think, realize the speed with which India and Japan are becoming great industrial countries. Now when a country becomes a great industrial country it means that factories spring up and that there is a material change in certain regions in the country. It equally well means that a thing called a working class has got to be created. You cannot have factories without workers, and you cannot have workers without what are called industrial problems. It is not very difficult to see that with a very rapidly expanding industry and with a population being turned into an industrial population in countries which have no experience of industrial life special problems and peculiar difficulties arise. It was natural that the Governments concerned should have been considerably perplexed as to the best methods of meeting these problems. Should labour organizations be encouraged? Should organizations of limited experience and unpractical aims be given an immense prestige by special recognition for the purposes of international representation? Could their untried leaders be sent without serious national danger as full delegates into an official Conference? Were the comparatively small and unstable movements which they led the stable constitutional recognized movements intended by the Peace Treaty to collaborate with proper responsibility with their governments in the appointment of a workers' delegate and advisers to the International Labour Conference? Might it not be possible to organize under Government supervision the inexperienced workers in the factories into some kind of general association which could elect a delegate to the Conference who would be familiar with the conditions of the workers? It was equally natural that, for example in Japan, the Japanese Federation of Labour should claim to be the only body to be consulted and should regard any such *ad hoc* organization of workers under Government inspiration as menacing its own authority and even existence. What might have been the result of this controversy in the absence of other elements it is impossible to say. What is certain is that its prolongation could not have been other than harmful. A solution was secured rapidly because of the right of the Labour Conference to examine the credentials of delegates and to refuse to accept those whom it deemed not to have been nominated in accordance with the provisions of its constitution. The Conference while not excluding the Japanese workers' delegate at its earlier meetings and while appreciating the difficulties of the Japanese Government, nevertheless gave a pretty clear indication of what its collective experience led it to believe to be the wisest solution. And finally the Japanese Government decided to make future appointments in agreement with the Japanese Federation of Labour. The collective experience of the Conference made it easier for the Japanese Government to realize more fully considerations to which it had no doubt already given attention, namely that the spontaneous organization of their workers was inevitable; that they could not hope to impose on it Governmental tutelage nor define its ideals; that while it must develop freely and formulate its own programme there was every advantage in letting it do so in close and personal contact through the International Labour Organization with the older and more experienced Trade Union movements; and that through responsible participation in the work of the Conference it would become committed to a programme which was the fruit of practical experience and which represented a common agreement of what was both possible and desirable.

Thus what was secured was this. The Japanese labour movement secured official recognition. The position of its leaders was strengthened. The Japanese Government was freed from the impossible task of attempting to build up an artificial labour movement under official tutelage, and at the same time it secured that the spontaneous movement should work in close and educative contact with experienced movements elsewhere, and thus escape, at all events to a large degree, the dangerous inspiration of inexperienced demagogues or subversive agitators. And since industrial anarchy in one country cannot but be harmful to all, this promise of greater stability in the industrial development of oriental countries, for an almost identical story could be told with regard to India, may be regarded as a definite gain to the world as a whole.

The development of industrial organization which has resulted from the existence of the Organization does not, of course, mean the disappearance of industrial friction. It may tend to diminish it, but we are yet far from the stage at which it can be avoided even in its most dangerous form. Nevertheless, when it occurs the regular meeting of the antagonists in the International Labour Conference is a new feature of industrial life which may be considered to have a considerable importance. When relations between employers and workers have been broken off in a particular country, or when as was recently the case in Great Britain the action of the organized labour movement is considered by the Government to constitute a direct challenge to its authority, there is surely an advantage in having the hostile leaders meet on a different plane for the transaction of common business in which they have a common interest. A striking example was furnished at the Labour Conference this year where Mr. Pugh who, as Chairman of the Trade Union Congress, had been the leader of the general strike in England only a week or two earlier, might have been sitting at the same table as the British employers and the British Government representatives, engaged for the space of a month in close collaboration for the achievement of a common end. The existence of the International Labour Conference, where leaders, who nationally practically never meet except to oppose conflicting claims, come together on another and a wider plane where their national differences fall into a different perspective, is undoubtedly a new factor in industrial relations the effect of which, though psychological and incapable of measurement, must be definitely beneficial.

In the six years during which the Organization has been in existence there have been nine international labour conferences and thirty-three meetings of the Governing Body, and in all those nine conferences and thirty-three sessions of the Governing Body organized workers and organized employers have continued to meet without a break. And it should be remembered that those six years have been years of peculiar economic difficulty, years in which in many countries there were violent fluctuations in the cost of living, and hence in real wages, with consequent urgent demands for readjustments of wages which from the nature of things could never be satisfactorily realized. They were years, therefore, in which industrial relations were inevitably strained and frequently broken. During all that exceptionally difficult period the contact and the collaboration in the

Conference and the Governing Body has gone on with never any hint of a threat of its cessation. It is clear, therefore, that the plane of those international relations is different. It might perhaps be supposed that absence of correspondingly severe tensions was due to the fact that the international plane is somewhat artificial, and that crises corresponding to the national crises have been avoided because the international discussions which take place thereon are too far divorced from reality, that there are no violent estrangements because there is nothing to be estranged about. Personal experience of a labour Conference would rapidly dissipate any such idea. Differences are as profound in the one case as in the other, but they are manifested in different conditions and they are also to some extent differently distributed.

In the first place the Conference does not meet because one or other group has a demand or ultimatum to present to the other. It is a meeting of a constitutional body sitting under a charter to which its Members have subscribed, and under which they have freely associated themselves to pursue certain defined common ends. The subjects it discusses have already been chosen in agreement. The annual meeting is a periodical and regular proceeding: not an accidental contact arising out of a claim or a grievance. The Conference thus starts with a favourable background. It does not by any means follow, however, that serious divergences of view do not exist and do not manifest themselves with energy and sometimes with vehemence. A stranger, following an international labour conference for the first time, might well be excused if during the first fortnight or three weeks of its proceedings he was left with the growing conviction that any agreed result was impossible. It would be difficult for him to perceive and analyse the cross currents which by finally coming together lead to a common course. They need not be analysed here. It will suffice to point out that while the reality of differences is manifested by the vigour of the discussions and by the number of amendments moved and the closeness of the voting on them, nevertheless the final result with few exceptions, for which special reasons can be given, has usually been secured with unanimity or something very closely approximating to it. The same is true of the more frequent and less formal meetings of the Governing Body. It is rare to find decisions carried against one of the three groups by the other two. There is always an effort towards compromise, usually successful. The mere existence of such an unbroken series of meetings with their lengthening record of agreements is surely something which represents a definite advantage.

There are, however, other results of a somewhat different and even more general character. The Labour Organization in comparison with the League may be regarded as working in a non-political field. It has therefore been perhaps freer to make experiments in international organization, experiments which may prove of immense value in the future development of its sister political organization. As the mass of international business to be transacted grows, or rather as the need for its transaction in order that modern civilization may give the full measure of its service to mankind is more fully realized, the pioneer work of the International Labour Organization in international methods may be of inestimable value. The League was set up when men's minds were appalled by the catastrophe of a world war in which their civilization had all but perished. It was fundamentally inspired by the desire to insure against a repetition of that final peril. And so the Covenant contained detailed prescriptions as to the steps to be taken in international crises to avoid the resort to war. It contained little or nothing on the procedure to be followed as regards that general international collaboration which is referred to in its preamble, or as regards the achievement of certain humanitarian objects which are mentioned almost incidentally in some of its later articles. It is true that it has displayed an immense activity in the realization of what may be called its secondary programme, and it is also true that in so doing it has contributed perhaps in the most effective way possible to its essential purpose. The more numerous the questions recognized as of international concern, and the closer the network of administration which strives to adopt or apply international conventions designed for their solution, the more widespread and the more resistant the relations which the threat of war menaces. But that effort to create effective international collaboration in the technical fields of transit, health, economics, finance, &c., had had to proceed on the old basis of international relations. It is hampered and cramped by the old methods of international relations because the constitution of the League provided no new ones. The old methods were based on theories which were deduced from an observation of the world as it was, a world of absolutely independent States, serene and aloof in a sovereignty which like the Divine right of Kings transcended human qualification or any other control but its own. The League is struggling to work out schemes of international collaboration between interdependent States by methods which were designed for the jealous preservation of distrustful independence. In the case of the International Labour Organization matters are very different. It took the League for granted.

It assumed that civilization would survive. And because it was created to achieve positive reforms its constitution provided new methods for its operations. It proceeds by way of treaties. Treaties had hitherto been the close preserve of professional diplomats and Foreign Offices. Their negotiation and conclusion were hedged around with much mystery and occult ceremony. However much these might be necessary as regards political settlements the authors of the Labour Organization were anxious to avoid them as regard Labour Conventions. They were afraid that the diplomatic witch doctors might not be over sympathetic towards a witchcraft somewhat outside their ken. They wanted more direct and more democratic treatment for the international engagements the Labour Organization might prepare. And so they devised a whole system of novel procedure based on the principle of international collaboration which marks in many respects a revolutionary break with the older method which was based on the principle of national isolation.

The experience of six years of the International Labour Organization has shown that this new system can be applied with success, and this aspect of the working of the Organization will no doubt be a valuable guide in the future development of international collaboration.

In the first place the Organization has abandoned in its procedure for the negotiation of a Convention the essential rule that flowed from the conception of the old sovereign State, the rule of unanimity. Labour Conventions are adopted by a two-thirds majority, and in spite of the many forebodings that were expressed as to the impossibility of applying any such rule the Organization has survived and has achieved the remarkable record of ratified Conventions which I have already discussed.

But the abandonment of the rule of unanimity involved another change which considerably simplifies international procedure. Under the older system, which still prevails as regards League Conventions, when plenipotentiaries have negotiated a Treaty they sign it. No one would argue nowadays that that signature has any great value. No one would argue for example that the signature of President Wilson affixed to the Treaty of Versailles in any way bound the United States to that Treaty. The value of signature nowadays is simply to secure an authoritative text, so that no subsequent dispute may arise as to the exact terms of the agreement arrived at in negotiation, but that agreement has no binding force unless and until ratified by the principals concerned. This formality of signature has, however, disadvantages, particularly when the subject of negotiation is technical and what may loosely be called non-political. It can only be accomplished by persons possessing ' full powers ' and the granting of this mystic capacity may mean delay. It may mean the holding up of useful settlements because of the intervention of purely formalistic considerations. The most competent official of the Department concerned may have negotiated a technical settlement, but the State cannot even be asked to consider its ratification until the paper on which it has been written has been signed by a quite different official unable to appreciate its substance, and therefore incapable of altering its form, but empowered by an obsolescent incantation to purify it for the consideration of the Sovereign Power. True, there is a tendency, especially as regards League Conventions, to merge the two individuals, the humble technician and the resplendent plenipotentiary, and to give the actual negotiator authority to sign with ' full powers '. But the intervention of a second department

as the custodian of those powers is nevertheless quite use-
lessly required, since the instructions of the negotiator have
usually been given at the beginning, and probably in all
cases confirmed at the end of the negotiations by a properly
considered Government decision.   Moreover, there is a tendency for an authority to sign to be accepted in practice
which would not pass muster by all formal tests, and so there
is a danger that technical objections might be subsequently
raised if circumstances should render them convenient.   To
that extent there is something to be said for a rigid application of the older system.   But it is cumbersome, involves
useless duplication, and has the disadvantages indicated
above, and no doubt as the nature and number of international conventions are multiplied a simpler procedure will
be sought.   That such a procedure can be applied is proved
by the experience of the International Labour Organization.
Once the rule of unanimity had been abandoned and the
democratic rule of decision by a majority adopted in its
place it became obviously impossible to apply the formality
of signature.   Delegates who had voted against a convention
could hardly be asked to sign it, and since all Members of
the Organization are under obligation to consider the ratification of all Conventions adopted by the Conference, it
would undoubtedly weaken that general obligation if the
Conventions were signed by the delegates of only some of
them.   The constitution of the Organization therefore deliberately provided a new and much simpler procedure which
need not be described in detail.   In spite of express provision
for it some difficulty was encountered in getting it generally
accepted.   Ritual, although it has ceased to correspond to any
reality, can still be tenacious of survival, and some of its
perfervid devotees were even prepared to argue that any

provisions abolishing signature were unconstitutional and therefore inoperative. These difficulties were, however, surmounted and there is now in operation, at all events as regards one class of treaties, a system of non-signature universally accepted which provides for all practical needs.

An innovation of much more fundamental importance, however, is that which deals with the procedure leading to ratification. The Covenant of the League forbade secret treaties and in so doing provided a valuable guarantee for democracy. But the democratic control comes after the *fait accompli*. States may hesitate to conclude treaties of a certain character knowing that they must be published and that there may then be a certain reaction of public opinion. But a much more serious guarantee is to secure that the ultimate national decision on an international treaty should be taken by a representative assembly and not by the executive decision of a cabinet or even of an individual minister. It has been found possible to provide for such a procedure in the constitution of the International Labour Organization. When an international labour convention has been adopted by a final vote which requires a two-thirds majority there is an obligation on the Government of every Member of the Organization, whether it voted for or against the Convention, whether it was present or not at the Conference at which the convention was adopted, to lay that convention before the authority in its particular country which is competent to give effect to it by legislation, i.e. to lay it before its legislative assembly. If that legislative assembly approves the convention the Member is then obliged to proceed to its ratification.

Here is a very real guarantee of a positive character. It may be impossible to extend it at present to all treaties, but it has other obvious advantages as regards the technical conventions negotiated by the League. At present when the League negotiates a Convention it does little more than express a pious hope in some detail. There is no specific provision in the Covenant obliging Members to take it into consideration, let alone submit it to their parliaments or assemblies. Members no doubt will never argue that because of the absence of such a provision they have no intention of giving consideration to League Conventions. But busy administrations are not to be blamed for giving precedence to definite obligations, and the enthusiastic vote of the Assembly has a very diluted influence by the time it reaches some overburdened or socially distracted clerk in a Foreign Office six months later. The system of the Labour Organization which definitely links the work of the International Labour Conference to the national parliaments not only ensures consideration for its decisions but brings them into the arena of the national representative assembly where the Government must justify its action or inaction before public opinion. It both educates public opinion, therefore, as to international problems and makes it the judge of the solutions proposed by the international institution. The former process is essential to the success of the international experiment and the latter is a salutary check on its operation.

It is of considerable interest to note with what a degree of smoothness and efficiency these innovations, which might have been considered as somewhat daring, have worked. But that they corresponded to the practical needs of a more intensive international activity is fully proved by the fact that in the experience of the working of the International Labour Organization States have spontaneously gone farther along the same line of development than it was thought possible to ask or require them to do. The innovations made, in one form or another, might have been combated on the ground that they instituted an infringement of national sovereignty. They were sometimes opposed as I have pointed out, but it was on considerations of ritual rather than of right. The argument of sovereignty was not invoked, but on the contrary there has been an evolution which involves an admission of an international accountability which is as surprising as it is hopeful.

Provision, as I have indicated, was made in the constitution of the International Labour Organization for the expeditious and public consideration of the Conventions adopted by the Conference. Member States are under obligation to decide within twelve months, or in exceptional circumstances, eighteen months, whether they will or will not ratify them. But that decision, to ratify or not to ratify, was regarded as a sovereign decision to be taken in complete and absolute independence without the possibility of question or the need of explanation. Neither the Office, nor the Governing Body, nor an individual Member, nor even the Conference itself was given the right to ask for the reasons which might have led a Member to decide not to ratify a given Convention, and it was thought inconceivable that such a right should be created. Any one following an International Labour Conference or reading its proceedings might, however, be excused for assuming that such a right existed. The Conference has before it at each Session in the Director's Report a detailed table of the progress of ratifications, and in the discussion of that Report complaints of the slowness of the progress realized are not infrequently heard, especially from the workers' group. The result is not, as might have been expected, that Government representatives retrench themselves behind the Treaty and point out that the Conference is not the organ of a Superstate, that it is only a body for the preparation of international settlements, and that it has no right to examine or to criticize the individual sovereign decisions of the Members with regard to them. On the contrary Governments seem eager to take advantage of this particular discussion to explain to the Conference the steps which they are taking, the hopes which they have of speedy ratification, or the circumstances which had led them reluctantly to the conclusion that ratification is impossible. Thus, in practice, they go beyond the obligations which are incumbent on them. They seem to have realized in an unexpected degree that they participate, not in a rigid mechanism, but that they are parts of a living organization developing its own personality, and entitled to display a natural curiosity as to the reasons which impede the full acceptance of the reforms it proposes. It may be long before a similar spirit is manifested as regards settlements of a more distinctively political character, but it is of immense interest and importance to note its spontaneous appearance within the Labour Organization.

It would be possible to examine other novel experiences in the working of this pioneer organization. Enough, however, it may be hoped, has been said, to show that its success should not be measured merely by the number of ratifications secured, but that some of its indirect results may in the long run prove an important contribution to the world's effort towards a higher form of international collaboration. In this connexion there is one last consideration which needs examination. Most thinking people are agreed that the world must find some means of maintaining peace or civilization will perish. Is the work of the Labour Organization an essential contribution to the solution of that primary problem? The machinery of Government is cumbersome and overburdened. Its powers of adaptation are dangerously slow. Should not what it can give towards international collaboration be concentrated on the fundamental problem, and is there not a danger of expending too great a proportion of our effort on the side-shows of Peace and so compromising success in the main field? In other words, is there a real organic connexion between the work of the Labour Organization and the work of the League or is the former in present circumstances just an energetic and successful irrelevancy not without peril? The answer is to be found in the consideration of the nature of the League and of the conditions upon which its success or failure ultimately depends. The League is a structure of States. Those States in greater or less degree, and in all probability in a degree which will tend to increase, are organized on what is called the democratic system. Their organization in this respect may not be perfect, but it exists in all cases in form, and in most cases in substance to some degree. Any attempt to secure and maintain the peace of the world must take account of that fundamental fact. If it were the task of the League to secure a peace of despots or even a peace of Governments we might well despair of its success. There is some hope only because Governments nowadays must count with the opinion of the mass. To say that two democracies would not make war would perhaps be straining the argument. What is certain is that war is less likely between democracies than between despotisms. One man in his anger or fear or ambition may be willing to risk his all against another whom he hates or fears or envies. But anger and fear and ambition suffer dilution when they become the motives of a group, and it is still more difficult to imagine them as effective when we think not of a group but of a people. It may be argued that there are historical instances to the contrary, the attitude of Rome to Carthage, and of France to Germany only a few years ago. But Rome was not a democracy as we understand the term, and the French masses condemned the Ruhr policy and all it implied as soon as a general election gave them the opportunity. But we need not examine the historical case. Democracy follows instinctively the law of self-preservation. In its bones it is opposed to war because war is opposed to its existence. War from its very nature must mean dictatorship, and dictatorship is the antithesis of democracy. Thus the democratic tide as it rises tends to lift the bark of civilization clear of the shoals of war—the ' tide rising in the hearts of men ' as President Wilson called it.

. What do these considerations mean in terms of the organized international effort to maintain peace. The answer is indicated by a host of national experiences. Every civilized Government having a democratic system, having a system of universal suffrage or something approximating to it, has as a necessary corollary recognized as a primary duty the provision of educational facilities. If every citizen is to have some share in determining the destinies of his fellows the State must see that so far as possible he is equipped for the task. Education in the democratic State is not a fad or a fantasy but a necessity. But education for this end does not mean the rules of arithmetic and the ability to read and write. If it means anything it means the giving to the child of the possibility of self-education after the school years are over—that is, when the working years have begun. If that possibility does not exist we get not democracy but despotism in its modern form. Interests and imperialisms, avarice and ambition, pride and love of power, can triumph as before. They only need to flatter and cajole an ignorant mob incapable of judgement till bemused it follows their unscrupulous leadership to its own destruction. The dangers of democracy are the real dangers of civilization. They are diminished by anything that increases the possibility of intelligent citizenship, that helps to secure conditions in which those who exercise political power may fit themselves for their great responsibility. Can it be denied that the efforts of the International Labour Organization to obtain for the worker leisure for the comprehension and exercise of his duties as a citizen, relief from the pre-occupations of uncertain employment, protection against industrial risks and their demoralizing consequences, security against exploitation of women and children, are a real contribution to the basis on which the democratic structure of the world now rests ? And is it not certain that in the degree in which those efforts are successful the chances of interested or unscrupulous political exploitation will be diminished and the guarantees of peaceful relations between peoples increased ?

At the end of the war men thought of Peace as the absence of war. Other generations will not know that violent reaction. The guarantee against war in the future will be an enlightened democracy. When the great majority of men have a material, an intellectual, and a cultural stake in Peace, they will have a peace worth having and therefore a peace worth keeping. If one could imagine the International Labour Organization wholly successful only madness could throw civilization again into chaos.

It is for this reason that the work of the Organization may be considered as an essential contribution to the effort of the League, and if the Organization should fail it may be doubted if the League's efforts could in the long run save humanity from supreme calamity.

SECTION II
THE LEAGUE IN ACTION

CHAPTER IV
ACTION OF THE COUNCIL OF THE LEAGUE OF NATIONS IN INTERNATIONAL DISPUTES

M. PAUL MANTOUX:

THE proper title of this lecture should be the Methods of the Council of the League in dealing with International Disputes. What I have to do is to show how the system which was outlined in a document called the Covenant has been working, and what practical methods are gradually developing and establishing themselves.

I will deal with the political activities of the League because that is my particular responsibility in the Secretariat. Although the time is perhaps coming when it will take less time to describe what the League is not doing than what it is, at the present time, and in spite of the fact that the League at present is dealing with all sorts of questions such as economic reconstruction, the protection of minorities, international health organization, the improvement of international transit, intellectual co-operation and so on, the original purpose and *raison d'être* of the League remains, after all, the settlement of disputes that might lead to war, and all the other activities of the League centre round that special and essential purpose. It is hoped to create between nations a feeling of common interest and a development of common methods in dealing with common problems, and it is because of that that the League has extended its activities

into such various fields. But we always come back to the
fundamental problem, which is the settlement of dangerous
disputes between nations.

What are the methods by which this is done? It is those
methods which I hope to describe to you. I had to deal with
this same subject a few months ago when I addressed the
British Institute of International Affairs, and in thinking
over what I should say on that occasion, it suddenly occurred
to me I had entirely neglected a document which was essential to my purpose—the rules of procedure of the Council.
It seemed rather strange for a student of procedure to deal
with his subject without looking at that document. I asked
my secretary, therefore, to bring it to me, and the first thing
that caught my eye in it was article 4, which read : ‘ The
President and the Vice-President of the Council will be
elected by the Council from among its members by secret
ballot and by majority. They will hold office for one year.’
To any one who has been following the Council Session after
Session, that is simply astounding. First of all, there has
never been a Vice-President. Next, the President has never
been elected by secret ballot or majority, because each member of the Council takes the Presidency in turn, and they
never hold office for one year, but only for one Session. I am
inclined to think that perhaps in this case, therefore, the
texts do not count for so much, but that it is rather the
methods which are gradually developing under the pressure
of circumstances which are important.

That does not apply, of course, to everything. I do not
want to convey the impression that the Council disregards
every article of the Covenant, and that each of them in turn
becomes a subject of ridicule like this provision in the Rules
of Procedure which has never been applied. The rules which

have been most scrupulously adhered to have, nevertheless, to be interpreted in the light of actual practice and unwritten constitution, which you would look for in vain in the text of the Covenant itself, but which could be found and understood by going through those much more ponderous and voluminous documents which contain the Reports of the Sessions of the Council itself.

My first point is this. The natural tendency of the general public who are educated in this particular science is, whenever any dispute arises in any part of the world, to ask at once what the League is doing, and if League action does not follow immediately or at all, they ask why. They say : 'Why did not the League stop the fighting between Poland and Soviet Russia, or between Greece and Turkey ? ' This brings us to the first point in the Procedure of the Council, which needs some explanation. The League is not and cannot be, in the present state of affairs, a sort of supernatural being hovering in space, as it were, and swooping down on a single nation. Its French title : ' Société des Nations ' must be taken literally : it is a society. It consists of members, and each of those members is a sovereign State which is not likely in the near future to form itself with the others into a federal unit. The action of the Council, therefore, cannot be automatic. The Council cannot meet if it is not summoned, and it cannot be summoned except by the initiative of one of the members of the League.

This is very clearly shown by the provisions of articles 11, 12, and 15 of the Covenant. An appeal must be made in each case, and addressed either to the Acting President or to the Secretary-General, specifying the object of the dispute and indicating, as far as possible, the article in the Covenant the application of which is desired. If no appeal is received from any member, no action is possible, because that action is not started by anybody, and the League cannot be accused if anything follows, because the responsibility of the League in fact resolves itself into the responsibility of each of its members. If none of the members of the League moves, the League itself cannot move. The League does not consist of a body of officials in this building. I agree we are extremely distinguished people, but after all, we cannot start an action which would bind sovereign States to appear before the Council, or which would oblige the Council to sit and discuss a case. We are the servants and not the masters of this institution. It is necessary to say this, because of misunderstandings which have sometimes found their way into the press.

The appeal is not necessarily made by one of the parties concerned; it can be made by any member of the League. This, of course, makes the situation easier. By paragraph 2 of article 11 of the Covenant, each member has ' the friendly right to bring to the attention of the Assembly or of the Council, any circumstance whatever affecting international relations which threatens to disturb international peace, or the good understanding between nations on which peace depends '. This is not a theoretical provision; it has been applied several times. Very early in the history of the League—in July 1920—the British Government made use of that provision for bringing before the Council the question of the Aaland Islands, which was likely to create trouble, and was creating considerable friction between Sweden and Finland. Neither Sweden nor Finland had formally asked that the case should be brought before the League. It is probable that Great Britain did not act without knowing that at least one and probably both of the parties would accept her initiative. But at any rate, the Power which brought the question before the League was not an interested party. A similar case occurred (and here again the British Government was the initiator) when the attention of the Council was called in November 1924 to the difficult situation and the risk created by the presence of Serbian troops in Albanian territory, the frontier of which was not at that time clearly defined.

I have quoted the second paragraph of article 11 of the Covenant. It can be used sometimes by the parties themselves. I have shown the advantage of the provision is that it enables a non-interested State to bring a case before the Council. The parties themselves, however, may find some advantage in using that article. The wording of the paragraph I read is purposely vague, and does not suggest anything too dramatic or tragic. It makes it possible to bring a case before the Council without appearing to say that the house is on fire. A party will bring a case before the Council before it becomes too bad, simply saying : ' I call the attention of the members of the Council to a situation which threatens to disturb relations between neighbouring States.'

There is, of course, a risk in this. The result might be to induce Governments to bring a case before the League without making any effort to settle it by direct negotiations or by means of conciliation, but, as I will show later, the practice of the Council is to discourage any appeal which, if the circumstances permitted it, has not been preceded by attempts to settle the case by direct negotiation or by some judicial or conciliatory procedure.

The Covenant, by many of its provisions, encourages direct understandings, and every method of conciliation, arbitration, or judicial settlement, the parties always being left to choose between such methods and an appeal to the Council. It might be said that there is no body in the world which has so little *amour propre* or professional greed as the Council of the League. It does not wish to deal with questions, and if any question can be settled without it, it prefers that that should be done, and it always encourages people who are on the point of coming before it to try something simpler first.

That is shown by the provisions of articles 12 and 15 of the Covenant, and the Council has repeatedly said that if there is any hope of settling a dispute by other means, it will not insist on the use of its authority.

This goes far to explain—although if the matter is to be studied historically, other considerations would necessarily have to be taken into account—an incident which has been very much commented on, the famous Corfu incident of 1923. Italian officers who represented the Conference of Ambassadors in Paris having been murdered near the Albanian frontier, and Greece, after the Italian Ultimatum, having applied practically simultaneously to the Council of the League and to the Conference of Ambassadors, saying to the latter body : ' You have been offended and we will accept whatever your decision may be ', and Italy having objected to the jurisdiction of the Council and accepted that of the Conference of Ambassadors, it was extraordinarily difficult for the Council of the League not to wait until the result of the procedure that had been accepted by both parties was known, and it was in conformity with precedent that the Council waited, and tried to facilitate a direct understanding on that basis. What it could do, and in fact did, was to help by making certain suggestions, and whatever judgement may be passed by independent persons on what happened afterwards, it is a fact that the incident came to an end, reparations were fixed, and the Island of Corfu evacuated.

If I mention this famous case, it is only from the point of view of procedure. The Council, in a rather difficult situation, created by the circumstances of the incident, was guided by a general principle which is contained in several articles of the Covenant, and had been applied in other cases.

The Council can act only on the application of one or other of its members. Those members are, of course, obliged to appeal to the Council by the fact that they have signed the Covenant if no other peaceful method is likely to succeed. There is no doubt about this from the point of view of principle, but doubts have arisen from time to time as to whether great and powerful nations, although theoretically bound by their adherence to the Covenant, would in fact bring their cases before the Council, other methods having failed. This gives particular importance to an agreement like that of Locarno. There is not much in that agreement which did not exist before in the Covenant, but it is a solemn repetition of the Covenant applying to certain nations which are likely, if any trouble arises between them, to find themselves in a more dangerous and difficult situation than many other nations, and it is an agreement between nations which, if they left any doubt about their intentions, might be suspected of forgetting some of the pledges they have taken by the Covenant under the pressure of grave circumstances.

This gives the matter supreme importance, even if you consider that the Locarno Agreement and others similar to it which may be come to in other parts of the world do nothing but repeat what is said in the Covenant.

The Council, of course, meets as soon as it can if the case

is an urgent one. It may be of interest to recall what happened when the first case to be dealt with as one of urgency occurred last autumn—the case of the dispute between Bulgaria and Greece. Bulgarian territory having been invaded by a small part of the Greek Army, the urgency provisions of the Covenant were applied. In a case like that, the Secretary-General has the right, as soon as he has received an appeal—an appeal, of course, must come : if there is no appeal there is no action—to summon himself the Council, without referring, as he does in other cases, to the President for the time being.

That is what happened. The President was immediately informed by telephone, and the thing was done so quickly that, the appeal having been received on Friday morning, it was possible to arrange a meeting in Paris for the following Monday, at which all the members of the Council were represented—the Swedish representative having come by air.

On that same day—Monday, 26 October—a resolution was taken, fixing a time-limit of twenty-four hours before the expiration of which the Council had to be informed that orders had been given on both sides of the frontier to withdraw the Greek and Bulgarian troops, with another limit of sixty hours for the complete execution of such orders. That was a very interesting rehearsal of what should happen in a grave case.

We have now passed the preliminary stage, and will suppose the Council has met. The next point is the presence of the parties at the Council Table. Their right to be present is recognized by paragraph 5 of article 4 of the Covenant. The parties receive an invitation to be present at the Session of the Council at the same time as the ordinary members of that body, and their representatives at the opening of the Session are invited by the President to take their seats at the table. A literal application of article 4 might mean that no meeting was possible without their presence, and that no decision could be taken without their concurrence. This would no doubt lead to grave difficulties. There is a practical contradiction between a provision of that kind, if applied with absolute strictness, and the practical necessity for consulting separately with each of the parties in order to prepare a compromise or a possible solution. Some means have to be found to reconcile the recognized principle with actual needs in each particular case. It may be said that there is no general principle, but there has been a practical method adopted, in accordance with the needs of each case. Sometimes the members of the Council have asked the representatives of the parties to withdraw, to give an opportunity to their colleagues to discuss between themselves. That, of course, is quite correct, because there is formal consent. This procedure was applied in the case I have just referred to—the case between Bulgaria and Greece last autumn. Sometimes this procedure is not followed, because the members of the Council cannot be denied their right of meeting, not exactly as a Council, but perhaps some, or almost all, of them together, to exchange privately their views and prepare their discussion. We have repeatedly seen this, because a private exchange of views between members of the Council may lead to progress much more easily.

What must be done, of course, in each case, is everything possible to prevent any suspicion of the use of secret methods against the interests of one or all of the parties. The parties themselves would be very unwise, however, if that suspicion made it impossible to take action the object of which, in fact, would be to make a solution between them possible.

It is impossible to find in the Covenant a general article saying that a decision in a case interesting to members of the League can be taken without their consent. Under paragraph 7 of article 15 it is said only that a Report is deemed to have been adopted unanimously by the Council if approved by all the members, excluding the parties to the dispute; but this particular provision does not apply to all cases. It applies specifically to the final conclusions adopted by the Council, and published when no terms of settlement have been agreed to by the parties. This is a particular application, but from that particular application the principle has been, in fact, extended, and without at any time laying down a hard and fast principle, but taking into account the particular difficulties of each case and leaving as much as possible to expediency and common sense, the Council has established the practice that it can and will determine and bring forward its recommendations without the consent of the parties. That consent, as I will show you in a few minutes, has to come later, because what is fixed in that way is only a recommendation, and a recommendation has to be accepted, so that that final reservation remains. It would, therefore, be mere folly to have a preliminary reservation first.

I have dealt with the case of members of the League having a dispute with one another, and coming before the Council of the League and being invited to sit at the Council Table as members of the Council. This, of course, is something quite new, and shows a great difference between the methods of the Council and judicial methods proper. It makes it possible to deal with cases where probably the parties would not agree to a decision being given unless they were members of the body giving the decision.

This principle, however, has been extended to States which are not members of the League if there is a dispute between one of them and a member of the League. This follows from article 17 of the Covenant, for one of the first things the Council deems just is to make the rights of each party correspond with the obligations they are asked to assume. If a State not a member of the League is asked to assume the obligations of membership for the purposes of a dispute, it must logically also be invested with the rights of a member of the League for the same period. This very natural principle has been accepted and acted upon from the beginning.

For instance, one of the early cases dealt with in the League was the one I mentioned before—the dispute between Finland and Sweden as to the fate of the Aaland Islands. At that time, Sweden was a member of the League and Finland was not, but Finland was at once invited to sit at the Council Table with the same obligations and also the same rights as Sweden. Similarly, the Turkish representative, when the Mosul question was discussed recently, was admitted on the same conditions.

Would the refusal of a State not a member of the League to appear before the Council paralyse the action of that body? It would, of course, create very serious embarrassment, and in this connexion I can instance an interesting case. In 1923 the Finnish Government called the attention of the Council to the alleged violation by the Soviet Government of Russia of its promises concerning the autonomy of Eastern Karelia, which is inhabited by a Finnish population. The Soviet Government was asked to send a representative to Geneva, but refused to do so. That was before a Russian representative had been murdered at Lausanne, so that reason could not be given for the refusal. The Council could do nothing but ask the members of the League who were in political relations with Moscow to offer their good offices for the opening of negotiations, which was a very mild way of dealing with the question. The Soviet Government declined to enter into any negotiations on a question which, they maintained, was solely within their domestic jurisdiction. Finland then asked the Council to consult the Permanent Court of International Justice on the question of whether the point was one of international interest or of an international character, and whether the assurances given by the Soviet Government to the Government of Finland in the Treaty of Dorpat concerning the autonomy of Eastern Karelia constituted an international act which should have international sanctions. The Council acceded to that request, and put the question to the Court, but the Soviet Government refused to appear before the Court or to send the Court any written documents. This embarrassed the Court very much, and it considered it could not give any opinion on a question regarding which one of the interested parties had refused to supply any information whatsoever. It can be said, therefore, that in this case the negative attitude taken up by the Soviet Government of Russia blocked the way and made it impossible to go any farther. There is, in fact, no means of bringing before the Council, against its will, a State which is not a member of the League, but it does not follow the League would be powerless against such resistance if it resulted in acts of violence. Nothing happens as long as the refusal to appear before the Council or the Court is followed by nothing else, but if such an attitude was followed by a resort to violence, the provisions of articles 16 and 17 of the Covenant would be applicable. While, therefore, the Coun-

cil cannot compel a State which remains outside the League
to answer its summons, and still less to accept its recommendations, it retains its full power to protect the members
of the League against any aggression which may follow
that refusal, assuming, of course, that the member of the
League in question accepts and carries out the obligations
it undertook in signing the Covenant.

What happens after the Council has met the interested
parties has to be shortly examined. The members of the
Council have before them an appeal made by one party, with
all the supplementary documents which they may choose to
lay before it. When the Council meets and the representatives of the parties have been invited to take their seats at the
Table the work begins. In each case the Council appoints
one of its members as rapporteur—a word borrowed from
French parliamentary procedure which is used in all League
documents in both languages. The rapporteur is the member of the Council in charge of the question. As a rule he
must be the representative of a State which has as little
national interest as possible in the dispute itself. That is
why, when the question of Mosul between Iraq and Great
Britain on the one side and Turkey on the other was discussed, the member in charge was the representative of
Sweden. Again, for the Polish and Lithuanian dispute the
Belgian representative, who had no interest in the matter,
acted as rapporteur. The rapporteur presents to the Council
an introductory statement, prepared with the assistance of
the Secretariat, not giving any views or suggestions, but
simply calling the attention of the Council to the main points
of the dispute before them, explaining its nature and adding,
if the case calls for it, a few legal comments. The rapporteur
also helps in any negotiations that have to be carried out

during the course of the dispute between the parties under the auspices of the Council. He follows the question stage by stage, and at the end of the procedure, after ascertaining the views of his colleagues, he drafts a final report and resolution, which, without any exception—considering how it is prepared—is always adopted by the Council. The rapporteur is an original feature in the procedure of the Council of the League, and has been found of great practical use.

Should a question be particularly difficult or delicate, or should the rapporteur not desire to have the full responsibility exclusively on his shoulders, the Council will appoint a Committee of its own members to examine and deal with the case—generally a Committee of three, but sometimes of four and five. That is what happened in the Upper Silesia and Mosul questions. In the latter case the Swedish rapporteur, in the later stages of the procedure, was assisted by other members.

Apart from such Committees as that, from time to time the Council uses other Committees or Commissions of different types. Sometimes the Council requires to have information collected on the spot. For instance, in the Aaland Islands case a Commission was sent to the Islands as well as to both the Finnish and Swedish capitals, to bring all sorts of information to the Council and suggest a solution. The members of that body were an American judge, a Belgian diplomatist, and an ex-President of the Swiss Confederation. Sometimes a Commission will not only be a Commission for information, but will also negotiate and prepare a solution. That was the case with the Commission presided over by Mr. Norman Davis, which was sent to Memel at the end of 1923 to prepare the Statute of the Memel territory. It not only went to Lithuania, Memel, and Poland, but came back to Geneva with a Lithuanian representative to discuss, article by article, a Convention which was eventually adopted and has been the basis of the settlement.

Another type of Commission is the Commission that was sent to Mesopotamia to study the frontier between Turkey and Iraq in the winter of 1924–5. Sometimes a Commission of that kind will also have executive duties. That was the case with the Commission presided over by a British Ambassador, Sir Horace Rumbold, which was sent to the Greek-Bulgarian frontier last autumn after the incident that occurred there, and which had not only to report on that event, but also to decide finally upon certain indemnities.

Sometimes a Commission has simply to follow the result of a resolution or recommendation of the Council. For instance, in the dispute between Poland and Lithuania, the first thing the Council did in the autumn of 1920 was to send a Military Committee to the spot, and that Committee actually stopped the fighting between those two countries, although the whole affair is not generally quoted as one of the successes of the League, because the relations between the two countries concerned have not become exactly friendly. It is, nevertheless, the case that that Commission succeeded in stopping fighting which had actually broken out, and by its presence in the contested territory for a number of months made a renewal of fighting on a large scale impossible.

I might, of course, quote other and less interesting types of Commissions, but you will see there is a great variety in the formation of and functions allotted to them.

When the Council finds in its way a difficulty of a legal nature which appears to be too serious for it to dispose of immediately, perhaps with the help of the Legal Section of the Secretariat, it will ask the Permanent Court of International Justice for an advisory opinion. I do not intend to give a lecture on that subject, however, because it would take too long and would deal with really a separate matter. I simply mention it as one of the various steps taken by the Council in the cases I am describing.

The first difficulty of this kind which was met by the Council happened at a time when the Court did not exist. It was at the time of the Aaland Islands dispute. The Finnish Government declared to start with, that though they accepted the invitation to appear before the Council, they would ask the Council not to proceed because the question was a purely internal one, concerning Finland alone. There was some disagreement between the inhabitants of the Aaland Islands and the State of Finland, just as there might be between the inhabitants of Long Island and the authorities of New York State, but, they said, it was not for any outside body to come between them. There is an article in the Covenant which, in such a case, makes it the Council's duty to declare it will have nothing to do with the matter. The other party maintained that the case was of international interest. It was found necessary to have a legal opinion on this subject, and the Court (the formation of which was provided for by article 14 of the Covenant) not being established at that time, a Special Commission was formed consisting of jurists of international reputation, who gave the opinion that, as the declaration by the inhabitants of the Aaland Islands, showing some preference for Sweden, had taken place at a moment when Finland had ceased to be part of the Russian State, and had not become recognized as an independent Power, it might be considered that the question was a judicial one, and called for an international settlement.

Since it has been established the Court has been consulted

several times on points which were considered as being of a legal nature, though they were sometimes closely mixed up with purely political considerations. To give you a typical example of the consultation of the Court by the Council in a small case which is of real interest, however, from the point of view of procedure, I will refer to the dispute between Czechoslovakia and Poland over the Valley of Jaworzyna, a small and picturesque valley in the Carpathian mountains, devoid of economic and military interest, but which had become a subject of bitter contention between the two States, and was endangering their relations. The question had been brought before the Allied Powers and before the Conference of Ambassadors, and many other ways of settling it had been tried and failed. The difficulty was that the Czechs maintained that the question was of a purely legal character. They said that a certain decision had already been taken which gave them that piece of territory, and that it was against any principle of justice to open the case again. The Polish Government carefully avoided discussing this, but pointed out that economic and other considerations made it more natural that the territory in question should be allotted to Poland. They refused to examine the legal aspect of the matter, and called attention rather to its substance. For this reason it was impossible to bring the case before the Court, because this could not be done without the consent of both parties. Those who thought the question was simply whether there was or was not a previous decision giving them that control were of opinion that the Court should decide, but the other party did not wish the Court to have anything to do with it, and maintained the question should be examined on its own merits.

The Council, after a preliminary examination of the case,

came to the conclusion that no progress could be made before the legal point had been settled, and Poland, having accepted the jurisdiction of the Council, could not refuse this recommendation. The Council accordingly asked the Court to give an Opinion on the point, and the Opinion of the Court was entirely in favour of the Czechs. The question then came back to the Council, and it was very advisable that it did, because, in spite of the fact that from the legal point of view the rights of the Czechs were indisputable, the economic and other difficulties pointed out by the Poles did exist, and it was possible for the Council, after recording the opinion of the Court, to add some suggestions as to direct negotiations between the parties with a view to making certain practical arrangements on small points, like communication between local markets, rights of passage of inhabitants, and the use of the territory for tourist purposes. This resulted in a very good local Convention which did more than anything else to do away with the bad effects of what had been a long controversy, and bring about a friendly feeling between the two nations. This is a very small case, but it shows how, things being as they are and considering the present mentality of sovereign States, something can be done by combining the two methods I have mentioned. This does not contradict what Dr. Scott said earlier this evening; I should like to quote his words: 'There is no limit to the possibilities of judicial settlement except the limits created by the willingness of States to submit to such a settlement.' This very irregular and purely practical method has been, in certain cases, and may be in the future, the way to obviate difficulties created by the present mentality of sovereign States.

The result of all the procedure I have been describing is

not resolutions binding on the parties in the strict sense of the word, but recommendations. A recommendation is something which can be accepted or rejected. The Council, if its recommendation is rejected, has no other means of action than to make a Report and publish it, retaining at the same time its right, if the party which has not submitted resorts to violence, to exercise other powers. It cannot, however, impose its will, because the Members of the League are sovereign Powers.

To say this at the end of a long explanation of procedure may create a feeling of discouragement in my audience. Sceptical critics will say that the Council's power is not very great if it is limited to settling disputes when the parties are willing to accept a settlement. I could, of course, cite a number of cases where the parties, before coming to the Council, pledge themselves to accept and execute its recommendations. In other cases it is not so easy. There is, of course, room for irony from people inclined to be ironical, but if we look at the actual cases which have been brought here and the results already achieved in spite, not only of the incompleteness of some of the provisions of the Covenant, but of the great difficulties which faced the League during its first years of existence when faith in the League was not at all general, and when so many difficulties and prejudices existed after the greatest conflict that has ever taken place in this part of the world, we may be rather surprised by the results already achieved.

The worst that can be said, after all, against the procedure of the Council for settling disputes, is that it presupposes a minimum of good faith on the part of the interested Powers. That is perfectly true, but if it is only a foolish delusion to build anything on such a foundation, why should

Treaties be signed or laws enacted, and why should commercial bills be circulated? No transactions whatever between nations or individuals would be possible without the assumption of a minimum of good faith, and no courts and no tribunals could have been built up if there was not something of that kind at the basis of them. The assumption that it is possible to build on that foundation does not seem to be so absurd if we consider that there are such things as organized, civilized nations, and active and effective systems of justice in the world. What is true is that the Council cannot hope to achieve results if it is not supported by the earnest will of all its members. It is for every nation which is pledged to observe and uphold the Covenant to reinforce the authority they have set up in that way, and in the countries which have adhered to the League of Nations it is for every individual citizen to see what his Government is doing in the way of observing the pledges it has taken.

CHAPTER V

THE PROGRESS IN EUROPE OF ECONOMIC
RECONSTRUCTION

Sir ARTHUR SALTER :

I HAVE been asked to give the best picture I can in the
short time at my disposal of the efforts which the world
has been making in these last eight years to recover from the
material damage caused by the war. It is obvious that the
choice of so large a subject for so short a time presents many
considerable difficulties, and I shall necessarily have to be
guilty of many serious omissions, and shall have to make some
statements in too absolute a form through lack of time to
make the necessary qualifications. To some extent the
picture I give can be no more than a personal impression.

I would like at the outset to say one word of warning.
It is my experience that many discussions during the last
eight years of the economic condition of the world have
been characterized by an exaggerated pessimism. Speaking as
I do after a year which undoubtedly represents something
like a set-back from the progress previously realized, I think
it the more important, so that you may have a fair perspective of the picture I wish to present, to give at once a general
warning against a too exaggerated pessimism.

Economists during the last eight years (and even during
the last twelve, since their mistakes began before the conclusion of the war) have been inclined to under-estimate the
extent to which man is an adaptable animal; they have
tended to consider the variations and changes in the medium
in which man has to work without allowing sufficiently for
the extent to which man himself is a variable factor and to an

amazing extent adapts and adjusts himself to the difficulties which confront him. We all know that men refused to stop fighting until years after the economists had told them they must be exhausted, and since the war men have in millions refused to die although all the economists told them they must be starving.

During the last eight years there has been too much ill-founded talk about the ' ruin of civilization '—a phrase which did express the legitimate apprehensions of the years immediately succeeding the war, but is an improper expresssion of any reasonable anxieties which should now be entertained or could reasonably have been entertained during the last three years. It may be that our civilization will perish, but if so it will either be through some follies which cannot fairly be ascribed to the last war or through the even greater folly of falling into another war. In that sense we have turned the corner : whatever difficulties we have ahead of us, we have not, as a necessary result of what happened during the war, to fear that the fabric of our civilization as we know it will this time fall.

To complete my present point, let me remind you—or perhaps inform you—of what I think is a very notable fact. Already by the year 1924, so far as it is possible to ascertain with exactitude, the total production of the world had not only reached pre-war proportions but exceeded them to as great an extent as the increase in population since the war. My figures are based on the production of basic commodities only, but I think the legitimate inference is that taking the world as a whole the total wealth, the total annual income, the total consumed wealth and, therefore, the total average of material comfort were already in 1924 as high as before the war.

Having said that, let me add that that does not mean we have recovered ground in every country or even in every continent, still less in every class in the world. The impoverishment of many parts of the world has been offset by the greater prosperity of other parts. It is true, of course, that the continent of Europe is, as a whole, somewhat poorer than before the war, and that the average wealth is probably somewhat less, while certainly some countries and some classes in many countries are very substantially worse off than they were before the war. These countries and these classes make up an absolute mass of impoverishment that still calls for serious attention, and it is the troubles that result from that impoverishment that I intend to deal with this morning.

Before I attempt to give the brief history of what has been done during the past eight years, or an estimate of the stage which has now been reached, I had better outline what it is that is essentially wrong in the economic condition of the world as a result of the war. We must first dispose of quite a number of red herrings. What is essentially wrong with the world is not, in the first place, an inadequacy either in the resources of nature or in the capacity of man to deal with them. The resources of nature at our disposal are much what they have been before, and the capacity of man to exploit them is continually increasing.

Nor is it that we have a world surplus population. It may be that that will arrive, but it is distant yet. There are large spaces in the world either unexploited or only partially exploited. At the most we have local blobs of surplus population here and there, and for the most part even those local surpluses are only relatively surpluses. The low level of production and of wealth, which itself is due to troubles of disorganization, reduces the total amount of material resources which those countries themselves might exploit were the causes of that disorganization removed.

Nor, in the third place, is it that man has shown, as people were inclined to think he very soon would show after the war, a special disinclination to work. You will remember Mr. Hoover's famous phrase, ' The demoralized productivity of the world.' You will remember the prophecy, which for a time seemed not unreasonable, that man would refuse to return to the daily routine of work after the disturbance of the war. I am not going to say that we all work as hard as we should, and certainly we do not all work as hard as we could. We never have, and we never shall, and personally I do not think we ought to. After all, man does not live by bread alone. I do think, however, that as one of the special causes of the impoverishment resulting from the war an increased disinclination to work cannot be properly assigned a major place.

Nor, in the fourth place—and here I come to a fallacy which has deceived many people—is the root-cause of our trouble due to a material destruction of wealth during the war. Let us never forget that the great bulk of material wealth that was destroyed during the war was created during the war, and by special exertions during the period of the war. Most fortunately the extent to which in any literal or physical sense posterity can be made to pay for a war is very limited, for the simple and conclusive reason that the shell which is going to be fired to-day must have been made yesterday and cannot be made to-morrow. If we hold firmly on to that simple fact we shall see our way through a great many of the fallacies that have gathered round the whole of the debt problem.

In what I am going to say now I am speaking, not of interallied debts or of any other kind of international debts, but of the great internal debts which oppressed the finances of almost every belligerent country after the war. Many people seem to think that the existence of an internal debt of some seven thousand million pounds in Great Britain means that the annual charge in respect of that debt is so much to be deducted from what would otherwise be the total consumable wealth of England each year. That is not so at all. The total consumable wealth of the world and, subject to external obligations, of any country, consists in what it produces minus something to be assigned for capital investment. The rest is consumed year by year as it is produced and is reflected in the average standard of material comfort enjoyed by that country ; and, except to the extent to which the existence of debts may discourage production, the amount produced and the amount consumed is not changed by the fact that there is a large internal debt. Its distribution is largely changed, but the average level of comfort is not necessarily changed at all. That does not mean that debts are not as such a regrettable fact and should not be removed if they can, but it does mean that it is an entirely wrong thing to take, as many people do, the burden of the debt of a country and say that, but for that debt, the country would be so much better off, and everybody would earn so much more per annum or per week. Debts, troublesome as they have been as an element in disorganization, have not themselves, apart from that indirect effect, been a major cause of that impoverishment with which we are now dealing.

If we have disposed of these red herrings, what then is the general character of that which has gone wrong as a result of the war ? In general it is really a problem of disorganization and not of destruction. The loss to the world due to disorganization is immensely greater than the loss due to actual material destruction which, great as it may be and is, in relation to the particular country which was the scene of the conflict, is small in relation to the productive capacity of the world as a whole. The disorganization due to the war, on the other hand, is a thing that through all these eight years has been, in practically every country in the world, reducing the standard of prosperity and of comfort which would otherwise have been attained.

What has happened essentially is that a world whose level of prosperity, whose standard of living, whose population itself, was based largely on a system which secured, in comparison with anything we have since known, an easy and frictionless interchange of the commodities of every part of the world with every other part, has had its total wealth reduced by the effect of every kind of impediment and maladjustment being placed between the producer and the consumer.

Let me just repeat that to make it clear. The level of wealth and of average prosperity throughout the world at any moment depends on three factors : firstly, the resources of nature ; secondly, the capacity of man to exploit them ; and, thirdly, the existence of a system which enables the products of one country or of one class to be exchanged without friction, without waste, and without cost, with the products of other countries and other classes.

The resources of nature are not reduced. The capacity of man to exploit them is continually increasing. But what has happened essentially since the war is that, through a number of causes to which I will refer in more detail in a moment, the system of interchange has been interrupted, arrested, impeded, and in some cases shattered. That is what has gone wrong in the world, and if, in following the history of these eight years and in attempting to estimate the stage we have now reached, we wish to arrive at accurate conclusions, we have always to bear in mind the conception not of destruction but of disorganization, the idea not of too little production, not of the inadequacy of man or of nature, but of the impediments to the interchange of goods between one set of specialists and another. If we do that we shall have a much juster estimate of what has happened and of where we have arrived.

What have been the causes of this disorganization? I think they have been of three different kinds. In the first place there have been the disorganizations due to the depreciation of currencies—to the financial troubles of the world. That is the first, and, during these eight years, perhaps the greatest of the causes of disorganization. In the second place they have been due to the character of the economic policies pursued by the different countries of the world during these eight years. And in the third place, apart from these two causes for which Government or central authorities such as banks are responsible, there is beyond that the intrinsic difficulties of individual adjustment. Throughout the world the bonds of custom and tradition, of steady demand and steady supply, which bound the customer to the producer, have been shattered. Needs have changed, old connexions have been broken, and it is a long and almost interminable process to reknit these snapped threads of international commerce. This is a thing which Governments and central authorities can do little to assist. It is a work full of innumerable details in which the numerous producers, customers, and working men of the world each have to take their part. It is a work which in the nature of things is too complicated to permit of exact description, but it is a work which, if it cannot be greatly assisted by direct and positive action from central sources, can nevertheless be, and has been, enormously impeded and in some cases rendered impossible, either by the omission of Governments to do things they clearly ought to do or by their positive action in imposing impediments that ought not to have been imposed.

These, then, are the three main causes of this world disorganization which in turn is the cause of the impoverishment that is now attracting our attention. Let me turn to each of them, and particularly to the first two.

We come now to the old question of inflation. I say ' old ' inasmuch as it is a question about which most of us have been thinking a very great deal in these last eight years ; although it is a new question in the sense that practically none of us had heard the word fifteen years ago. What is inflation ? What has been happening in the world these last eight years ? What has really happened in a few words is this. When the war finished practically all the finance ministers of the belligerent countries and of many others found reluctant taxpayers and enormous current needs. They could not at once compress their expenditure nor could they extort current revenue sufficient to meet it. In those circumstances, one after another, they resorted to the device of printing papermoney. As this money was printed its value necessarily and inevitably fell. During the early stages this process seemed to have, and indeed had, if we put aside questions of justice, very considerable advantages. It provided the Finance Minister with the ready-money he could not otherwise obtain, and it relieved his country, overborne by the enormous internal debt incurred during the war, of a great deal of the real burden of that debt, at the expense it is true of the bond-holders who held it.   In the third place it had the effect, perhaps unfairly so far as competitors were concerned, of stimulating trade.

The trouble with inflation, however, is that, considerable and real as may be its immediate advantages, it is extraordinarily difficult to stop it once it has begun, and the longer it goes on the harder it is to stop it ; while, if it is not stopped it ultimately and inevitably involves the ruin of all concerned.

Most of my audience I suppose come from countries which have known something of the disadvantage of increased prices, and may have known something, as in England, of a somewhat depreciated currency, but have not experienced what it means to live in a country whose national currency has gone utterly to pieces.   To most of us in America and in England the foreign exchanges are a matter of real interest perhaps to bankers, financiers, economists, and so on ; but hardly to other people.   When you live in a country where the currency has gone utterly to pieces, however, and where it may be, as it has been latterly, not an extravagance but an economy, to light your cigar with a bank-note rather than with a match, and where bank-notes have been printed when their value after printing was not one-fiftieth of that of the paper and ink needed to create them, it is another matter. When you get to that stage, as, unless the process of inflation is arrested, you do get, you discover for the first time the extent to which the whole of your economic life depends on the existence of some practical and reliable medium of exchange between what you are creating and making and what other people are creating and making which you would like to have in return.   When you get to that stage, a stage at which the value of a currency may fall, as in several cases it has fallen, by 50 or a 100 per cent. between 10 a.m. and

2 p.m. the same day ; when, as Mr. Keynes said, what the economists call the velocity of circulation attains its most vivid illustration in the picture of a man who, having been paid, let us say, in old German marks at 10 a.m., no sooner gets them than he runs as fast as he can to a bank to change them for good foreign exchange—when you get to that stage of affairs you have something that necessarily impedes, reduces, and arrests the whole productive life of the country.

Over a large part of Europe we have had an experience as extreme as that. Over a larger part of Europe we have had a demoralization of the currency which, while not so far utterly destroying the system of internal exchange within the country, has been sufficient to wreck, or arrest and distort, the external foreign trade, and incidentally to inflict great loss not only on the country whose currency is demoralized but upon other countries with whom that country's international trade normally takes place.

What, generally speaking, has been the course of the world's efforts in dealing with this first and greatest of problems during these last eight years ? The League of Nations itself early recognized that it was a problem which had very important international aspects, and it summoned the Brussels Conference in September 1920, and there there were drawn up several resolutions which for years afterwards served as a guide for those who, in one country after another, were attempting to re-establish and reform their currencies. Unfortunately, valuable as the result of these general resolutions was, it proved not to be sufficient. Some countries, indeed, succeeded in stabilizing, but for the most part in the years that followed currencies continued to depreciate and the problem of inflation got worse.

In the year 1922 a great effort was made by the Genoa

Conference and the negotiations which preceded it. For some months the world had sufficient confidence in that Conference to think that its problem was solved, and perhaps for three months about that time practically all the currencies in Europe remained stable. The Conference was held, and, though it had some incidental results of minor value, it was after all a failure, and, immediately after its conclusion, the steady downward progress continued ; so that, by the end of the same year—1922—some currencies had not only depreciated very much further, but had become utterly disorganized. We have had the utter disorganization of the Austrian, the Hungarian, the German, the Polish, and the Russian currencies. By the end of the year 1922 it was impossible to foresee what would be the end. Obviously, unless the process were arrested in those countries it meant ruin in those countries themselves and widespread ruin in other countries also. Obviously too, most, if not all, of those countries were incapable of effective reform by their own unaided efforts. It was at that crisis that the League supplemented the assistance it had already rendered by means of counsel and advice by a practical demonstration of what could be done in the great experiment of the reconstruction of Austria.

I do not propose to describe that experiment to you in detail this morning. I will only remind you that in 1922 it seemed the most hopeless case in the world, and that, by contrast, just two months ago the Council of the League of Nations was able to certify that the financial stability of Austria was assured.

That first successful experiment in Austria was followed by an equally and, in some respects, even more successful experiment in Hungary, and two months ago, at the same date, the Council was able to certify that the financial stability of Hungary was also assured.

Largely as a result of those two successful experiments, and particularly of the first, it became possible in the year 1924 for the even greater case of Germany, where the currency had been even further demoralized, and where the extent and character of the ruin was even greater and more serious, to be dealt with. It was possible at last to arrest that process, first of all by internal efforts made in Germany itself, and then by the efforts of the Dawes Committee, without which it is quite clear the internal effort of Germany by itself would not have been successful. I have no time now to point out to you the way in which at nearly every crucial point in the work of the reconstruction of Germany use was made of the experience gained in the two great League experiments that had preceded it.

Largely encouraged by the results in those three cases, other countries whose currencies had gone to pieces made a great effort to pull themselves together. In particular, Poland, watching closely the Austrian experiment, made a most remarkable effort to secure the stabilization of her currency, which for over a year seemed completely successful. More or less at the same time (though I cannot claim under a similar inspiration !) Russia, whose currency had gone to pieces, established her chevonetz, related to gold.

You therefore had, in the years 1923–4, the remarkable fact that all the currencies which had gone utterly to pieces had been brought back to stability and were, for the time being at least, related to gold. It began to look as if this first great step in reconstruction was successfully completed. Whereas in 1923 currency depreciation had been the principal obstacle to international trade, in the year 1924 the fluctuations and depreciations were within very narrow limits. There was not a single currency in the world whose average value in January 1925 was lower by more than 5 per cent. than its value in January 1924.

A year ago to-day it really looked as if we were within sight of complete financial stabilization. Not only had the currencies which had been utterly disorganized been brought back to an apparently permanent stability, but other currencies, not absolutely stable, had confined their fluctuations within such narrow limits that for the time it was possible to say that this greatest of all impediments to international trade had ceased to impede the traffic of the world.

It was at that time and in those circumstances that the League of Nations thought the time had arrived for at least preparing for the second great effort at reconstruction, and accordingly arranged, in September last, for the preparation for an Economic Conference ; such a conference being only likely to be valuable and practical, as I shall explain shortly, if the first stage—that of financial reconstruction—is safely passed and out of the way.

I regret to say that during the past year there has been a very notable and serious set-back in the progress that had been reached a year ago. It has been a set-back curiously coincident with and corresponding to the somewhat similar falling-off we have seen in the general international political position of the world from the time of Locarno and during the subsequent year. It is not my intention to refer to the political aspect at all, and I will only say this : that just as I believe the set-back in the economic sphere, serious as it is, is only temporary, so do I believe that the set-back in the political progress of the world, serious though it has been, is only temporary.

In the financial sphere the set-back has for the time been undoubtedly serious. During this last year or so we have seen a renewed crash of the French franc. We have seen an attempt to stabilize the Belgian franc, followed by a tragic failure. We have seen the Polish zloty, after remaining stable for over a year, fall to half its value. We have seen weaknesses in the Russian currency, and a fall in the Greek drachma, and we have seen troubles elsewhere which I need not describe in more detail, just as, outside the financial sphere, we have had revolutions in two countries, and even more frequent and complete changes in governments and the characteristics of governments, and in my country a great and disastrous strike. We have, we must recognize, had a serious set-back during the past year, though, as I say, I am convinced that, taking a long view over these eight years as a whole, it is rather a temporary eddy than a change in the general tide of progress.

So much for the first great cause of disorganization. I would now like to say a few words about the second.

Undoubtedly the level of prosperity possible to the world has not been attained during these eight years, partly because of the character of the economic policies which have been adopted by the different countries of the world. You will not expect me, an official of this organization, to explain in great detail and in regard to each country what I think is wrong with the economic policy of that country. I will just say this, quite generally : whatever may be the reasons which lead to a country imposing an impediment to the free exchange of goods between one set of producers and another, and however real the advantages which may be derived from such a policy, it necessarily means a loss to the world as a whole ; and, therefore, the more that policy is pursued throughout the world the lower must necessarily be the general average level of prosperity throughout the world.

As soon as we have got past the stage of financial reconstruction it is quite clear that there is a great work before the world, and perhaps particularly before the League of Nations, in attempting to survey the field of economic policies and problems as we have attempted earlier to survey the field of financial policies and problems. It is with this idea that the League has arranged for the preparation for a great Economic Conference, which will have two principal aims : to search out what it is in the policies of the world that will tend to increase the material prosperity of the world, and to search out what changes in the economic policy and practice of the world will tend to increase the chances of maintaining peace in the world.

Fortunately those two problems, when you look into them closely, are seen to have very close analogies. Nobody who has given serious thought to the matter would contest the fact that on the whole the kind of change in the policies of the world that will increase the world's prosperity as a whole are also just those changes which are likely, on the whole, to conduce to the peace of the world, and that apart from the fact that if peace is not maintained any economic progress previously attained will be ruined.

Quite clearly economic causes are among the major causes of possible future wars. Quite clearly we have, in economic divergencies of interest and economic conflicts, the strongest of possible explosive forces. If you ask what is the policy to pursue in dealing with such dangers, I can only say, speaking generally, that if you have a boiler which works at very high pressures you had better see you have an efficient safety-valve.

To indicate the lines which policy should pursue, I will

refer you to a few great and authoritative statements which I think an official of the League may properly quote. Article 23 of the Covenant lays down as a principle that there should be equitable treatment for the commerce of all Member States. You have in the provisions of the Mandates system as applying to colonies of the Central African type a principle obviously capable of much wider application—the principle of equal opportunity for the commerce of all nations. You will remember that one of the Fourteen Points refers to the removal of trade barriers. You will remember that more than a century ago George Washington described his ideal of an economic policy as one ' which would hold an equal and impartial hand, neither seeking nor granting exclusive favours or privileges '.

In those quotations you have not, indeed, the description of an economic policy which will achieve the economic recovery of the world and maintain the peace of the world, but you do have, I think, something which, like a compass, suggests the direction in which the policies of the world will have to proceed if we are to achieve either of those objects. It will be, I hope, the role of the forthcoming Economic Conference to assist considerably in that task.

I have only a few words to say as to the third cause of the disorganization which has led to the impoverishment of the world—individual maladjustment in the different industries as between producers and customers throughout the world. During these eight years there has been, in spite of all the impediments resulting from the two major causes to which I have referred, a steady process of building-up from below. The individual worker, merchant, and manufacturer has been reknitting the snapped threads of international trade, and the degree with which he has succeeded is to some extent indicated by the general figures I quoted to you as applying to production in 1924, and, therefore, to the sale and consumption of the world.

That is a process which must go farther if we are to see a really satisfactory standard of prosperity throughout the world, but it is a sphere in which already very considerable progress has been made and is continuing ; and personally, looking to the future, I look forward with considerable optimism, always on the supposition that the world does not slip back into another disaster such as that of 1914–18. We can, as I have said, already say that the last war no longer continues to threaten our present civilization with actual ruin. The foundations of our civilization have been shaken but not shattered. But if that is true (as I think it is) it is equally true and equally obvious that our present civilization, as we know it, can never stand the strain of another great war with the increased means of destruction we learned of during the last war and since. In my opinion it is perfectly clear (and I believe every economist in the world would agree with me) that European civilization as we have known it during the past hundred years will be ruined, as many another great civilization of the past has been ruined, if we allow ourselves to fall back again into the crime and folly of another great war. After the next war, if it comes, we shall indeed at the end have a peace without victory ; it will be a peace without victory because, in the old Latin phrase, it will be a peace which will be a devastation. We shall be confronted at the end of that war with general and universal ruin, in which victors will be indistinguishable from vanquished. The whole of civilization as we know it will lie in equal and general ruin.

CHAPTER VI

CURRENT PROBLEMS AND PROGRESS IN DISARMAMENT

Señor S. de MADARIAGA :

I DO not propose to deal with some of the more intellectual and abstruse sides of this question of Disarmament, because I understand that there is, in your midst, a considerable number of men who would certainly better me upon this aspect of the question. I would rather understand my task as that of bringing to your knowledge, or, perhaps, better than that, bringing to your consciousness, the realization of some of the aspects of Disarmament with which you are, in the nature of things, bound to be less familiar than we are in Geneva, where the representatives of the various nations come to concentrate at regular intervals—sometimes far too short, I must say, and other times perhaps a little too long—upon the different matters which are intertwined under the heading of Disarmament.

For clarity, to begin with, I will make a rapid historical survey. The drafters of the Covenant wrote down the duties with regard to Disarmament, at the very outset of the list of articles which, in the Covenant, deal with the functions which the League is called upon to perform. The first seven articles only deal with Organization and Constitution, and, therefore, we may take it that in our own Charter, Disarmament is considered to be the predominant subject which must always be in our minds. As you know, article 8 defines these duties of Disarmament, and article 9 provides the Organization which the Council, which is especially entrusted with the duties of Disarmament, is to have at its disposal, for dealing with the various difficulties connected with the subject. This Organization, the Permanent Advisory Committee, familiarly known as ' P. A. C.', was constituted in detail—the Covenant having only defined its outline—at a Council meeting which took place in Rome in 1920. It is composed, as you all know, of one military, one naval, and one air representative from each of the States members of the Council, and, therefore, it includes three members from each of the nations, members of the Council, in all thirty men chosen by the national military defence departments of the States concerned. These men represent, on this Committee, the minds of their Governments, or, perhaps, more correctly, the minds of the General Staffs, once it has been approved by the Governments. The Assembly which immediately followed this meeting of the Council considered that Disarmament presented other aspects than merely military ones, and it decided to advise the Council to appoint a Commission, which was eventually styled the Temporary Mixed Commission. That Commission differed in two very important respects from the Permanent Advisory Committee. In the first place it was not composed of military men, although it included six of them, who were chosen by the P. A. C. for liaison purposes. It was composed of a certain number of general men—people with political experience—and a certain number of economic and financial experts, and labour experts chosen from the Organizations of the League and the International Labour Office. That is the first way in which it differed from the Permanent Advisory Committee. The second way was that instead of representing the points of view of the Governments, it represented the points of view of the several men who composed it. It was, therefore, a Committee of men speaking their own mind, and though in actual practice most—though not all—of them were in very close touch with their Governments, the fact is that this Commission had, so to speak, greater freedom of movement, because its members did not directly and officially represent the Governments of the countries from which they happened to come. You will all remember that it was that Commission which prepared the Treaty of Guarantee. The Treaty of Guarantee, the result of the fourteenth resolution which was drafted by Lord Cecil and by M. de Jouvenel, was an effort to solve the question of Disarmament *en bloc*. It was inspired by two ideas : Guarantee and Disarmament. As you will remember, in the resolution there was the principle that no Disarmament was possible without Guarantee, and that no Guarantee would be given without Disarmament. But what was the Guarantee to be ? It was a Guarantee of Security. The difficulty that arose at that moment when the Commission was preparing the Treaty was : How could a Guarantor State give a Guarantee to another State which might be attacked (owing, perhaps, to its own fault), without the Guarantor State being able to control the wisdom of the policy of the would-be attacked State ? All these questions boil themselves down to the definition of the word ' Aggression ', and if you turn to your documents on the matter, you will find that there is annexed to the Treaty of Guarantee a Memorandum, prepared by the Commission, with a view to guiding, so to speak, the opinion of the Council whenever a declaration of Aggression was to be made, to the effect that one very important consideration for the Council, when finding out which of the States at War happened to be the Aggressor State, might be the refusal of that State to bring the conflict to arbitration at any one of the stages which led to the conflict. So you see that in spite of the difference in name—and historically also—and in spite of the differences in the way in which these Treaties were received by public opinion in some countries, the Treaty of Guarantee, and what was later called the Protocol, differ much less than might be imagined, because they contain—though perhaps in different percentages—the three principles without which no one imagined then that the general solution of Disarmament could be brought about, namely, the principle of Disarmament, the principle of Guarantee, and the principle of Arbitration. You all remember how a change of spirit in several European countries (due perhaps to a change in internal politics) brought about the transformation of the Treaty of Guarantee into the Protocol, mostly by a considerable change in what I have just called the percentage of these three elements, that is before a considerable increase in the proportion of Arbitration, to the point that Arbitration became the foundation upon which the rest of the Treaty was erected. I do not propose to retrace the history of the Protocol, because you all know it well, and it is relatively recent; I will not say more than this, that, as was said in the Assembly which finally shelved it, the Protocol only died in the flesh, but lived in the spirit, as is proved by the fact that practically every treaty that has been concluded since (and certainly the group of Treaties of Locarno) would be unthinkable, not merely without the ideas that were embraced in the Protocol, but without the movement which was created in the world by the fact that the responsible Assembly of fifty-six States considered, created, and put on the table such a thing as the Protocol. I am convinced that these things are more than ideas; they are vital things which penetrate into the consciousness of public opinion, and which have in them a driving virtue or force which makes them act in the direction and through the channels of international politics in a new way altogether.

I now leave this historical survey, with just one word more. The last Assembly thought it necessary to get on with the preparations for Disarmament in anticipation of the time when the general feeling of security was sufficient to guarantee that an international Conference would be practical, and having discarded the Temporary Mixed Commission (because being so near the moment of realization the work had to be done in close co-operation with the responsible services of the Governments concerned) a Preparatory Commission was set up for an International Conference on Disarmament. This Commission is composed of the representatives of twenty nations, most of them members of the League, and one particularly important and friendly trans-Atlantic nation, with which some of you are familiar, who are not members of the League. They are all working here in a very amiable and friendly atmosphere and, having seen the main difficulties which have to be dealt with, they are, like the mills of God, grinding very slowly, very exactly, and very hopefully in order to prepare the ground for an international Conference which will be convened as soon as the Council thinks that the international atmosphere is ready for it.

. . . .

Now let me come to a point which our Chairman has mentioned. He said that the League had done very little in the field of Disarmament. While that is true in a way—as is often the case with statements of a general nature—it is quite untrue in another way. Remembering that we have had here quite recently that great European, Einstein, I propose to-day thoroughly to avail myself of the advantages of

the theory of relativity. In an absolute way, the work of the
League of Nations, so far as Disarmament is concerned, is
paltry ; but in a relative way it is very honourable indeed.
Perhaps I might attempt to justify this statement by a review
of some of the obstacles with which we have to deal. To
begin with, that which in my mind is perhaps the most
formidable is the vagueness and the haziness of our ideas and
our sense of Disarmament. Paradoxical as it may seem, the
work on Disarmament has been embarked upon, just as
Christopher Columbus embarked upon discovering a new
world, without knowing what it is, or what it means. Now
what is Disarmament ? The dictionary, very wisely—in fact
it might have been drafted by a member of the Temporary
Mixed Commission—says that it is the ' reduction of the
armaments of a nation ' ; it does not limit its meaning to the
' abolition ' of them. Now that is a very wise thing for a
dictionary to say ! If you dwell for a moment upon this
conception of Disarmament, namely, the ' reduction of the
armaments of a nation ', you might at first sight assimilate
it to the reduction in the temperature of a man who has
fever. But that will not do, because the temperature of a
man who has fever can easily be measured by a thermometer ;
there is something which goes up and down which you can
read and easily compare. You can say that So-and-So has
a temperature of 102° and So-and-So has a temperature of
98°. There is sense in that ; but there is no sense whatever
in saying that one nation is more armed than another. There
is, perhaps, a subjective idea, or a subjective feeling, but
there is no scientific way of measuring the level of the temperature in the case of armaments' fever in any nation
whatsoever. As regards the state of a nation whose armaments we want to reduce, we find it composed of a concept

which is relative, but relative in a twofold way : relative in
its relativity. The first way in which it is relative is that it
is in itself a mere relation. The concept of the armaments of
a nation or the state of armament of a nation, might be considered as a fraction, or as a relation, with a numerator and
a denominator. First of all you have the armed power of the
nation, which would be the numerator, and you then have
its requirements which would be the denominator. Let me
give an example ; let us take a nation of one million square
miles with two hundred million inhabitants, and an army of
eight hundred thousand men, and another nation with
twenty thousand square miles, one million inhabitants, and
an army of eighty thousand men. It is no use saying that the
nation with eight hundred thousand men is more armed than
the one with eighty thousand men, because the other conditions, the area, and the population, which would be among
the elements composing the denominator, would so considerably alter the relative proportion, that you could not
possibly attribute to the first nation the same degree of
armaments as you could attribute to the second.

But then the degree of relativity due to the fact that
armaments are a fraction is enormously complicated from
the fact that both the numerator and the denominator are
extremely complex ideas. Take the numerator, the armed
forces. I do not propose to enter into a very close analysis of
the two elements of our fraction because it would take not
one lecture but a course of lectures in order to do that
thoroughly. The armed forces of a country can, without
much analysis, be distinguished by what I call the three M's
—men, material, and money. You can imagine all sorts of
possible combinations of armed forces in which men, material,
and money enter in different proportions. How can you

possibly compare quantities composed of three elements all of which are important, in fact primordial in armaments, and yet entering in different proportions. If we take men, how can you compare the French soldier who serves 365 days in a year and who is a compulsory service man, and goes home when he has spent eighteen months or two years in the army, according to the law of the time, with the English soldier who is either a professional soldier for life, or a Territorial who takes the army as a sport and yet is a good soldier, or even with the Swiss soldier who is an ordinary citizen working at his office or at his works with his gun at home, and who goes out every now and then for a bit of shooting. A comparison between men of those three types—and there are many more types—is wellnigh impossible.

Now let us take material. Our technical men have been working now for months in trying to define what is war material and what is not. Is a military kitchen war material? Is the bed of a soldier war material? That, however, is a small point. Take war material *stricto sensu*. Take the material which would not be manufactured in any form whatsoever if there were no wars. Take, for instance, a machine gun, or things of that kind. How can you compare the number of machine guns held by a nation which, if it had no machine guns, could build those guns at three months notice, with the number of machine guns held by a nation which could not build any such guns simply because it had not the works for doing so. That is a difficulty which has to be considered.

Take the question of money. The question of money spent on armaments is most complicated. We have at the present time two Commissions dealing with the matter, and they are studying this question very precisely. Can the armed forces of two nations be compared by comparing their military and naval and air budgets? The number of difficulties which arise as soon as this question is put to experts, either military or financial, is overwhelming. What is a military budget? Where does it start? Is a subvention given to a territorial force to be brought into a military budget? There was a time, and I believe there still is, when the British Government paid money to the officers training corps in some universities and colleges. Is that military money or not? Is the money given to a purely civilian society engaged in the training of strong young physical men military money? Where is the line to be drawn?

Apart from that, it has been suggested that a good method of comparison would be the division of the total sum spent in national defence by the total sum paid by the State in its total budget. That is a question bristling with difficulties. I may remind you, because it is an amusing incident, that the Head of the Swiss Federal Military Department speaking not long ago to an assembly of officers mentioned this difficulty in a very intelligent way, as of course a man in his position naturally would. But what he said was twisted by some papers in Switzerland and at least in one case in England, and it was published under headings such as ' The Swiss Federal Authorities give the lie to the statistics of the League of Nations '. Those papers made that authority say that the League had published statistics in which the Swiss nation appeared as the fourth in the list of spending nations by that test of dividing the military budget by the total budget, while an accurate calculation showed it to be the fourth from the last. The trouble is that the League statistics have appeared in a very stout volume in which there is a very well thought out preface which explains that on no account are nations to be compared by such a test because they cannot be compared. Whoever put Switzerland into the fourth place, therefore, did it not only unauthorized by the League statistics but against their express warnings.

Let me take the case of Switzerland, because it is an interesting example. We find that there are some Cantons of Switzerland which give small sums of money for objects which may fairly be considered as co-operating in the military budget. Then what are we to do? Are we to add those small items from the budgets of the Cantons into the military budget of Switzerland or not. If we do not, the sum total of what Switzerland spends in military defence is not accurate. If we do, you cannot compare that figure with the total budget of Switzerland without adding to the total budget of the Federation the total budget of the Cantons. You will see from that that the position is extremely complicated.

Added to that are the difficulties of currency. How are you to compare budgets in the present fluctuating state of the exchanges, the difficulties with regard to the purchasing value of money, and even if you reduce to one common gold standard all the countries of the world, would their money buy the same value? Is their standard of life the same? Could not food be bought for ten soldiers of a given nation with the same amount of money that would be required to buy food for one soldier of another nation?

Let us take now the denominator of the fraction. We say that reduction of armaments means the reduction of a complex idea composed of the armed forces of the nations in proportion to their requirements. We have so far dealt with the armed forces. Let us now deal with the requirements.

As you will remember, article 8 says that the nations of the League recognize that it is in the interests of the world to reduce all armaments to the minimum compatible with their national defence and with their international obligations. The requirements, therefore, have been taken into consideration by the men who drafted the Covenant. National defence is a very formidable subject. How can you compare the requirements of an island nation with those of a nation with a good frontier, or with those of a nation with a bad frontier, the requirements of a nation placed on the edge of the sea with those of a nation which is land-locked in a continent? The cases are entirely different. How can you compare a nation with a very long flat frontier without any natural defences with a nation which has magnificent natural mountain and river defences? You have the case of a nation like the United States which has on its borders a nation like Canada with which it cannot be imagined or dreamed that it will ever be in hostility, and, on the other hand, you have the case of a nation which has a long historical feud with another Power. These are essentially subjective ideas. But if we come to international obligations, the subjectivity of international obligations is even greater than the subjectivity of national defence. It is evident that no one but ourselves can define the role which we play in life. Most of us consider our own role in the world as exalted and majestic. What is good for the individual should be good for the nation, and if one particular nation thinks that its own role in the world is exalted and majestic why in the name of anything should not other nations think exactly the same about their own role in the world? You will thus realize that the idea of international obligations, which is in black and white in the Covenant, and which every nation has a right to invoke in order to defend its own military establishment, is one which cannot be separated from another idea which is still more subjective. I refer to the idea of prestige. There is no doubt that in some kinds of armaments the idea of prestige is fundamental. A nation has a battle cruiser just as a woman has a silk dress, or as a man has a dress suit. It is worn as the custom. These which might be called unsubstantial feelings are perhaps the most powerful springs of international relations.

This brief survey of the idea of armaments suggests two conclusions. The first is that with regard to what I call the numerator of the idea, armed forces, it cannot be measured by objective standards. The second is that the denominator requirements can only be measured by subjective standards. The result, as you may guess, is pretty hopeless.

One word about what might be called the psychological origin of all this. How is it that we get in the world this urge for disarmament? I think you might trace the very powerful and complex current which it has become to two fundamental streams—although that does not mean that there are not other contributory streams. One stream is of a financial and economic origin, and the other is what we might call the pacifist stream. The financial and economic influence can be easily explained because the burden of armaments in the world is something appalling. I think I have said enough to make you feel that in matters of armaments figures must be dealt with and considered with great care and circumspection. But there is one particular numerical example which I think may be safely quoted because it deals with general figures and does not descend into detail, and yet I fancy it is very telling. It is a fact that if the total amount of money spent in the world on armaments in a single year were set aside it would provide money enough to meet the present budget of the League of Nations for about six centuries.

Yet I do not know that the purely budgetary expenditure

is the worst feature in this order of things. Perhaps there is a still more dismal feature in the knowledge that so many men in the world are kept idle in so far as creative work is concerned, and still worse, that so many men are every year kept busy in doing work which implies, at least potentially, distrust and destruction. In that way the financial and economic current touches the pacifist current, to which might be applied the quotation that our Chairman gave us from Lord Grey, that it is arms that make wars, arms create a feeling of distrust and fear, and fear generates war. Perhaps another argument within the pacifist idea is the argument which might be derived from inverting the well-known English saying that ' The wish is father to the thought '. The General Staff of the Army is thinking about war so often that the thought becomes father to the wish, and by dint of thinking of the beautiful chess-play, which a good campaign would provide, it might be imagined that on occasion in the past General Staffs had been tempted consciously or unconsciously to bring about wars in order to participate in their games of chess on the actual chess-board of the world. I cannot help thinking, however, that the pacifist tendency is apt to overlook an argument which is exactly inverse to that. It may be true, in fact I think it is true, that the existence of arms is a danger in that it tends to bring about wars, but it is no less true that arms exist because wars do take place. War has to be considered as a disease which, like malaria, has times of subterranean quiescence, which develop now and then into periods of hostility and aggression. War is perennial in human nature, but it is only now and then that it breaks out into actual hostilities. The spirit of war is active wherever the spirit of co-operation is inactive, and that to my mind is the key to the situation.

An interesting point about these two distinct ideas, one that arms generate wars, and the other that wars generate arms, is that they have led to two schools of political thought. The first idea that arms generate wars has led to the school of thought which lays stress on disarmament. The second idea that wars generate arms, has led to the school of thought which lays stress on security. Disarmament and security are, therefore, two ideas which are not merely the outcome of different political situations, but depend largely on the temperamental psychology of the people and the races which hold them.

Now what is security ? Or, if you like, what is insecurity ? Insecurity is the feeling of danger that arises out of the feeling that the order of things in which we live is unstable, and the instability of that order of things may be considered to be due to a lack of sympathy and a lack of coincidence between the facts of life and the wishes of the world. What is the remedy ? Obviously the remedy consists in foreseeing the prospect of conflicts, studying them continuously, methodically, and impartially, and providing a solution for them on the level of international justice. From that analysis you come to the conclusion, therefore, that the work of disarmament is intimately linked with the work of the international organization of life, not merely with the purely technical, straightforward convention on the limitation of armaments, but with the wider aspects of the organization of the world in all its fields—territorial, economic, financial, juridical, and racial.

To my mind we shall never achieve anything in the way of disarmament except by modest and slow though important steps until this wider issue is tackled. We must attack the problem of the international organization from all its angles at the same time. There is no wholesale solution for the ills of the world. The ills of the world require a constant working and nibbling at, and they require to be understood steadily and as a whole. The root evil is, I should say, the lone hand with a sense of the urge of power. Where there is power without co-operation there is the enemy of disarmament.

I should not like to think I had conveyed the impression that in matters of disarmament I am a pessimist. I am not a pessimist. I am a convinced optimist. Here again, however, I should like to avail myself of the advantages of relativity. The trouble is that the world has been arming for centuries during which its ideas of speed were slow, when the world went leisurely on and the normal speed of human motion was marked by the gallop of the horse ; and now the world wants to disarm in a period when the motion of the world is very active, when things move very quickly, and when a man's sense of speed is marked by racing motor-cars. You cannot expect the world to disarm at the same speed as the speed which has been ingrained into our very spirit by the fact that we possess to-day magnificent machines for transporting ourselves from one place to another on the surface of our globe. The speed of the spirit is always the same ; it is only the speed of matter that can be increased.

The CHAIRMAN :

I think you would like me to thank M. Madariaga, as you have already done by your applause, and to say how very much we appreciated his address. I think he did exactly what we wanted him to do. He went quickly and lightly over the earlier part of the subject, which is familiar to most of the people in this room, and then told us what no one else could have told us in the same way about the exact present position of this vital problem.   There are some people here who do not know the earlier part of the story, and perhaps there are one or two points which might be emphasized for their benefit.

It must be remembered that disarmament and security are absolutely linked up with one another in connexion with this problem.   As soon as the League tackled the question of disarmament it realized that it was no use saying to the nations : ' disarm ', because that might have led to the last state of the world being worse than the first.   As M. Madariaga told you, this problem is psychological almost through and through, and the nervous nations said, ' if you are going to ask us to reduce our armaments, you must give us some other security that we shall not have aggression on our frontiers ; that is to say, you must guarantee our security '. Therefore, it will be seen that disarmament and security are absolutely linked together.

Supposing in the 1780's, before there was a United States of America with a big ' U ', but just thirteen small united States with a little ' u ', the Pennsylvanians and New Yorkers had said : ' We have to keep up an army of such and such size because we are afraid that the British will come back, or more likely that the Indians will cause trouble on our frontiers ; let us cut our forces in half and agree that whenever there is trouble on the frontier of either, the forces of both States will assist in the defence.   In this case we shall be just where we were, because there will be the same army to face the aggression wherever it occurs, and any one who contemplates aggression knows that he has not only to defeat this army, but has to defeat the whole resources of both States instead of only one.'   Therefore, the deterrent effect of an army composed of two nations may be even greater than an army of the same size composed of only one nation ; the result may be that you are able, in two States of about the same size, to cut their forces into half, because each looks upon the force of its neighbour as ready to suppress aggression wherever it may occur on the frontiers.

If you extend that idea to a continent like Europe, of twenty-six States without Russia, you see that a very large amount of reduction of armaments is possible if only you can get the nations of the different countries to look upon the forces of the other countries, not as prospective aggressors, but as ready with their own forces to suppress aggression whenever it occurs.

The problem is this : how are you to get the necessary change in peoples' minds ? It is a psychological problem, and the change is needed in different ways. In France, for example, it is necessary to realize that armaments are the danger ; in England the difficulty is to get English people to realize that they will only get disarmament on the continent if their forces are ready to go anywhere to suppress aggression along with the rest of the armies of the world, wherever that aggression may occur.

I am not going to detain you with further reflections, and that is a point which might be discussed later on, but this business of disarmament and security is the sort of thing we were thinking about in Europe five or six years ago, and it may be good for some of us to be reminded of these earlier ideas on the subject. M. Madariaga finished by saying that the spirit of war is active wherever the spirit of co-operation is inactive. It seems to me that it is the spirit of co-operation which is the chief thing lacking, and it is in this direction perhaps that we may be able to help most when we return to our own countries.

CHAPTER VII

THE LEAGUE AND INTERNATIONAL INTELLECTUAL CO-OPERATION

Mr. ALFRED ZIMMERN :

THE intellectual side of the work of the League of Nations dates from 1921. There is nothing about it in the Covenant, and in the work that led up to the formation of the League of Nations you will find little or no reference to it. In 1921, at the instigation of M. Léon Bourgeois, the Council of the League set up a Committee of eminent scholars which now consists of fourteen persons selected from fourteen different countries. They are not selected as representatives of those countries, but simply on grounds of intellectual distinction. Professor Bergson was the first Chairman, and among the other members may be mentioned Professor Gilbert Murray, who is now Vice-Chairman, Professor Laurenz, the distinguished Dutch Physicist, who has now succeeded Professor Bergson as Chairman, Dr. Einstein, Madame Curie, and others. They are representative of the best scholarship in the world.

For some years this Committee met twice a year, and attempted to deal with a number of subjects. But it worked under great difficulties, because it had only a very small staff at its disposal in the Secretariat, working under Dr. Nitobé,[1] and that staff was charged also with other duties. Early in 1924 it therefore issued an appeal to Governments and other agencies for help, and in the summer of 1924 the French Government generously offered money enough to place at the disposal of the Committee an Institute in Paris,

[1] Dr. L. Nitobé, Japanese, Under-Secretary-General and head of the Section that deals with intellectual co-operation.

housed in the old Palais Royal, working under the Committee on a completely international basis. It is that Institute, which after its rules had been passed and its international character safeguarded by the Council and the Assembly, opened its doors six months ago.

What is the work we are trying to do? It is twofold. Firstly, our object is to promote the meeting of minds, or if you like, to promote practical intellectual co-operation between living persons. Secondly, our object is to improve the tools of the intellectual worker, to improve his instruments or work, and to facilitate intellectual work in all its wide range. I want to talk first about that second part, and then I will come back to the meeting of minds.

Up to the formation of the Committee, there had been no organized contact between the world of scholarship and the world of government. Before the war and until the formation of this Committee, scholarship and government moved in separate orbits, and they had no way of coming into contact. I think that was due in large measure to the suspicion among scholars that if they came near government in any way their freedom of thought might be corrupted, and their integrity might suffer. It was also due to the fact that scholars and other intellectuals did not realize that with the growth of international organization they would come more and more to require the help of Governments, and to require action by Governments in order to have their needs satisfied. In other words, scholars and intellectual workers to-day, just as is the case with manual workers, need international conventions. International conventions are needed to deal with intellectual questions, like the exchange of official publications, or larger questions, such as we are hoping to reach later on, and which out of discretion I forbear to mention. The way to reach such conventions is assuredly that which is shown by the organization of the International Labour Office; that is, to have a body of experts who will meet the wishes of the associations of voluntary workers concerned in this field, and who will draft them in the form of conventions and see that the Governments sign and eventually ratify them. We are, in fact, technically speaking, a point of junction between all the various organized bodies of intellectual workers and Governments, the Governments which alone can frame and carry through international conventions dealing with intellectual matters.

That is the importance of our relationship with the Council of the League.

The Institute works under the Committee, and the Committee is an Advisory Committee of the Council. Its work is passed by the Council and the Assembly, but the eminent scholars who form the Committee are the sure shield and protection to save us at the Institute, and intellectual workers generally, from the intervention of the political influences of which scholars used to be so much afraid. We are remote from the political side of the League, as is shown by the fact that from the very beginning the United States and Germany have had members on the Committee, and there is nothing —so far as I know—to prevent a scholar from Soviet Russia being made a member of the Committee. At present, Dr. Einstein represents Germany, and Dr. Millikan, the distinguished Physicist, the United States.

I should like to say a few words now on the nature of our detailed work. I could read you the Director's Report on our first half-year, but instead I will just give you a few headings, because I do not want to weary you. The question was raised some years ago of having an International Library where all the books and documents in the world could be collected and made available. That is obviously a Utopian ideal, but we are trying to realize it in a more practicable way by co-ordinating the existing centres of documentation and research. We have sent out a questionnaire to every important library in the world, asking in what subjects they have special collections, and whether they are willing to supply an Information Service to correspondents who wish to make use of such collections and whether, if they have not money enough to do so, they would be ready to do it if funds were available. We have received a large number of replies, and have unearthed a number of interesting facts about the resources of libraries in various parts of the world. When our report is published, I think it will be of great practical use to scholars.

Another matter with which we are dealing is this. No one has yet tried to apply the principle of international co-operation to museums. There are thousands of museums in all parts of the world. Many of them have printed catalogues, but they do not always send those catalogues to one another. Many are over-rich in some respects and deficient in others, and they would be glad to know how to make exchanges so as to improve their position. Many would be glad to know how to get photographs, casts, &c., of works in other museums. We have circularized the museums and the replies have been so encouraging that we are setting on foot an International Museum Organization which will provide those facilities, and for the first time bring together curators and others interested in museums in different countries. They will thus come into contact with their professional brethren throughout the world.

Another extensive field of work is that of bibliography.

The field of bibliography belongs strictly to the international learned societies, but they work under great difficulties. Sometimes they are ill-equipped with funds, and sometimes they better meet the needs of the larger and richer countries with more widely-spoken languages than the needs of smaller countries. Some central clearing house was required. In certain cases we have done more than merely survey the field of bibliographical work opened up by others : we have initiated bibliographical work ourselves by promoting conferences. A case in point is the Conference of Experts in the Social Sciences and Economies, which has just presented its report of its first meeting to the International Committee.

In our university section we have taken up the whole problem of the exchange of students and professors—a subject on which a good deal of material exists in many countries. That material needs to be collected, and above all appreciated, so that countries which are beginning an exchange system may know under what conditions such systems work, at what age the exchange is most advantageous, for what length of time it should last, and so on. We hope that before long that material will be available to those in all countries who are setting up such schemes.

Dr. Nitobé, in co-operation with us, organized last Easter a Conference of International Students' Associations, where for the first time representatives of seven International Students' Associations were brought into contact, and thrashed out their common problems, attempting in a certain degree to delimit their respective fields of action. We have adopted an expedient of the same kind, but of a more frequently recurring character, at the Institute, by forming a Committee of International Associations interested in education. We have a standing Committee which meets every six weeks. It is composed of the Secretaries or other representatives of some eighteen International Associations interested in education, who had no regular way of meeting before and were in some danger of overlapping one another, because they were engaged in closely related activities. Now they know one another, and are co-ordinating their activities and learning how to co-operate practically as well as ideally.

Another matter we have taken up is the question of translations. Hitherto it has largely been a matter of accident whether a book was translated, and many important books were overlooked. In collaboration with international literary societies, such as the P. E. N. Club, we are trying to put that subject on a satisfactory basis.

The last matter I will mention is one which interests your Institute—that of the study of international relations. It was put on our agenda in the form of a project for an international university, but analysis soon showed that what was practicable was not a university covering all the various faculties—natural science and so on—but courses embracing those particular studies which are related to international affairs : history, international law, economics, and so on. Also, at a higher stage, there should be professional schools for assisting those who are going to take up an international career. An international career to-day is a term that covers a far wider range than in 1914. Before the war, any one who was asked what an international career was would have replied that it was diplomacy, but to-day there are the officials of the League of Nations and the numerous persons working for voluntary international organizations. There are large numbers of people whose professional activities require them to be in touch with international affairs—engineers, bankers, and so on. There are people in businesses of various kinds who need the same kind of training. In fact, the international career is now a definite career in the world, and needs to be provided for by professional training. Such training should be carried on, if not in an international institution—which, perhaps, it is too early to hope for—then in institutions in the different national centres which should be co-ordinated one with another, and which should work in close harmony so that students can pass freely from one to another.

Finally, I should like to mention the fact that there has been a remarkable improvement in the international intellectual atmosphere during the past twelve months. I do not claim any credit for the League of Nations or the Committee on Intellectual Co-operation or the Paris Institute in that regard; I merely put it on record that whereas a year ago the international learned societies were still troubled by problems and prejudices arising out of the war, to-day what some one has described as the academic Locarno is an established fact. The international learned societies have agreed to make no distinction between those who were fighting on different sides during the war. We have, therefore, one consolation for the failure of the March Assembly, namely, that it has enabled the scholars to go ahead of the politicians, and allowed the academic Locarno to be an accomplished fact before the political Locarno.

THE LEAGUE AND THE WORLD TO-DAY

CHAPTER VIII

GERMANY'S INTERNATIONAL POSITION SINCE LOCARNO

Dr. ARNOLD WOLFERS:

LET me impress upon your mind, before entering into my subject, that I am a citizen of Switzerland, a German-speaking Swiss who has lived and worked in Germany for many years, but yet a Swiss. I say that because Germans coming abroad and speaking to a foreign audience would be thinking all along how they might help create an atmosphere of international confidence. They would want to make you feel their, and their country-men's, desire to promote international understanding. I am well aware how important it is that Germans should be able to take such an attitude. My position, however, is a freer one. My task, I believe, in speaking to you lies on a different line. You want information. You want it, if I understand correctly your intentions in coming here, as objective as possible. I trust that your desire for international friendship is such that any obstacles I may have to show you on the path to peace will only strengthen your endeavours. A knowledge of difficulties will arm us against disillusion, and harden our energies for times of crisis.

If I am to discuss Germany's international position to-day I cannot help leading you a little way back in history. The important facts have not occurred since Locarno. We must try moreover to analyse the Locarno Treaty in the light of the developments which took place beforehand.

For Germany—as for France—Franco-German relations are of such primordial importance that they overshadow all other factors in her foreign policy. Franco-German relations for centuries have turned in a vicious circle. When the day will have come for this circle to have been finally broken then we will be entitled to speak of the beginning of a new era in Europe. It seems incredible that two nations, both contributing wonderfully in their own way to the development of that European civilization which they largely share, should have to be continually at war with one another. It is yet more astonishing if one comes to believe, as I sincerely do, that neither of the two has to-day, or ever had before, a primary design either to conquer the other's soil or to become the other's master. The vicious circle of which I spoke is one of fear, fear leading to violence and predominance, and these in turn leading to a new fear and revolt, a revolt calling for more fear and a new violence.

Take France first : The French people, you are told, long for peace and security, so as to be allowed to develop their gifts and their welfare. But deeply rooted in the French mind is the fear that if Germany too was to develop itself in independence and unity, France, weaker in population and economic forces, would be menaced. Such feeling naturally leads to aggressive forms of self-defence. Again and again in history it carried French armies forward to the Rhine and over the Rhine, and, by promoting separatist movements in Germany, tried to bar the way to German unity.

Then look at Germany : Here you find a highly differentiated nation in the centre of Europe, struggling in vain for centuries to re-establish its unity. In the minds of this people you will find the conviction that it was France who had all the time been out to perpetuate this disastrous disintegration of her neighbour. They think it quite natural, therefore, that Bismarck should have had to establish the German empire by bringing about a victory over France. Fear again led victorious Germany to such aggressive self-defence as would call for revolt and revenge on the part of France.

France's victory in the world war turned the tables. The old and terrible game, however, did not come to an end. Fear did not end, and with it the whole vicious circle went on. As long as the mere existence of the neighbour was believed to be a threat you could either desire that he be annihilated or you had to acquire such hegemonial predominance as to be sure to be able to keep the other down.

Millions of men and women in every country had counted on President Wilson to put an end not only to this, but to all the vicious circles inherent in a system of international anarchy and aggressive self-defence. Wilson saw the root of the evil. Nations could not trust their neighbours as long as national sovereignty was looked on as an arbitrary right to do whatever national egoism demanded. He felt that only in a league of nations could fear give way to sympathetic co-operation. Why then was the league, which Wilson succeeded in establishing, not capable of solving the problem? It need not be explained why a league of victorious nations, excluding the vanquished, could not do anything but make matters worse. But that is not the question. We must ask why the League did not, according to its real meaning, open its doors to all, and replace, for so-called dictated peace treaties, mutual friendly agreements based on justice. Wilson seems to have believed that however unjust some clauses of the Treaty might be the League would revise them and settle matters later on. He did not see that a Treaty which in so many of its essential clauses continued in the course of the old vicious circle would necessarily call forth all the old reactions and so bar the way to the very development of that spirit by which a League could alone hope to gain efficient power.

The Treaty did not satisfy France. In wounding Germany's national pride and honour it was certain sooner or later to create revolt. In view of this France had reason to fear again. France therefore was demanding more definite security. The Allies were refusing to give her hegemonial predominance. They refused her the frontier of the Rhine, the guarantee-pact, the disintegration of Germany. Victory again was for nothing then. The vicious circle going on, victory had not eliminated the future dangers.

For Germany, I need hardly say, the Treaty was a painful disillusion. The old fight was to go on with the tables reversed. France would live at Germany's expense ; the most that could be hoped for would be to avoid a total breakdown. A long period of dishonour and suffering would have to be faced. All hope would have to be concentrated on some new catastrophe in a far future, some unavoidable new war which might open a way again for Germany to fulfil its destiny among the nations of the world.

The total breakdown was near coming about. The reparation problem allowed France to move forward, to occupy the Ruhr, to promote separatism. No wonder that in the days of the Ruhr conflict a wave of unparalleled pessimism swept over Europe. France herself had become the prey of forces over which she had no control. The vicious circle was dictating her steps. The French realized the deadlock. Each step forward made security less possible. The world was beginning to look at France as a disturber of peace and economic reconstruction. Financial pressure was being brought to bear on France. The franc dropped. By March 1924 France, though victorious in the Ruhr, was not much less desperate than her newly-vanquished opponent.

Fortunately new men came into power, men with sufficient imagination to try new ways and methods. Macdonald was made Prime Minister in England, Herriot succeeded Poincaré in France. First they had to grapple with the problem of reparations from which such an acute crisis arose. You all know how in August 1924 by the so-called Dawes Plan a modus was found that saved Germany economically, establishing the stabilization of the mark, making impossible further French sanctions on behalf of reparations, and laying down methods for future peaceful revision of the plan in case of need. The reparations were thus taken out of the dangerous realm of political Franco-German relations. They became an international matter under the control and leadership of the United States of America. However painful the paying of reparations may be, and whatever in future the burden may be, the Dawes Plan certainly at the time saved Germany from imminent disaster. Had the Franco-German conflict been only one of reparations it would have been practically eliminated by the plan. But it was of another order. The fear was not taken from Germany that France would find other clauses in the Treaty by which to continue the destruction of Germany's unity and existence. France, on the other side, felt less secured, since the Dawes Plan had put Germany back on its feet and had put France to a large extent at the mercy of Anglo-American finance. _France, therefore, was looking out for new and stronger allies, and trying to persuade Great Britain to enter into an alliance for the defence of France's security. In all sincerity the strongest military power of the continent was begging for more security. Germany, as must be expected, was seeking for help too. She had little to offer and therefore little to hope for. She had for a time expected that England would come to her rescue so as in her own interest to avoid the establishment of French hegemony on the continent. But when, during the Ruhr conflict, England looked on and did nothing, the eyes of Germany began to turn towards the East. Russia seemed to be the only power that might take sides with Germany. Had Russia been strong at that time, as strong as some people liked to think, the temptation to fall into Soviet Russia's arms might have become irresistible. Some people say that it was capitalistic solidarity between the German and the western bourgeois democracies which prevented such a decision. Capitalistic interests were certainly strong in the matter, here as everywhere. Yet they alone did not lead the other way. Apart from radical groups the great majority of the German bourgeois and labour classes was disinclined to any desperate and revolutionary policy. After terrible years of political, moral, and economic crisis the Dawes Plan had just given a chance to economic regeneration. The relations with the Anglo-Saxon countries were such that they gave hope not only of credits but also of some assistance along political lines. All of this would have been jeopardized if the Franco-German conflict had once more been allowed to tear Europe apart into two enemy groups. Germany, disarmed as it was, would by such a policy have condemned itself to become the future battle-field of Europe.

England refused a separate alliance with France ; Germany

did not decide in favour of Russia. Other solutions had to be found. Macdonald and Herriot, while at Geneva in September 1924, were led to think that this time the League of Nations would be able to help. The Geneva Protocol was framed and was welcomed with enthusiasm by the assembly of the League. I cannot in this lecture discuss the Geneva Protocol. It was not accepted and therefore never was able to prove its merits. I will only say in passing that I personally did not look at it as a workable solution at the time. It seemed to me to be repeating Wilson's mistake of wanting to build up international lawfulness and peace on a foundation that was breeding bitterness, revolt, fear, and violence. On the basis of a dictated Treaty the nations of the world would not be able to risk pledging themselves to defend the *status quo* even against a well-determined ' Aggressor'. Would they know whether at any future moment they would feel to be normally bound to use violence against this ' aggressor ' rather than against those who were refusing to bring about necessary peaceful revisions of the *status quo* ?

What then could be done if the League again was bound to fail ? A revision of the Treaty, pure and simple ? Nobody dreamt of such a possibility. A return by some other means to the ' balance of power-system ' which after all had kept Europe at peace from 1871 to 1914 ? Yes and no. The ' balance of power ' is necessary to Europe, but taken by itself it is not sufficient. The pre-war system was a sort of armistice, keeping enemies out of war by letting them feel that the other had nearly an equal chance. In a state of anarchy what other way is there of avoiding war than by mutual fear and equal risks ? The other nations, according to this system, would have to combine against the stronger party, forcing it by every possible means, for the sake of self-defence, to aim for hegemonial predominance. In the situation of 1924 such an attempt would simply have urged France to quick and preventive action, thus leading to an immediate disaster for Germany.

At this moment Germany took the initiative which may prove to have shown the right direction. In offering to France a ' pact of security ' she proposed that France and Germany might seek to guarantee to one another the security they had so long in vain been seeking against one another. In the ' Locarno Agreement ' this idea has taken legal form. Much has been said and written about what has been called the ' atmosphere ' or the ' spirit ' of Locarno. So much so that one is inclined to become sceptical as to an agreement where so much is said about atmosphere at a moment when most realistic acts and deeds need to be accomplished. Yet we can understand that it should be so if, under ' atmosphere ', we understand a new attitude, and the will to seek a solution in a direction opposite to that of former times.

The Locarno pact says two things : Germany and France agree to have no further conflict regarding their boundary-lines. They further pledge themselves to settle whatever other conflicts may arise between them by arbitration. If this be so, does it not seem as if Franco-German relations had definitely stopped being a problem of World-Peace ? If there is to be no war between them in any case what else is there to be achieved. In view of reality, however, this seems to me to be too optimistic an interpretation.

Germany has given up her claims on Alsace and Lorraine. France will not have to fear a war of revenge on behalf of these territories. France having less to fear can loosen her grip. Germany then will not feel threatened any more in regard to its own self-development inside of its new frontiers. There is a chance for the two neighbours to have a new experience, namely, that of getting along side by side without being a menace to one another.

But, after all, Germany had other grievances than the loss of Alsace-Lorraine, or the violation of its western frontier by French sanctions. Has Germany by the Locarno Treaty given them all up and forgiven them? has she put up finally with France's military predominance and with the other clauses of the Versailles Treaty against which up to now she had so bitterly protested? Many Germans to-day may be in a mood to give up every claim for the sake of peace. In the long run, however, I firmly believe, that the Locarno Pact like every other agreement for the peaceful settlement of international disputes will only stand if it really leads to peaceful and satisfactory readjustments. To make it more plain, treaties of non-violence and arbitration will abolish war if they lead to revisions of a status brought about by war and in that case only. A German to-day would most likely avoid speaking of revision and changes of status. But I said at the beginning that I do not intend to encourage illusions. Whether we speak of disarmament, of the occupation of the Rhineland, of minority problems or Eastern boundaries, nobody can make me believe that friendship and peace can be guaranteed if agreements cannot be reached as the time goes on to change present conditions. The real meaning, therefore, of the Locarno Pact is that of the two nations consenting to co-operate in bringing about such a state of equilibrium as may serve as a stable and righteous foundation for a coming new European order. An agreement such as this will certainly put all the nations to a heavy test. Is it audacious to hope that they will stand up to the task ? If we were to rely on nothing but their mutual sympathy we would yet have reason to be rather disheartened. In Germany certainly, after so many discouraging experiences, people would hardly be willing to expect other nations to make sacrifices on their behalf. Yet there is a growing feeling that community among nations is becoming stronger than the wishes and independent interests of each single nation. There is a growing readiness to acknowledge the existence of such community, bitterly or gladly according to temperament. The other nations of Europe no doubt are having the same experience. It may, however, be typical for the German mind to believe that nations will be more willing to bring sacrifices and to show moderation if it be demanded for the common good of a Commonwealth of which they form a part than if it be asked for in the name of some other nation. Whatever interpretation we give to the facts there certainly is in Europe a formerly unknown consciousness of mutual dependence and the urgent need of a more stable European order. Economic, social, and cultural factors are leading up to this same conviction.

This brings me to the point where we must take in account the relations of Germany with other nations and with the League. Logically the Locarno Treaty must lead up to Germany entering the League. Should by any misfortune— or intrigue—Germany in September again not be accepted, little, I believe, would be left of the Locarno Pact by autumn. The League is the organization best fit to bring about the series of agreements to which the Locarno arrangements must necessarily lead up. The re-establishment of a well-balanced European order, it is true, is to some degree a purely European matter. The idea of giving certain issues over to a European section of the League may soon come up for discussion. But there are other agreements for which even the whole present League is insufficient. I think, in the first place, of questions like disarmament. Here American and Russian co-operation proves indispensable.

We must now try, therefore, to analyse the significance of the Locarno Treaty respecting Germany's relations both with Russia and with the United States. I must apologize for leaving aside the intricate problems of relations between Germany and Poland or Czechoslovakia. I am aware of the fact that they may at any moment prove to be most urgently in need of a satisfactory settlement. It has seemed impossible, however, to cover so wide a field in one lecture. Some words must be said in regard to England.

The promoters of Pan-European ideas and other groups working on similar lines are expressing the opinion that the Continental powers of Europe should form some kind of separate union. Neither Russia nor Great Britain are to be included. They believe Franco-German relations could become more intimate if there were no third great power involved in their agreements. They can point to the fact that in history England has often been able to profit by dissensions between France and Germany, and has been able to use these two powers against one another. Most Germans, however, I think, would agree that there is little hope for Germany and France being able really to overcome their mutual suspicions and fear if England were not there to help bridge the gulf. The dangers pointed out above would seem to them the smaller evil. Great responsibility therefore comes to lie on England's shoulders. She can choose either to separate or to unite the nations of the Continent. Germany cannot expect England altruistically to forget her own

M

interests. But the benefits to England resulting from European stabilization by Franco-German friendship, it is hoped, will prove superior to those promised by the Latin proverb : Divide and thou shalt rule.

With England forming a part of the European combination the danger of friction between a continental *bloc* and Great Britain is being avoided. Some people point out, however, that another and greater menace to peace is not being sufficiently considered. They see the continental powers becoming a weapon in the hands of England against other powers. For Germany this would mean that she would become the country in which armies are to fight for England. You will remember that the Russian problem was in everybody's mind in the days of Locarno. Germany's attitude toward Russia was then, and has often since been, misinterpreted. It looks as if it were dictated by some sentimental sympathy. The so-called Berlin Treaty which was signed between Germany and Russia last April seems to give much more to Russia than it does to Germany. Germany promises not to take part in any war of aggression against Russia. It pledges itself furthermore never to become a partner to any anti-Russian coalition, formed with the intention of bringing about financial or economic boycott against Russia. Russia promises the same kind of neutrality. But practically this is of far less importance. The probabilities of the near future anyhow lie far more in the line of wars against Russia. What benefit then does Germany expect from the Treaty ?

The Berlin Treaty must be looked upon as an official German interpretation of the Locarno agreements. Germany wished to make it clear that she could only co-operate with the western powers, if, and as long as, they gave up any intention they might have had in the back of their minds to attempt aggressive war against Russia. Germany has most to fear from the re-commencement of a vicious circle between Western Europe and Russia. She would, of course, lose whatever political or economic backing she may be getting from Russia. In addition to that she would be continually threatened with becoming Europe's battle-field again as in centuries gone by. The great international importance of Germany definitely opposing any aggressive policy on the part of the combined Locarno powers lies not in the assistance given to the Soviet system. It is to be found in the fact of the Anglo-Franco-German agreement thus being interpreted, in one very important direction at least as a purely defensive alignment.

Nobody, I suppose, would assert that the foreign policy of the big European powers up to the present day has been anything like purely defensive. I would not like to prophesy that the tendency is for it to become so in future. But I do believe that if England, France, and Germany really want to stabilize the European order they will have to give up much of their aggressiveness in regard to the rest of the world. On a policy of aggression they will never be able to agree. Agreements between them therefore make for peace not only in Europe. The result of such a check put on their foreign policy most likely will be a tendency to strengthen their efforts in making the League a universal organization. If countries can no longer settle conflicts with other nations by aggressiveness and violence, without risking the destruction of important neighbourly agreements in doing so, there is every reason for them to wish to arrive at definite modes of peaceful procedure with all other nations. Here again I must point out the extreme difficulty of the task. The big powers are heavily engaged in colonial disputes. Capitalistic

and nationalistic imperialism and boundary-lines fixed by
violence have brought about terrible antagonisms all over
the world. I cannot see how the League could be expected
to deal efficiently with the problems that are sure to arise
unless she finds a way of inducing both the United States and
Russia to co-operate regularly with her in matters of universal
importance.

The more America gets to know of all the difficulties yet
to be overcome in settling Europe's post-war troubles, the
less tempting it may seem to her to become entangled. But
is it really a question to-day of whether America wishes to
become entangled? The feeling in Germany is that a
statesman over here can but rarely take a decision of importance without having America in mind. America's financial
and economic predominance has deeply impressed the people
of Europe. It is even being exaggerated to a point that
makes for bitterness and resentment. At such a moment the
question is no longer whether the continents shall go their
way in splendid isolation. There is a choice as yet whether
the existing and unavoidable mutual dependence shall be
organized in common or whether it shall be allowed to
expose the world to all the risks of anarchy. Germany, I
need hardly say, feels largely dependent upon America's sym-
pathies. I have not felt that there is much resentment
about it. It is even astonishing how little in that respect is
left over of the war-psychology. There is much talk, of
course, of future revisions of the Dawes Plan, but everybody
feels that they can only come from the free consent of
America. People in Germany have been asking themselves
whether it might be to the profit of their country if America
should decide to use its financial predominance either for
enforcing disarmament, or for bringing about a reduction of

reparation claims on the part of European creditors. Opinions are divided. Knowing of the disastrous effects of what I have called the vicious circle, I believe, if I were allowed to give my personal opinion, I would warn any one of expecting good from a policy of mere pressure or violence. Germany especially has experienced again and again since the war that it is always the first to suffer when France or England have serious difficulties with other nations. The best she can hope and work for is that America may take its full share in helping to bring about a more stable balance of power by all-round friendly agreements. It is for such agreements to lead up to disarmament and debt settlement by free consent.

I have spoken of Germany, France, and other nations as if in each of them public opinion were unanimous, uniting all classes and political parties on one political programme. You all know how little this corresponds to the real situation. The Locarno policy, nevertheless, has been able to unite a larger majority in Germany than any other issue has been able to do since the end of the war. Far into the ranks of so-called nationalist and socialist circles conviction has spread that the present situation made necessary such new methods. Some, of course, greeted them with enthusiasm, others have had to resign themselves to accepting them. In France, if I am not mistaken, Briand's policy is also finding so large a support, that he is able to survive the crises of various cabinets. This does not mean that the majority of Germans and Frenchmen have suddenly turned pacifists. It shows, moreover, how urgent the need and how strong the interests are that demand co-operation between the two countries. We must, however, not overlook the groups both to the right and to left of the Locarno majority—if I may speak in terms of parliamentarism—that do not agree or that bitterly oppose the policy of their present governments. The communists are convinced that it is hopeless to seek for peace in a capitalistic world. The 'Bourgeois' agreements, they believe, are but forms of capitalistic conspiracy changing competition among exploiters into exploitation in common. To the radical nationalists agreements such as that of Locarno appear only as a method for establishing more firmly the domination of the powerful nations over the weak ones. Both groups, I believe, are a real challenge. They are sure to grow, and even to become predominant, not only in Germany, if the new agreements should ever be allowed to become nothing more than ideological screens behind which capitalistic or nationalistic violence may hide itself. The radical groups have again and again been in a position to unmask economic and other interests abusing the words and organizations of peace. It has taken a long time for German youth to regain confidence, after having so deeply experienced deception by fine words, behind which there was no reality. Nothing could strengthen the radical groups at present as could hypocrisy in regard to the achievements of Locarno. It will serve the cause of peace far more if its sincere promoters be the first to denounce any fraud committed in the name of peace. Why not call a disarmament conference by the name it deserves, if the outcome is but a new sanction to armaments? I have taken this as a purely imaginary example. I hope it is not a prophetic vision.

The German people are far from expecting wonders or quick results. France has her good reasons for wanting to step carefully. The Germans do not pretend to be angels of peace and moderation. But the same, I think, is true the other way round too. Conferences may fail, even when they pretend to be accómplishing great progress. If the friends of international co-operation, however, will courageously expose failures and yet not lose their faith and energy, I am certain that an ever-growing number of Germans will come and fill their ranks.

CHAPTER IX

THE FOREIGN POLICY OF THE UNITED STATES SINCE THE WAR

Mr. CHESTER H. ROWELL :

THE foreign policy of the United States, so far as it influenced the Treaty of Versailles, began with the foundation of the League of Nations, and I am proud, as a Republican, to be in an institution on whose walls President Woodrow Wilson is commemorated.

The foreign policy of the United States since that time has been an interesting study in the psychology of reactions. There was first the reaction against the war and the administration of the war period. It provides an example of that curious mixture of tenses which seems to make up so much of popular American psychology. That confusion of tenses comes out to-day in what has become the most exciting subject now under discussion in America. Nearly all the political agitation in America at this time is on the question of whether the United States shall adopt the eighteenth Amendment. You observe a certain mixture of tenses there !

About the time when the Peace Treaty was being concluded, American psychology began to discuss the question ' Shall we enter the war ? ' A considerable element in the population of America, including some very active politicians in the Senate of the United States, decided that future tense question in the negative, and proceeded to act accordingly. There was first, therefore, this reaction against the administration of the war, and criticisms, both legitimate and illegitimate, on war policies and their details and operation.

There was next a personal reaction against Mr. Wilson

himself. Mr. Wilson had all his life been a person of certain psychological fallibilities of temperament. His colleagues in the University were familiar with those fallibilities, and the strain and responsibility of the Presidency did not decrease them, while sickness greatly increased them. These fallibilities of temperament ran counter to other fallibilities, less excusable, in the United States Senate, and President Wilson did not understand how to deal effectively with the pettiness and egoism of the senators.

The result was the calamity that an insignificant minority in the Senate of the United States, when much more than two-thirds of the senators were ready to vote for entry into the League of Nations, made the Senate vote against entering the League. A majority of the senators voted for entry, but that majority fell short of the requisite two-thirds. That was due to lack of tactfulness on Wilson's part.

Whether you regard that as a major or minor psychological phenomenon depends on your estimate of the different qualities of the human mind and character, but as an historical phenomenon it was one of the great tragedies in the history of the world. I will not apportion the degree of guilt between the psychology of a sick man in his bed in the White House, and the psychology of petty men playing the small tricks of minor politics in the Senate of the United States.

There were also wider public reactions. We must be careful to distinguish between the reactions of the people and the playing of the game of the senators. The senators skilfully used the reactions of the people as one of their tools in the game. There were two different reactions against the Peace Treaties. There was, first of all, that legitimate reaction which was voiced in the objections of British Liberals, and which in America produced all the intelligent arguments used against the Treaty of Versailles. It produced arguments, many of which have since been justified by history. Among people of your class in America there were many who sympathized with those views, but they found no voice in the United States Senate. In the Senate criticisms of the Treaty of Versailles and of the Covenant of the League were based not on the only too-evident follies of those documents, but almost exclusively on their virtues. The chief objection to the League of Nations in the country was that it was not yet possible to make it a complete and powerful inter-State organization, and that it was not yet competent to do all the things which idealists dreamed it might do. The objection to it in the United States Senate, however, was that it was too competent and might possibly do some of those things. When my friend Professor James Harvey Robinson, in the opening chapters of his book on *Mind in the Making,* compared the argument of two wayside mechanics repairing a motor-car with the arguments on the League in the United States Senate, very much to the disadvantage of the latter, he was only too correct.

What I have been describing are the reactions which took place against the war itself, and against the very idea of America ever having entered into it. That reaction is an emotional one. You will find very few persons who will acknowledge it intellectually. The general reaction against the Peace Treaties, however, was manipulated with extraordinary skill by certain elements in the country, and particularly in the Senate, and that caused the first great step in the development of the foreign policy of America after the war, which was her non-ratification of the Treaty of Versailles. That Treaty was not ratified simply because it contained the Covenant of the League of Nations.

Popular psychology also had its reactions owing to the cosmopolitan nature of America. Those of you who are Europeans and who live in homogeneous countries must come to America before you can realize what sort of people, what sort of congeries of people, there are there. During the war there was absolute uniformity of action and of expression— that is the tyranny of all wars—but those who had been suffering from these repressions and inhibitions immediately after the war began to make their influence felt again in the new atmosphere of freedom. There was the reaction of the Irish, who are always a potent element in American politics. Those of you who are not Americans should realize that by far the greatest Irish city in the world is New York, and there are many more Irish in America than there are in Ireland. Even to this day, in my own city San Francisco, meetings are held by Irish people in the name of Irish politics and patriotism which, if held in Ireland, would be repressed by the Irish Government as treason against Ireland. In the recrudescence of Irish influence in American politics the League of Nations was objected to because Ireland was not in it, and that objection is still maintained although Ireland is now in it.

The Italian group is now becoming a very important force in American politics. I know of one Assembly district in San Francisco and of several Assembly districts and one or two Congressional districts in New York where there is every year a violent contest between two Italian politicians as to which one shall represent that Italian district, and the only real issue between them is as to which Irishman's Italian shall represent the district. It is simply the old Irish politics not yet extinguished and the new Italian politics not yet mature exerting their influence. There was also the recrudescence of suppressed pro-Germanism, and a recrudescence of fear of pro-Germanism on the part of American politicians. All these things arose out of our congeries of still unassimilated peoples, and produced confusion in the American mind. They led to a lack of confidence on the part of American people and American politicians as to the possibility of America taking an intelligent part in foreign affairs.

It is curious how this inferiority complex shows itself when one nation thinks of its relations with others. We constantly hear in America that our representatives abroad are no match for the skilled diplomatists of Europe. I happened to be in Japan, on the other hand, at the time the invitation was extended to that country to attend the Washington Conference. I talked to some Japanese who were very doubtful about attending it, and they wanted to know what trick we ' smart Americans ' had up our sleeves to impose upon the innocent, frank, and straightforward Japanese! That opinion of ourselves as innocent and gullible people is one which other peoples seem to share in regard to themselves, and to speak about with a certain amount of pride, comparing their own simplicity with the skill and astuteness of their rivals. That feeling also led to isolationism.

Thus the isolationism of America grew and grew. I do not believe it has extended to the whole of our people, and I do not think it ever will. But I do think that that isolationism, plus indifference, would probably represent at this moment the mathematical majority of our people. Let us hope such a state of affairs will not continue. It cannot be denied, however, that the enormous majority of the American people do not know and do not care anything about the subjects we are considering.

I have just come from a country [1] where every one is a

[1] Russia.

politician and an economist and in which every person is intensely interested in politics, and I found they were astounded when Douglas Fairbanks visited them to discover that this great man did not know anything about politics. Having just come, as I say, from a country of that sort, I can appreciate the fact that the mathematical majority of our people are completely uninterested in the whole business.

You must add to that the reaction which has arisen and produced isolationism. That isolationism has as its effective organ a small but very powerful body in the United States Senate, but the isolationism manifested there is no mere psychological reaction; it is a determined personal policy on the part of a small group of the most skilled manipulators of the political game in the United States. That small group, although possessing not nearly one-third of the votes in the United States Senate, defeated the Treaty of Versailles, and only last year tried to defeat the adherence of America to the World Court. In that it was not successful, as there was no sick President in the White House to deal with, but the group in question was successful in loading American adherence with conditions which Geneva next month will have to consider, and, should any one nation out of the forty-eight present members decline to accept those conditions, this insignificant group in the United States Senate will have won a victory against all those who compose the present administration, and against a huge majority of their own colleagues as well as practically the whole American people. It is a curious illustration of the effect of mechanics and of skill in the operation of Government. These men are skilled men, determined men, and in a perfectly legitimate sense reckless men, as one may well be if one takes only a negative part in affairs. If you wish to construct this building you must put every stone and beam in its exact place, and you have to be very careful about it. If you wish to pull this building down, however, it is a matter of indifference at which end you begin ; the final result will be the same.

A certain amount of isolationism exists throughout the country generally, which it is, however, exceedingly difficult to measure. We have had two opportunities of gauging it recently, one of which was the measure of public support given to American adherence to the Permanent Court of International Justice. In the earlier stages of the proposal to adhere to that Court there was no measure of the public support it would receive, but it was soon found that all the leaders of the people almost without exception were in favour of that policy. It was favoured both by the Republican and the Democratic parties and by labour and capital in their organized capacities, and it was supported also by the various religious sects, organized bodies of women and so on. In the end every articulate voice of organized opinion in America supported the proposal with the single exception of the small group of senators to which I have referred, the Hearst newspapers and the *Chicago Tribune*. If that did not represent American public sentiment then all our organizations, formal and informal, for its representation are misrepresentative.

Then came the fight led by Senator Borah in various senatorial campaigns to make this the issue before the people, and that fight is now going on. I have been out of touch with American affairs for the last month and so I do not know how things are going, but a month ago it was still doubtful mathematically which way the census would go and almost more doubtful whether that alleged census meant anything. On the other hand, there has been a tremendous effort by politicians who think it is good for one more election to raise this issue and to test the proposition that the American people are of one mind in the face of the fact that all their leaders and trusted representatives are of the other.

There is also a very great reaction based firstly on the question of American debts, and secondly upon the American opinion that Europe has no use for America except for what it can get out of her. On the subject of American debts there has been, as you will have appreciated, a conflict of the two psychologies based on the fundamental error of human nature of treating all questions as if they were moral. There are some questions which are not moral. The multiplication table, for instance, is not moral. Economic laws are not moral. The laws of economics operate very much like the law of gravitation. You can pump water uphill but it takes more power to pump it uphill than it will produce by coming back. You can sometimes reverse the laws of economics by main strength but in the long run they operate.

Our people have not always known that and the people on both sides have thought that this question of debts was not an economic but a moral question. The French say ' It is morally wrong that Germany should not pay us '. It is morally wrong, but mathematically it is impossible that they should pay them. The French say ' It is morally wrong that we should have to pay to America sums of money expended for ammunition we shot away to protect America, and that we should have to pay America when Germany does not pay us.' On the other hand, the Americans say ' This is a business world and there is nothing in this world but business. There are no principles in this world but business principles. Accepting these axioms, if people owe us money they should pay and it is immoral that they should not.' Gradually in the hard school of experience both sides are learning that economic questions must be settled on economic principles. France has been learning that. French experts have known from the beginning what had to be done and what should not be done, but they have had to do things which they know should not be done so that by actual experience of their failure their people might discover they would not work. America has to go through that school to learn by experience what it would be infinitely cheaper to learn by intelligence.

There has also been a moral reaction in America against Europe. We have made the unexpected and shocking discovery that the European nations are selfish, that each nation in Europe is out for its own ends and that each nation is trying by intrigue and trickery to get all it can. We, as a virtuous people who have none of these defects, are very naturally indignant at the exhibition that Europe made of itself here in this city last March, although I very much question the right of America to get excited over it. These things, however, have gradually developed in America a very large psychology of isolationism, a psychology that is perhaps somewhat analogous to the other psychology I have just come from—the isolationism of Russia.

Russia has isolated herself from the League of Nations because she feels isolated from the rest of the world in every other respect. Russia has made debating points against the League of Nations which can be used for argument but mean nothing in substance. America has done the same thing and I think that except for purposes of political manipulation we may very well omit all the debating points of both. The real reason is the instinctive feeling of both nations that they are both so great, so self-sufficient, and so different from the rest of the world, that the League of Nations might be allowed to degenerate into a Western European alliance to solve its local problems. That is a very common opinion in America. One needs nothing beyond the glimmering of an idea of logic to see how false that idea is, but amongst a great and intelligent people who devote one-tenth of 1 per cent. of their thought to this question (when they are doing extra well) it is an opinion which is widely held since matters are not properly thought out.

Among those who had adopted the isolationist view and afterwards became ashamed of it various attempts were made to substitute something for the League, some of which were merely futile but some more substantial.

First of all there was Warren Harding's campaign. Some of us may remember the peculiarly ingenious speeches which Harding made. I started out in the campaign with the idea that Mr. Harding's mental processes were somewhat slow and crude. Many things which occurred afterwards confirmed me in that impression, but not these speeches. These speeches were composed with a degree of astuteness of which no person of dull intellect would have been capable. One-half of the speeches were for the League of Nations if you read them hastily, but if you read them with care every word of them could have been read critically as against the League of Nations. The other half were violent speeches against the League of Nations if you read them carelessly, but if you read them critically every one of them could be interpreted as in favour of the League of Nations. Incidentally my friend Mr. Hiram Johnson took each of those speeches against the League of Nations and translated it into unambiguous language and Harding was not in a position to repudiate that translation and was held to it afterwards.

After these ingenious speeches whose *raison d'être* was the entirely intelligible desire to secure the votes of both sides

Harding brought forward a proposal for an association of nations. I heard of a similar proposal from official sources in Russia last week. The history of America since has shown the futility of it. With the best will in the world Harding could not even formulate on paper any location on earth in which to put his association of nations which was not already covered either by the League or by nations who would not go into the League or into ' an association '. Nevertheless, it was an ingenious method of confusing American thought for the time being.

There came afterwards two more intelligent and successful gestures, the first being the Washington Conference. The Washington Conference undertook to do two things and did do one-half of one of them, and did it very well. It undertook to consider the whole problem of disarmament, but France declined to discuss land disarmament at all. In the direction of a reduction of land armament America had nothing to offer, since her whole armed forces would not be equal to the police force of New York and Chicago and were barely equal proportionally to the amount of armed forces to Germany. France was invincible in her determination that the question should not even be mentioned at the Conference.

On the naval side we were successful in disarming the race for naval armament in major vessels and we were successful for the simple reason that we could apply the sole method by which such proposals can be made to succeed. We had the most to give up and we gave it up. If by a generous gesture the nation with the greatest army were to say ' We are ready to disarm ; we will disband one-half or two-thirds of our army if others will do the same ' the proposal would instantly be accepted. America could and did make that proposal with

regard to major vessels of war. It did not succeed in regard
to minor vessels of war. It did not even start doing anything
about air armaments. Nevertheless, it performed a tremendous
service in stopping the ruinous race for building the greatest,
the most expensive, and most wasteful objects of the modern
world, thus saving money for nations which had plenty of
other things to do with it and supporting a sentiment of
peace.

I have told you something of the atmosphere in Japan,
when Japan was invited to the Washington Conference. I
had an opportunity of talking to the Japanese Commissioners
when they were on their way back to Japan. They were like
men who had gone through a moral regeneration or religious
conversion. They had discovered to their astonishment that
Mr. Hughes was an honest and sincere man and to them that
was one of the greatest revelations in human nature they had
ever had vouchsafed to them. They were glowing with
enthusiasm at their discovery.

Finally came the question of the World Court. The
World Court, as you know, is an essential part of the system
for the unification of mankind. In its practical operations
it is very important, but American membership of it, with
all the reservations which were adopted in the Senate, gives
to her adherence, if accepted, what cannot be regarded as
more than a purely sentimental value. Provided we are
generously allowed to adhere to the Court on our own terms,
I think, however, that that step will prove to be of great
practical value. Its only present value, if consummated by
the acceptance of our reservations, is as a public gesture towards a renewal of co-operation with the world from which
we have temporarily withdrawn. What will happen to
America's proposal will be known, I hope, in the course of

a few weeks. At any rate, if America finally finds herself in the World Court, formally, publicly, and officially in one world organization, it will open a wide psychological door to the possibility of adjusting American sentiment to fuller co-operation. That is the objection raised against it.

Here again there is a distinction to be observed between debating points and reasons. A debating point made was that American adherence to the World Court would be the first step towards American membership of the League of Nations. Formally and technically that is not true at all. Formally and technically the terms of the American adherence to the World Court do not involve her even in such relations as the World Court has to the League of Nations. We might remain fully fledged members of the World Court for ever yet never have any relations with the League of Nations. While this is true technically and legally, every one knows it is not true psychologically. Every one knows that having once broken down the taboo of any sort of international relations, the question of any other sort of international relations becomes at least possible to discuss. It was the fear of this psychological opening of the American mind rather than the pretended fear of opening the door to this building that caused the desperate opposition to the World Court on the part of Senators who knew perfectly well that the terms of America's adherence made our action at least harmless to anybody and probably almost useless to everybody.

We have also had our own domestic problems, amongst which I should first mention the question of normalcy. That again is a case of confusion of tenses. The old world was regarded as the normal world, the ideal world. The America of whatever date when we were young was regarded as the final culmination of the progress of humanity. Everything that had happened before that was good and nothing must ever happen after that. Historically as a nation we are very inclined to put that date at 1789, and we think no new political thought later than that date. Economically, we are likely to put the date at whatever was the culmination of the industrial revolution—in the eighties or nineties of the last century for instance—and personally, we put it at whatever date we stopped, at the age of adolescence, the thinking of a lifetime.

So we elected Mr. Harding on that programme and we proceeded to adjust ourselves on the assumption that nothing had happened and nothing must happen. As a matter of fact for the time being that was probably the wisest thing to do in our fiscal affairs. The first requisite was to pull down the great war machinery and retrench the great war expenses and put ourselves governmentally to the sordid task of running the Government as cheaply as possible, while individually facing the interesting task of restoring our business as usual. These are not inspiring ideals, but I think they are justified for a few years after the war.

Because this was a domestic problem it turned our eyes inwards. You are well aware that in the early days when we faced the Atlantic foreign relations were not only part of the policy of the United States, but of the consciousness of the people. Then for three long generations we conquered a great continent and turned our minds inward. Only recently have we turned them outward again and when there came the slightest provocation to turn them inward the process was both easy and natural.

There was also the fear of Japan—a fear of any sort of relations with Japan. There were the real rivalries of interest and policy between America and Japan and the Bugaboo rivalries which in both countries set up bogeys every other week, and led to fears of war when neither country has either a cause, the physical capacity, or a desire for war. Nevertheless, the bogey of Japan has occupied a large place in the minds of some Americans. I would have no objection to that bogey if the question were really thought out, and it was realized that no matter how isolated America may remain from Europe, America never has been, and never can be, isolated from Asia. I would not mind if it was realized that America's neglect of and scorn for the League of Nations may lead to that body shrinking to an alliance of Western Europe so that there will be three great alliances in the world and the situation which made the great war in Europe will once more occur on a world-wide scale, making a world war inevitable with my own State of California as its first battle ground.

Unfortunately people have not thought the matter out so fully as that. They still think in the old terms of new problems to which those terms do not apply.

Certainly the reaction is already beginning. I think this small group of isolationists which in the Senate has never been anything but a fanatical minority is now coming to represent a fanatical minority of the people. It is a very intense minority and like its leaders will probably fight to the last ditch, but the people of America are coming to realize more and more that America is not isolated and that this shrinking planet has no longer room in it for any one to be isolated. That has manifested itself in certain concrete ways. It has manifested itself in a constantly increasing degree of co-operation between the United States and the outer edge of the League of Nations.

The position is a very curious one. The Republican Part has been in power ever since the war and there have been two factions within that party on these policies throughout that time. All the noise has been made by one of those factions. In spite of that the majority of the members of the Cabinets of both Harding and Coolidge have adhered to the other faction. I think that if at any time a free vote had been taken in the American Cabinet on the League of Nations, it would have been found that their opinion was in favour of the League during the whole of this anti-League of Nations administration.

The policy of both Presidents, though it began rather timidly during the first part of Mr. Harding's administration, seems to have been to go as far as they thought was safe in co-operating with the League of Nations. By safe I mean without causing an explosion in the Senate. They sent delegates to the Opium Conference and to the Disarmament Conference, and they apologized for sending representives to the Disarmament Conference by saying the Conference was futile and would not do anything so that there was no need to be afraid of it. They have informal representatives of all sorts attached to the various organs of the League. They even answer letters from the League nowadays, at least to the extent of acknowledging their receipt. There was a time when literally they were afraid to do even that.

I am perfectly sure that Coolidge and the dominant members of his Cabinet would go very much farther than that except that they wish to succeed in whatever they do. If they can move forward an inch at a time and bring most of the Senate with them and keep the rest of it quiet they may even perhaps be able to move forward another inch. Personally I should prefer a bolder policy, but they may be right since they have to deal with such an explosive and reactionary party as the so-called progressives in the United States Senate now are.

American politics consist largely of paradoxes.

The gesture in regard to the World Court was very largely some sort of apology to ourselves for something we had grown ashamed of. Neither party dared leave it out of its platform. The house of representatives in shame voted 11 to 1 in favour of it. The Senate finally voted in favour of it by an enormous majority and then cast its anchor to windward by adopting reservations. Nevertheless, what has been done is a step forward.

The question is what hope there is for the future. I think we may place our faith in the eternal progress of events. You can put that faith in a mystic religious form if you like. Certain laws must inevitably be fulfilled sooner or later, and certain prophecies may perhaps be based on the inevitableness of events. There is no escape from the conclusion that the isolationist policy will become in the hard school of experience visibly impossible. It has already become so in so many details that isolationism is now an emotion and a theory ; it is no longer a fact. If we could merely follow the policy of having no theories at all and dealing with each emergency as it arose, the direct result of such a policy would be progress. I am convinced that that is the present policy of the American Government in the strictly technical sense of the word ' Government '. It is not the policy of the Opposition. We have some very peculiar features in our constitution which people from Great Britain may find it difficult to understand. The policy I have mentioned is not the policy of the Opposition. I think in both Houses of Congress (and especially in the Senate, which is the only one which has to do with foreign relations) the Opposition are in control as representing the majority party of all the strategic committees. If you had in Britain a conservative government with a conservative prime minister, and in that conservative party there was an insignificant group of persons opposed to the conservative party and their policy and who constituted in fact its most violent opponents, and then you made your ministry exclusively of them, you would have a situation which would exactly resemble the present situation in the Senate of the United States. The perfectly sensible policy of the administration of having no policy at all—and British people ought to understand that—and of simply doing each time the practical thing regardless of whether it involves inconsistencies, will inevitably lead towards an abandonment of the isolationist policy, but it will have to be carried through, if it is carried through, against the opposition in the Senate, which means that it cannot flow in its natural channels and must sometimes leap exceedingly difficult rocks.

CHAPTER X

THE FOREIGN POLICY OF THE UNION OF SOCIALIST SOVIET REPUBLICS

Mr. MICHAEL FARBMAN :

ONE feels naturally a little perplexed on being asked to give an account of the foreign policy of the Union of Socialist Soviet Republics. This arises first of all from the fact that the new Russian State has begun only quite recently to evolve anything which can be fairly so described ; for it cannot be disputed that for the first years of the Revolution Russia, while possessing a Foreign Office, could not be said to have a foreign policy. Foreign policy had been superseded by foreign propaganda. Just after the Revolution the Department of Foreign Affairs in the Soviet State was purely a department of foreign propaganda. In October 1917, when Trotsky became the first Commissar for Foreign Affairs the belief current among the Bolsheviks obviously was that the Foreign Office was a bourgeois prejudice and had no place in a proletarian state. 'I accepted this post of Commissar for Foreign Affairs', Trotsky said on one occasion, 'just because I wanted to have more leisure for party affairs. My job is a small one : to publish the secret documents and to close up the shop.' But even long after Chicherin had replaced Trotsky at the head of this Commissariat, and Chicherin's attitude to foreign affairs and to this particular position was, as we all know, much more serious than Trotsky's, the Foreign Office continued for quite a considerable time to be a mere department of foreign propaganda. The change from foreign propaganda to foreign policy was a very slow and painful process. But of the causes and the development of this change I shall speak later. My immediate business is to proceed to an explanation of the second difficulty that confronts one in dealing with Russia's foreign policy.

Soviet Russia has obviously a peculiar aim in her foreign relations, and without doubt has evolved a peculiar method of realizing her aim. But both aim and method are so entangled, so seemingly contradictory, that it is by no means easy to resolve them into anything like a system. Whether this is due solely to lack of experience on the part of Soviet diplomatists or to their employment of a diplomatic language strangely interspersed with revolutionary jargon, or to both, it is hard to say. At any rate, in all Bolshevik diplomatic declarations, still more in all pronouncements of policy intended for internal circulation, one cannot help detecting contradictory principles. The result is that declarations and pronouncements are so indefinite in their wording that the maximum latitude of interpretation is always possible. These are the main difficulties that one encounters in attempting to define the foreign policy of the Soviet Union. Notwithstanding, we see now clearly enough that the new State is pursuing a line of policy more or less consistent, and, if we use a little patience and persistence, we may, I think, be fortunate enough to arrive at a fairly correct interpretation of this policy.

It is not my intention to detain you with a *réchauffé* of the history of the Russian Revolution; but a few words in explanation of how and why revolutionary propaganda abroad has been replaced in Moscow by a more or less traditional foreign policy are, I fear, unavoidable.

We are now fully aware that the Bolsheviks, when they found themselves actually in power, shared the opinion of the outside world that they were a mere episode and had not come to stay. They looked upon themselves not as the Government of the country, but simply as leaders of one of the armies of the World Revolution. How thoroughly and how sincerely they may have believed in the imminence of the expected World Revolution is a matter of some dubiety. But of their belief that, without a World Revolution, they would be unable to retain the Government in their hands, there cannot be the slightest doubt. To them there seemed only this alternative possible : either the arrival of the World Revolution, which would establish them in power for all time or, in case the World Revolution failed to arrive, their own disappearance with, as Trotsky said, ' as big a bang on the door of history as was possible '.

In this envisagement of the situation there was obviously no room for anything like foreign policy. Their attitude to the outside world was bound to consist of nothing more than downright revolutionary propaganda. But history is full of surprises, and the Bolsheviks, who had established themselves in the Kremlin as the general staff of the World Revolution soon found themselves compelled not only to rule their country, but to fight for the re-creation of its integrity. And then the most unexpected thing of all happened ; for the Bolsheviks proved to be mistaken in both of their anticipations. The World Revolution failed to arrive, and yet they failed to go. To their utter surprise they continued to exist at the head of the country. More than that, with the termination of the policy of intervention, the Western Powers began to be more and more inclined to come to some understanding with the Soviet State. The Bolsheviks were, however, for the time so sceptical as to the possibility of securing any terms with the capitalist world

that, while ready enough to take part in diplomatic negotiations, they still trusted in the main to revolutionary propaganda as the chief guarantee for their security. But the
more they began to feel themselves secure from internal
opposition, the more they began to long for the security of
the State from external aggression. And the more they
began to feel that the capitalist regime of the world, which
in their earlier view had been tottering, was in process of
stabilization, the more they themselves began to be eager
for coming to terms with it. Previously their main aim had
been to make friends and to establish relations in foreign
countries with the Left, with Labour, and with the forces
of the future revolution. Later they were attracted by the
desirability of making friends and of establishing relations
abroad with Governments, with financiers, and with the
forces of Capitalism.

The beginning of the new policy we can trace to the
negotiations of the first trade agreement with Great Britain
of 1921 ; while its first great achievement was the conclusion
of the Rapallo Treaty with Germany in 1922. But, even
when the plunge had been taken and a solemn treaty of
friendship had been ratified between capitalist and bourgeois
Germany and Soviet Russia, all traces of the old policy, or,
shall I say, of the habit of conducting revolutionary propaganda abroad, could not at once be wiped out ; such radical
changes are never sudden and immediately complete. Moreover, in the minds of the Bolshevik politicians the idea still
lingered that revolutionary difficulties might possibly occur
in the West and in the East.

The big change in Russia only began when the Bolsheviks
finally realized that the post-war unrest in the world was
overcome, and that the capitalist régime had been, to use

their own phrase, ' stabilized '. Obviously, some of them had been early aware that the crisis of capitalism was only temporary, and they warned Bolshevik Russia time and again that the theory of the mortal sickness of capitalism should not be taken too literally. But most of the Bolshevik leaders were bound to regard such leniency towards capitalism as heretical. They were deeply committed to a belief in the imminency of a World Revolution. Moreover, they were in no mood to abandon their dream of a transformation of the world in which they would appear as the Messiahs of the age.

The conviction that capitalism had withstood all post-war attacks and was sound enough to be likely to continue in the West for quite a considerable period naturally then took some time in gaining general currency in this quarter. But, once admitted, it was bound to influence the entire policy of the Soviet State. And to-day it is not only admitted by the Communist Party, but has become official doctrine and the basic principle of their policy. In fact, Stalin, the General Secretary of the Communist Party and the High Priest of Communist Orthodoxy, actually made the stabilization of capitalism the text for his political report to the last Congress of the Communist Party (December 1925). The significance of this changed attitude is hard to exaggerate ; it really implies and necessitates on Russia's part the adoption of an entirely new orientation to the West. Stalin indeed, discussing the foreign relations of Russia at the Congress, declared without hesitation that what had been considered by Lenin a temporary respite or a truce was now likely to inaugurate a long period of peaceful relations between Soviet Russia and the Capitalist States.

There is probably no better way of indicating the tremendous change that has taken place in the psychology and outlook of the Russian Communist Party than by reminding you that only a few years ago those unfortunate Communists who dared to whisper that there were signs of the stabilization of capitalism in the West were promptly ' combed out ' from the Party as infidels, or were condemned as ' opposition '. Whereas at present the infidels and the opposition consist of leaders like Zinoviev and Trotsky, who venture to express some doubt as to this alleged stabilization. The recent controversy in the Russian Communist Party was indeed mainly if not entirely due to the fact that Zinoviev, Trotsky, and some minor leaders of the Third International are totally at variance with the majority of the Central Committee of the Party on two vital points. Still adhering to the belief that World Revolution, though postponed, will arrive ' in our time ', they refuse to take it for granted that Capitalism has been stabilized in the West. This may seem simply an academic disagreement. So it would be if the Russian Communist Party were not burdened with the responsibility of Government. But in this case, where the Central Committee has to dictate policy for the State, such a theoretical disagreement becomes a disagreement in immediate practical policy and threatens to break the unity of the party. And in fact in all questions of internal and foreign policy the Zinoviev-Kamenev-Trotsky opposition offers a solution which differs very considerably from that adopted by the majority of the party. Take the internal policy for instance. It is obvious that every measure adopted in any branch of domestic policy, fiscal, industrial, or agricultural, will differ radically according as it is dictated by a trend to revolution or a trend to stabilization. The Left Wing, which is still true in a certain degree to the doctrine of World Revolution, is naturally very apprehensive about the development of State Capitalism in Russia, which in its opinion is more and more diverging from the straight and consistent path towards Socialism ; while the Central Committee, convinced in their mind that the revolutionary wave is abating in the West, believes that the growth of State Capitalism and of trade relations with the West and the introduction into the country of more and more foreign capital is the only sound way of promoting Russia's internal development. Big as this change in the psychology and the outlook of the Russian Communist party is, this is not the only or even the biggest change that has taken place in Russia during the last few years.

But before proceeding farther I should like to take advantage of this opportunity to express my conviction that, at the root of the difficulty of understanding and judging the situation in Russia, lies the unwillingness or inability to realize that the process of evolution and change in that country is real and is proceeding at a more accelerated pace than it is in the West. In the West, where evolution continues at a normal pace, ten years mean very little in the way of changes. But in Russia during the nine years of the so-called Bolshevik régime we have witnessed at least three changes so radical and so diametrically opposed to one another, that each one ought really to be regarded and studied by itself. My complaint then is that people in the West are misled by the continuity of the Bolshevik personnel into believing in the existence of a similar continuity of Bolshevik policy. Bolshevism in fact has been so much identified with militant and terrorist methods, with world revolution and the Cheka, that some observers, especially those who have studied this aspect of Bolshevism at close quarters, find it difficult to believe that the same persons, continuing at the head of a revolutionary Government and seemingly wielding unchallenged authority, can be conceived as having changed their methods, their programme, and their mentality. I was talking the other day to an English officer who had left Russia in the most tumultuous period of the revolution, and had only recently returned there for a visit. He told me that until he saw Russian soil again it was most difficult for him to realize the strides which the country had made since he was last there. To him, indeed, in 1926 it seemed almost like a new country. Unfortunately, however, the counsellors of the Western Governments are those unhappy people who suffered from confiscation and terrorism under militant communism, and who left the country with impressions which they cannot forget. The only Russian reality in which they can firmly believe is that which has fortunately disappeared. Moreover, even those who know and admit that a new stage in Russian development has begun are obviously unable to realize either the extent or the reality of the evolution of the Bolshevik Party. The result is that opinions formed in previous stages hold the field and prevent even unbiased persons from getting a proper evaluation of Russian realities to-day. The very fact that the Bolshevik party has given up the belief in the imminence of the World Revolution and has realized that capitalism has become comparatively stabilized in Europe should in itself be sufficient proof that its policy has suffered a thorough and radical change. For this new outlook must render inevitable a thorough revision of all the planks in the party's programme.

But, as I have already indicated, this is only one of the big changes that has taken place in Russian policy recently. The other, and by far the biggest, is the economic rehabilitation of the country, which began three or four years ago. It

o

is this economic revival, the outstanding fact in Russia to-day, which any one considering Russia as a world political problem has to take into account and which the leaders of the Bolshevik party most certainly recognize. The social conditions and the outlook of the people of the country are being changed by this basic fact. The difference between Russia of to-day and Russia of yesterday is indeed the difference between destruction and reconstruction, between an ever-increasing poverty and a commencing and progressive prosperity. Any one who compares either from personal experience or from knowledge of Russian literature pre-revolutionary Russia and Russia to-day must be struck by the change in the mentality and the aspirations of the people. The main element in this new mentality is activity instead of dreaminess, the utmost degree of self-confidence in place of diffidence and humility, and the desire to get on and to make money in place of a longing for spiritual and artistic perfection. The tendency to make good is so amazingly developed and cultivated among Russians of to-day that one gets the impression that Russia is speedily acquiring the American spirit. But the most striking feature of this situation is the glowing approval which it receives from the Bolsheviks. They disapprove of the United States as the most blatant of capitalist communities ; and yet they glory in the Americanization of Russia. Bukharin, for instance, the foremost of the Bolshevik theorists and propagandists, not only welcomes it but actually encourages it as a patriotic duty. He has even gone so far as to give the masses a new and striking watchword : 'enrichessez-vous', 'get on', 'accumulate'. True in making this amazing declaration Bukharin was repudiated by the cautious Central Committee of the Party, which explained that it was public and not private accumulation that it considered desirable. In any case, the fact that such a remarkable piece of advice should have been offered by a member of the Political Bureau of the Communist Party is sufficient proof that Russia and the Communist Party are living in a period very different, not only from that of the militant communism of 1918–20, but even from that of the new economic policy of 1921; and this holds good in respect not only of Bukharin's advice, but even of the Central Committee's interpretation of that advice.

We see then that there are two big factors which are changing the spirit of the ruling party and of the Government as well. First, the recognition of the stabilizing of capitalism in the West, and second a marked capitalist development in Russia itself. But there is also a third factor closely allied to both, and this is the peculiar position of the Russian Government as a sort of huge business and trading corporation, the centre, indeed, and chief mechanism of the economic life of the country. You must realize that the Russian Government concentrates in its own hands nine-tenths of the country's communications, manufacturing industries and foreign trade. This peculiar position, so dissimilar to that of the Government of any other country in the world, claims, I think, special consideration. That it cannot fail to colour the psychology of the Bolsheviks in their attitude both to home and foreign politics seems obvious. It is, indeed, only reasonable to assume that the leading Commissars are already more influenced by their position as the chief industrialists of the country than by their purely political and governmental functions.

Even those among the Bolshevik statesmen who personally conduct no business of any kind, diplomatists for instance, are imbued with the reconstruction fever. Diplomacy is obviously only the means to the end, and the end is what is rightly styled the Great Economic Revival, the building up of Russia. But this new orientation is not simply matter of preoccupation with business and with the necessary work of building up the country. It is a manifestation, I claim, of a sort of *reconstruction complex*. The Bolsheviks are developing a social as distinct from a class conscience ; and here you have the key to the understanding of the present Russian political situation. The Russian Communist Party could not have faced the shipwreck of most of their dreams without moral decay and a speedy dissolution had not the idealism which animated them at the beginning of their political domination been replaced by a new and maybe a more lofty, at any rate a more practical, conception of their mission.

The obviously unchallenged existence of Bolshevism in Russia to-day must remain a puzzle to you unless you realize that the Bolsheviks have become devoted to the new task of leaders in the economic revival of Russia. Individually and as a party they continue to cherish a belief in the ultimate realization of their communist and world-revolutionary dreams ; but this I am inclined to think is what the Germans used to call Zukunfts-Musik, the dream-music of the distant future. To-day the Bolsheviks are practical statesmen and plain builders of Russia ; and we must admit that they are bringing a considerable measure of efficiency to the performance of their new task. This and this alone furnishes us with an explanation of why they are allowed by the people to continue at the helm. Nations seldom trouble themselves about the principles and ideals which their Governments may cherish in provision for the future. Governments are allowed to dream any sort of dreams they like if they only continue *to do* the right thing.

The case of the Bolsheviks is, however, by no means quite novel. Let me remind you of the Saint Simonist School of Socialism in France. We all came to Geneva by the great Paris-Lyon Mediterranean Railway, but probably only a few of us realize that this railway was planned and built by the Saint Simonists, who believed that the economic development of France was the most essential step towards socialism. The scepticism of their critics, who used to accuse them of introducing capitalism instead of fighting for socialism, the Saint Simonists met with the same argument which Lenin and his followers have constantly employed since the inauguration of the new economic policy. ' You see only ', the Saint Simonists used to say, ' the scaffolding. Wait until we have finished our task and are able to remove the scaffolding and you will see the magnificent edifice of socialism in all its glory.'

But this I am afraid is a digression, and I must refrain from occupying your time with a more detailed description of the character, extent, and significance of the changes that have recently taken place in Russia. I have given you, I hope, such an account of them as will convince you that the process of evolution in Russia is real and constant. But, in order to reach my main conclusion, that the immediate stage of Russia's development must of necessity be a period of peace, I must ask your indulgence while I give you an explanation of what I consider the chief phenomenon of modern Russian history. In my view the solution of the agrarian question, and as a consequence the change in the State's attitude towards the development of the internal market, is the most essential and characteristic difference between pre-revolutionary and post-revolutionary Russia.

The new status of the peasants, indeed, gives Russia for

the first time in history a real opportunity for the development of the internal market. Imperial and semi-feudal pre-revolutionary Russia, with its scanty industrial activities, was always feverishly bent on expansion and on conquering new markets. Up to the very last day of its existence it was dreaming of new openings east and west. The chance of getting Constantinople was the last and most ambitious of these dreams. But this strange and illogical quest for foreign markets was only due to the fact that the potentially enormous domestic market was scarcely open. Many political considerations were responsible for this inability to develop the home market. The chief cause, however, was the impossibility of increasing the purchasing capacity of the peasants one iota without satisfying their hunger for land. The vested interests of the landowners absolutely precluded any possibility of a national development of the internal resources of the country. Indeed, it is no exaggeration to say that the solution of the land question opens before Russia magnificent prospects of progress and prosperity.

The success of the agrarian revolution may fairly be said to have put an end to Russia's century-old policy of expansion; her insatiable appetite for new territory and new markets has now grown languid. Revolutionary Russia was the more easily able to relinquish Imperialist dreams in Asia and to agree to the secession of the Baltic provinces just because the bottom had been knocked out of the policy of expansion. It is often asserted of the Bolsheviks that they are themselves Imperialists; an assertion which seems to be based on the fact that they pose as the champions of the suppressed races of Asia. But this championship can hardly be identified with Imperialism, which implies the idea of conquest and exploitation. As a matter of fact, the Bolsheviks have abandoned adventures and concessions alike in Persia, in Mongolia, and in China. The Bolshevik propaganda in Asia is a danger to Western Europe, not because it countenances but becauses it opposes Imperialism. The aims of Imperialism are the acquisition of new markets ; and without a race for markets there can be no such thing. It is safe to predict that the next stage in Russian history will be pacific and non-militarist. And this not because the rulers of new Russia are pacifists and non-militarists. Personally they may be said to be rather tainted with the militarist spirit. But a nation which has no desire or need to conquer new markets, and which is mainly concerned with the development of its internal resources, is predisposed to a pacific policy and is unlikely to engage in wars of expansion or aggression. The difference between nineteenth- and twentieth-century Russia is that, while the former was the era of an appetite for territory and expansion, the latter is destined to be the era of internal development. It is only natural then that the new Russian State should be greatly concerned, both in internal and external relations, with peace, security, and stabilization. Of this longing for security internally I need not speak to you to-day. But will you permit me to say just in passing that the almost panicky fear shown by the Bolsheviks when they are threatened even with the slightest disruption of the unity of the party is, in my opinion, largely due to the unsettled state of Russia's foreign relations. The difference between the tendencies in Russian domestic and foreign policy is in my view mainly this : that in the former the fear of insecurity is only *one* of many factors ; in the latter, that is, in foreign policy, this morbid sense of danger is the dominant, almost the only factor.

If the policy of the West is to discover some plan of

accommodation with Russia and ultimately to bring her into the League of Nations this Russian apprehension of menace will have to be taken into account. It is not enough to be conscious ourselves that this apprehension is fantastic and baseless. It will be necessary for the Western Powers to adopt such a policy as will tend to eradicate this impression of menace from the minds of the rulers of Russia. At present every diplomatic step taken in the West appears to them as a deliberate challenge to their country's integrity. This sort of feeling is, of course, irrational; but unfortunately it is in no sense novel. Moreover, it by no means precludes aggressive desires on the part of the country which is the victim of such a misapprehension. On the contrary it often happens that the very aggressiveness is dictated by panic. As an example I may remind you that the most violent periods in the struggles of the Russian revolution have been justly attributed to the then prevailing sense of panic. I think it is no exaggeration to say that the history of international relations is full of instances which show that aggressiveness is dictated by panic.

If I remind you of the mentality of France in the years immediately succeeding the armistice, when every Frenchman seemed to be getting hysterical about the alleged insecurity of his country, I think I indicate more or less the state of mind of Russia to-day and the main inspiration of her foreign policy. The similarity is, indeed, remarkable. There is one difference only: that, while France was afraid of the possible designs of one neighbour only, Russia seems to be suspicious of all her neighbours and, indeed, of all the world, which she imagines as in process of being leagued in one united front against her. The primacy in this alleged coalition of the world against Russia is, as you are all aware, assigned by the Bolsheviks to Great Britain, firstly as being the biggest and best organized of the capitalist countries of the Continent, and secondly as being the traditional and secular enemy of Russia in Europe. Consequently, everything which the British Foreign Office does or fails to do is interpreted as primarily anti-Russian. You probably all remember the excitement in Russian Government circles which was caused by the advent to power in Great Britain of the Conservative Government.

When the British Foreign Secretary went on a trip to Paris and to Rome the Russian press, if I may be allowed to say so, saw suddenly red. The object of these conversations between Sir Austen Chamberlain, Monsieur Briand, and Signor Mussolini could have no other purpose but that of constituting a European *bloc* against Russia. At the same time the Bolshevik press discovered British Foreign Office activities in the Baltic and in the Balkans, all designed to bring about the isolation of the Soviet State. When nothing came of all these alleged activities the explanation furnished by the Soviet press was that this was due to no lack of industry on the part of the British Government but to the insuperable difficulty of reconciling the interests of the larger and the smaller European Powers.

But even to-day the Bolsheviks still cherish the belief that Great Britain is actively and consistently engaged in an attempt to confront Russia with a united and antagonistic Europe. Having failed to make trouble for Russia in the Baltic and in the Balkans Great Britain decided to achieve the same aim by other means and forthwith proceeded to attract Germany within the orbit of her influence. This is the Bolshevik interpretation of the origin of the Treaty of Locarno, which they regard as the most serious and so far the most successful attempt to isolate their country. It is worth while noting in this respect that, with a certain ingenuity, they ascribe the whole credit of the success of Locarno to Great Britain. In their opinion France was the loser in these negotiations. They flatly refuse to credit the official interpretation of the Locarno Treaty as an attempt to give security to France. France's security was, in their view, a mere empty pretext. According to them the meaning and the aim of Locarno was to reinstate Germany in the European concert and by this means to effect a separation between herself and Russia. The Bolsheviks admit, of course, that the Treaty was designed to effect smaller aims as well, such as the weakening of the continental alliances and the political weight of France ; but they insist that the one circumstance which renders this Treaty historical was its attempt to create a united front of the bourgeois powers against Soviet Russia.

The foreign policy of the Bolsheviks for the last two years, that is from the moment of the repudiation of the Anglo-Russian agreement by Mr. Baldwin's Government, has been dictated solely by the conviction that Europe, under British leadership, is consolidating the forces of the West against Russia and by the determination as far as possible to defeat this plot.

I am quite aware that this attempt of mine to define the foreign policy of a Great Power as dictated solely by the sense of insecurity is bound to be challenged. It must seem incredible that a country like Russia should cherish and pursue purely negative aims. But, honestly, I cannot detect signs of any other motive in recent Russian diplomatic pronouncements and activities. In support of my contention I think I can do no better than quote for your benefit a passage about the foreign policy of the Soviet Union which occurs in that political report of M. Stalin which I have already mentioned : ' Now, about the aims of our party in foreign policy,' said the General Secretary of the Bolshevik Party,

' In the first place our aim is to conduct a campaign against all wars, and secondly, to cultivate peaceful and so-called normal relations with capitalist countries. The basic principle in the policy of our Government—the foreign policy—is the struggle for peace. This struggle for peace, this struggle against new wars, the exposure of all steps taken with a view of preparing new wars, the exposure of all steps which, though covered with the flag of pacifism yet in fact aim at preparing new wars (Locarno for instance), this is our task. That is exactly why we don't want to enter the League of Nations ; for the League of Nations is an organization designed to be the screen for the preparation of new wars. In order to enter the League of Nations we should have to make a choice, as Comrade Litvinov justly reminded us, between the hammer and the anvil. Well, but we will neither be the hammer of the strong peoples nor the anvil of the weak. We want neither the one nor the other. We are out for peace. We are for the exposure of all measures which lead to war, despite the pacifist flags with which they are screened. It is all the same to us whether it is Locarno or the League. We are not going to be deceived by false flags.'

This is then the official, exact, and most authoritative pronouncement of the aim of the Soviet Union foreign policy. The guiding principles, as we see, are almost entirely negative. The only positive element in them is the declared desire to cultivate normal relations with capitalist countries. What remains is a policy of measures, counter-measures, and manœuvres based on all round suspicion of the outside world as given up to warlike designs, intrigues, and plots against the Soviet Union under the guise of reconciliation and pacifism.

I submit then that when you come to analyse the pronouncements of the Russian Government you are confronted by an outlook so narrow and limited as to be almost astonishing. The prevailing, I may really say, the fixed idea is a morbid fear of plots, intrigues, and war-like designs against the integrity of the Russian State fomented by an antagonistic world. It is only natural then that when you examine the activities of the Russian diplomatic service you are invariably struck by the same strange narrowness and morbidity exhibited and concentrated in an incessant effort to counteract such alleged plots, intrigues, and designs.

At this stage of my lecture I cannot pretend to give you anything approaching to a *résumé* of the activities of the Russian Foreign Office under the Bolshevik régime. I think our object will be better served if we concentrate on a brief enumeration of the diplomatic steps taken by Moscow since and in connexion with the summoning of the Locarno Conference.

The first action taken by Chicherin was, if I am not mistaken, an offer of a pact of non-aggression to Poland. It was obvious that, with Germany included in the League of Nations and pledged therefore more or less to an anti-Russian policy, it would be necessary for the Western Powers to make also some similar arrangement with Poland. The Russian offer of a pact to Poland was designed to secure Poland's neutrality in the event of an open rupture between Soviet Russia and the West. We know well that the conversations at Warsaw had no practical result; but they undoubtedly had the extraordinary effect of indirectly paralysing the progress made at Locarno. I think we may assume that the Polish demand for a permanent seat in the Council of the League of Nations, and the sudden and obviously irrational consent of France to this demand was due to the alternative offer received by Poland from Russia. In this hall I think I need not emphasize the disastrous effect which this promise of a Council seat to Poland had on the vital question of Germany's admission to the League.

The next step taken by the Bolsheviks to counteract the result of the Locarno Treaty, as interpreted by them, was to attempt to force Germany to take up an unequivocal position as between Russia and the West. The question put to Herr Stresemann was, ' Does Locarno supersede Rapallo, or if not, is the German Government to declare itself unfettered in its relations to Russia by the Locarno Treaty and the League's Covenant?' The conversations of Chicherin in Germany were triumphantly successful: it was an easy victory for Moscow; for the German diplomatists welcomed the Russian pressure as helping them to make their position doubly secure, that is, as enabling them to gain British without forfeiting Russian friendship. The German Government, therefore, on the very eve of the departure of their representative to Locarno astonished their well-wishers in Great Britain and elsewhere by signing a complete commercial treaty with the Soviet Government. This was a sufficiently spectacular sign of friendship. But the German Government went even farther. In Locarno itself they declared that they were ready to enter the League but under one special reservation, namely, that in no circumstance should they be asked to participate under paragraph 16 of the covenant in a League of Nations campaign against Soviet Russia. This German protest completely achieved its object; for it elicited from France, Czechoslovakia, and Poland such a joint interpretation of paragraph 16 as allowed Germany to plead its particular military and geographical position as an excuse for not participating in any such military activities. On this reading of the paragraph

Germany undertook to join the League of Nations. But Moscow continued to be alarmed ; for obviously this renunciation on Germany's part of any obligation to join in military action against Russia could not prevent the League from demanding her participation in an economic boycott of Russia. In order then definitely to dispose of any danger which might arise from Germany's entering the League, the Bolsheviks insisted on the Germans signing a special treaty of friendship and neutrality. This treaty was signed in Berlin in April 1926 ; and it is claimed that this document finally annuls any anti-Russian consequences alike of the treaty of Locarno and of Germany's entry into the League of Nations.

Added to the text of this Treaty are two diplomatic notes which make it quite plain that the League of Nations will not be in a position to compel Germany in any conflict in the future to join the League in declaring Russia an aggressor (a necessary condition of her being outlawed by the League), or to take part in any action, military or economic, against her. A similar treaty of neutrality has also been concluded by Russia with Turkey; and it is important to note that the Soviet press expressly interprets this treaty as a move for guaranteeing the security of Russia's Caucasian territories in case of conflict with Great Britain or the League of Nations.

The aim of the foreign policy of the Soviet Union to-day is obviously to extend these series of engagements and to persuade all her neighbours, western and southern alike, who are members of the League, to agree, in return for a mutual guarantee for non-aggression, to remain neutral in case of a conflict arising between the League powers and Russia. With this aim in view an attempt has been made to arrange for a pact with the Baltic succession states. Latvia,

Esthonia, and Finland have in consequence found themselves in a rather equivocal position. They cannot refuse to accept an offer from Russia of a treaty of non-aggression ; on the contrary they would naturally be glad to have their independence guaranteed by such a treaty. But the idea of offending the League by contracting out of their obligation to it is a step they are very reluctant to take. Moreover, it is no secret that pressure is being put on them by the Western powers with a view to preventing them from adopting any such course. In this pressure Poland, which is no longer contemplating or being offered a pact of non-aggression by Russia, is obviously taking a leading part. The Baltic States then are in the unenviable position of having to manoeuvre between these two antagonistic sets of powers. So far they have succeeded in shelving the question of a pact of non-aggression with Russia by inviting the Soviet Union to meet the three states not separately but in concert, a suggestion that is obviously not agreeable to Moscow.

In the Baltic there is evidently a conflict going on between two schools of political thought. One leans towards an agreement with Russia which will relieve the budgets of the tremendous expenditure on armaments. The other looks towards the West and believes that the integrity of the Baltic States can best be secured by their entering into an alliance with one another, and by their forming a closer understanding with Poland, Rumania, and the Little Entente. Which school is likely to gain the upper hand I should not like to say, and happily it is not my task to make any prediction on this point.

In these attempts to conclude alliances and pacts we can again detect a resemblance between the Russia of 1926 and of France of a few years ago. It is a case of action and reaction. If the Western powers, in their attempt to pacify Europe, draw a line, discriminate between nations and try to effect what looks like a piecemeal reconciliation, they need not be surprised if the nations behind the pale get restive, interpret these pacific activities as war-like designs, and attempt on their part to create alliances which, as is only natural, are calculated to alarm the rest of Europe.

I have practically finished, and yet I have said nothing quite directly bearing on Russia's relations with the League of Nations. The official attitude of the Soviet Government to the League is well known. It is, as I have indicated in the passage I have quoted from M. Stalin, one of downright and uncompromising repudiation. But I personally believe, although I have no documentary evidence in support of such belief, that this official attitude does not represent Russia's absolutely last word on the subject. Germany, too, you may remember, for years protested that she could have nothing in common with the 'League of Conquerors'. We know well what made Germany change her attitude; partly it was that her own mentality changed. But we are all aware that the attitude of the League powers towards Germany changed too.

Russia, as I have tried to show you, is changing. To bring about her entry into the League it will be necessary that the attitude of the League Powers towards her should change also.

HISTORICAL PARALLELS AND PRESENT PROBLEMS

CHAPTER XI

THE JUDICIAL SETTLEMENT OF INTERNATIONAL DISPUTES

Dr. James Brown Scott:

I. Introduction

Arbitration precedes and culminates in judicial settlement.

THE problem still confronting the States of our day is how to settle disputes between nations in such a way as to prevent a resort to arms by parties in controversy; in other terms, war between them, which, as a recent and chastening experience has only too clearly shown an amazed and unthinking world, tends to spread like a flame to other and distant nations, causing them to pass through the fiery furnace of war, and threatens to reduce our common civilization to a heap of ashes.

The problem is as old as the world, or rather as society, and the same as that confronting every organized or unorganized group of men and women whether united by natural ties or artificial bonds of their own making. For force is force whether it be weaponless as the fingers between angry disputants of the smaller group, between men armed to the teeth in larger and more progressive groups, or between

P

nations pledging their ultimate resources to their Government in case of war.

We cannot expect to continue the appeal to arms lest it impoverish nations without administering to their safety, and we cannot expect to advance in the things of the Spirit if we give ourselves up to material devices and destructive processes. Yet, on the other hand, we cannot reasonably expect that the order of things with which mankind is only too familiar shall change in the twinkling of an eye or even overnight. We must interrogate history, which is, as I conceive, the application of human nature to the concrete facts of life, individual, national, and international, and if we do so, the reply is that internal order and national peace result from the application of law to disputes of individuals; that the disputes of nations can, therefore, be settled by the application of law, and that the principle of law is identical in either case; for it is not endurable, in the long run, that the law of a state will be unlike the law applicable to individuals of which all states here, now, and in all times have been composed. There is but a single standard for state and individuals—justice expressed in rules of law to meet new and changing conditions.

Within the State law has stopped the hand of self-redress; within the States of the American Union law has superseded the resort to force, and between nations law is slowly but surely obtaining the mastery.

To each of these phases of a long and universal development I ask your attention.

We are fortunately familiar with the origin, nature, and history of the one great system of law from its formal beginnings throughout the period of the Kings, the Republic, and the Empire of Rome—a system at once the law of the ancient world and the source of the law of modern Europe—and a system which still appeals to our imagination and directs our reason where its authority has ceased to exist. And the most superficial examination of the system shows how self-redress in the dawn of Roman history had given way to arbitration by agreement of the private parties, which later, in its turn, became judicial proceeding in the modern sense of the term by the appointment of judges and the execution of their judgements by the intervention and authority of the State.

The primitive procedure is wrapped in the mists of antiquity. Knowing as we do that the future is but the development of the past, the jurist can, by an examination and simplification of later practice restore primitive conditions just as the geologist pierces through the layers of strata to reach the primitive life which lies below the surface of things.

Therefore, let me analyse a familiar passage from the Institutes of Gaius, one of the greatest Roman jurists who flourished some time in the second century of the Empire.

Two Roman citizens are at odds about a slave. The plaintiff claims the right of possession ; the defendant denies the right of the plaintiff and himself claims the slave under the law of the land. As neither is willing to renounce his claim in behalf of the other the disputants agree to go before the Praetor, the law officer of the Republic and Empire. Before this magistrate the slave, as object of the controversy, is brought. The plaintiff states his claims and touches the slave with his lance. The defendant denies the plaintiff's claim, insists on his own right and touches the slave with his lance. Thereupon the Praetor intervenes, orders the parties to step aside, and addressing the defendant asks him upon what he founds his claim. To this question the defendant replies that he perfected his right when he touched the slave with his staff. The plaintiff thereupon denies the defendant's claim and challenges him to a wager on the well-foundedness of his contention. The defendant accepts; the issue is raised and the right of one or the other decided by the award of the sum of money which each has wagered. 'The staff or straw', Gaius informs us, which was used on such occasions in his day, ' represented a lance, the symbol of absolute right, as the best title to property was considered as derived from conquest.'

It does not tax overmuch the imagination to restore the original scene. Two parties quarrelling over the possession of an object; the claimant violent in the assertion of his right; the defendant insistent on his possession, and both surrounded by their friends and partisans. The lance was not then a wand or straw, but a weapon of iron in strong arms and ready to strike. An outsider rushes in, separates the claimants, counsels moderation and either offers himself as arbiter of their differences or acts as such at their request; or it may be that bystanders stay the hands of the combatants, and that through their intervention a man of wisdom and of repute in the community is proposed and accepted as mediator and arbiter.

In any event we are in the midst of an affray which is stopped by an agreement of the disputants to submit the controversy to an indifferent person possessing the confidence of both, and an agreement to abide by his opinion as to the rights of one or another. In terms of law the agreement is a contract to submit the controversy to an arbiter and a contract to accept his pronouncement. The act of the parties is voluntary if they have themselves submitted the dispute in first instance; their action is none the less voluntary if, yielding to the persuasion of a bystander or the community, they have chosen an arbiter and agreed to accept his award. Self-redress is renounced on condition that the loser will accept and give effect to the proposed settlement; otherwise, the party in whose favour the award is rendered is free to execute it with the approval of the community. At an early date the community is represented by the praetor before whom the plaintiff brings the defendant and through his intervention, if need be, the agreement is reached; but the arbiter is chosen by the parties, one or the other proposing an acceptable arbiter, if they have not agreed in advance, and, in case of failure to agree, the arbiter is eventually chosen by lot.

Plaintiff and defendant may be accompanied by their respective partisans, but they are no longer real or prospective combatants; they are at most but witnesses of an arbitral proceeding. The arbiter is a private person; he is neither lawyer nor judge, and his opinion is that of a private person, not the judgement of a public official.

The award is not a judgement and is not executed by the state or the community. If the defeated claimant fails to comply with his agreement to accept and perform the award the victor may take him into his possession by force if need be; if he imprisons him it is in his own home, not in a public jail; and whatever steps he takes to secure the fruits of his victory they are the private acts of a private party in a private affair. The Tribune could not intervene or forbid the execution of the contract; for the award was the opinion of a private person, not of a public magistrate clothed with the imperium of the state.

In the course of time the state appointed a number of persons to act as arbiters, and finally an equal number of senators, knights, and plebeians were chosen, their names entered on the *album judicum* and published annually. From this list or panel of arbiters the parties made their choice, and it was only in the reign of Diocletian that the state selected the arbiter or judge, and that the award became a judgement to be executed by the state.

Arbitration by the agreement of the parties gave rise to a judicial proceeding: the arbiter became a judge; the award a judgement, and the power of the state replaced the persuasion of the successful litigant. The court of justice had come into being and the state, instead of the individual litigant, took charge of the administration of justice.

In every modern nation and in every modern state courts of justice exist, and through them the disputes of their respective subjects or citizens are redressed within, and the national order and the peace of the state maintained. The victory of judicial procedure had been so complete that, in the later period of the Roman Empire, the development of judicial from arbitral procedure was so forgotten that the commentators of the period spoke of arbitral procedure, to which certain controversies were referred at the request of the parties, as a method based upon and derived from the procedure of the courts. We, like them, seem to have forgotten that arbitration preceded judicial settlement and gave birth to courts of justice; yet we must bear this in mind if we are to see how arbitration between nations and states is developing before our very eyes into judicial procedure in courts created by nations and states for the decision of their disputes.

The history of mankind is but the history of individuals on a larger scale; the arbitration of private parties is the precedent of arbitration between nations just as arbitration between nations is the forerunner of judicial proceedings of nations in Courts of their own creation.

The process is simple and it is inevitable.

Why could not self-redress between nations be restrained as it was between the citizens within their respective jurisdictions? Because between equal states there was no tribunal to which they could submit their controversies.

War between them was so deeply rooted that they overlooked arbitration, although canonists, theologians, and philosophers insisted that a suit between states should only be prosecuted by force if its cause were just, so just, indeed, as to have entitled, in their opinion, the complaining state to a judgement in its favour if such a court had been in existence.

On this phase of the subject I shall invoke the authority of Francis of Vitoria who in 1532, at the University of Salamanca, of which he was a professor, delivered two readings of a formal nature some forty years after the discovery of America. These dissertations deal with the rights of the Spaniards against the Indians of the New World, and his contention is that the Spaniards had no greater rights in America than the natives of the New World would have in Spain; that both would have the right to visit and to dwell in the lands of the other provided that neither should harm either, and to trade with one another. These rights, he maintains, are secured to states by the law of nations, which he defines and applies to the question at hand, and, especially, to the right of the Spaniards to wage war against the natives and principalities of America. The law of nations, he first defines, *quod naturalis ratio inter omnes gentes constituit*, and that he is referring to peoples or states is evident from the use of the word ' nations ' in the same connexion. This first modern and accurate definition of International Law· is applied to the respective rights of the Spaniards and Indians in these disquisitions which, taken together, form the first adequate discussion of a concrete international question. In so doing Francis of Vitoria created the Modern School of International Law of which Grotius was destined to be the most distinguished member.

Inasmuch as arbitration as a system between states was first adopted in the modern world by American States I have thought it advisable to take the statements regarding this phase of the question from the two readings of the Spanish professor as they indicate the law at the discovery of the New World, which, in the fullness of time brought new rules into being to meet new conditions.

On the threshold of his undertaking, Francis of Vitoria puts and answers the difficult question : May Christians engage in war ? He is quite sure that force may be resisted by force, that is to say, that defensive war is permissible, that the sword may be drawn against domestic wrongdoers and seditious persons and also in certain cases against external enemies. The great authority for the schoolmen on this point is St. Augustine who held wars to be just : ' in order to arrange a wrong done, as where punishment has to be meted out to a city or state because it has itself neglected to exact punishment for an offence committed by its citizens or subjects or to return what has been taken away.' That is to say, a war to obtain possession of property unjustly seized, to exact reparation for a civil wrong or tort, as we say in technical language, and the punishment of a crime either committed by the foreign state or its subjects which the state in question refuses or fails to punish. It will be observed that these are precisely the grounds for a suit in a national court of justice if citizens of the country are accused of their commission.

It may be difficult to decide whether a war is just in its causes ; it is, however, possible and in a way easier to reject causes as palpably unjust. Thus, according to our friend Francis ' difference of religion is not a just cause of war '. This statement is a commonplace to us in 1926; it was a brave pronouncement in 1532. ' Extension of Empire is not a just cause of war '—a doctrine which, if accepted and applied, would go far to keep the world at peace. ' Neither the personal glory of the prince nor any other advantage to him is a just cause of war '—a judgement upon the princes of the day and especially upon François I of France and Charles V, then Holy Roman emperor, and, as king of Spain, the sovereign lord and master of Francis of Vitoria.

If these be unjust causes of war what are and may be the just causes ? In the opinion of the great and good Father Francis, Dominican and Spaniard, ' There is a single and only just cause for commencing a war, namely, a wrong received,' and the wrong is the threefold wrong of which a national court of justice can assume jurisdiction and award the proper remedy.

May the individual smarting under a wrong himself redress the injury which he has received ? Yes, at the moment of unlawful seizure of his property or to repel force by force ; otherwise no, because he has the court of the prince, the common superior alike of plaintiff and defendant to which he may resort. The prince is thus the judge within his lands, and he administers justice through the court of justice established for this purpose. He has authority over foreigners ' so far as to prevent them ', Francis asserts, ' from committing wrongs, and this by the law of nations and by the authority of the whole world '. The appeal is here to International Law in its modern sense and the practice of civilized states as evidence of this law. But the Spaniard has also in mind the foreigner beyond the prince's jurisdiction, and the way to subject the outsider and through him the foreign state to the prince's jurisdiction.

The appeal is now to the very nature of things. ' Nay, it seems ', Francis continues, ' to be by natural law also, seeing that otherwise society could not hold together unless there was somewhere a power and authority to deter wrongdoers and prevent them from injuring the good and innocent.' How is this to be done, and through what agency ? ' Everything needed for the government and preservation of society exists by natural law, and in no other way ', Francis hastens to add, feeling that he is at the end of his argument, ' can we show that a state has by natural law authority to inflict pains and penalties on its citizens who are dangerous to it.' This may be so, but how about the foreign state ? Francis meets the difficulty by contemplating a society of nations with power over its members, and the wronged state as its agent in redressing the wrong which it has suffered. ' But if a state can do this to its own citizens' society at large,' whether it be the Union of American States or the League of Nations, I venture to interpose, ' no doubt it can do it to all wicked and dangerous folk, and this can only be through the instrumentality of princes.' ' Therefore it is certain ', continues Francis without an interruption, ' that princes can punish enemies who have done a wrong to their state and that, after a just war has been duly and justly undertaken, the enemy are just as much within the jurisdiction of the prince who undertakes it as if he were their proper judge.' That the

Dominican was thinking of nations as forming parts of a larger whole, if not actually merged in it, is evident from a passage to be found in his reading on the Civil Power in which he says : ' It is not to be doubted that the whole world, which is in a certain sense a single community, possesses a right to prescribe equitable and appropriate laws for its members, like those which constitute the law of nations. Hence it is ', he adds by way of example, ' that the violators of international law sin mortally as well in peace as in war, and that in important matters, like the inviolability of ambassadors, it is not lawful for any nation to refuse to observe the law of nations.'

In any event the prince was, in the opinion of the enlightened Spaniard—and he did not stand alone among his countrymen and the catholic theologians of his own and an earlier day—the visible agent of an invisible and undisclosed principal in redressing wrongs and restoring rights. His prince was in very truth a judge, and as such he was bound to know the rule of law involved, to act upon it and to apply it to the concrete case. War was only justifiable if its cause would have justified a court of the community of nations, had one existed in his day, to assume jurisdiction of the offence and to render judgement. It is, therefore, of interest, in the light of the progress which we are making in this direction, to dwell upon the matter somewhat ; for the views of Francis, of his predecessors and contemporaries, are the foundation and justification of an international court of justice. It is not enough for the prince to believe that he has a just cause, because princes as well as private persons are prone to error. The wise man's judgement is requisite, and to reach this it is essential that ' an exceedingly careful examination be made of the justice and causes of the war and that the reasons of those who, on grounds of equity oppose it, be listened to . . . for truth and justice in moral questions are hard of attainment and so any careless treatment of them easily leads to error, an error which would be inexcusable, especially in a concern of great moment, involving danger and calamity to many and they of our neighbours, too, whom we are bound to love as ourselves '. Here we have men learned in the law, as counsel for and against the case before the prince as judge. But even more is needed to cause the judge to act. ' Senators and petty rulers and in general all who are admitted on summons or voluntarily to the public council or the prince's council ought, and are bound to examine into the cause of an unjust war.' The lawyers might be wrong, therefore it is, as Francis assures us, that ' war ought not to be made on the sole judgement of the king, nor, indeed, on the judgement of a few, but on that of many, and these wise and upright men '.

So much for the just cause, of the question of jurisdiction as we might say. What of the judgement which the prince as judge should render ? Precisely what the judge in a lawsuit, instead of a forcesuit, might render between private parties. ' To recapture everything that has been lost and any part of the same.' This is a decree for the restoration of property unlawfully detained. ' To make good out of enemy property the expenses of the war and all damages wrongfully caused by the enemy.' This is damages and costs of suit, and that these are the very items which Francis has in mind is evident from the language which he uses in this connexion. ' This is clear ', he says, ' for the enemy who has done the wrong is bound to give all this redress.' Why ? Because ' When no other way lies open, a private creditor can seize the amount of his debt from the debtor.' We might think that the analogy between the law and the forcesuit was an exaggeration of our day and not a fundamental principle with Francis and his contemporaries ; for it cannot be too often repeated that his is not an isolated figure among catholic canonists, commentators, and churchmen. Therefore, I ask you to weigh and ponder the words of the noble Spaniard speaking for his countrymen and his church : ' If there were any competent judge over the two belligerents, he would have to condemn the unjust aggressors and authors of wrong, not only to make restitution of what they have carried off, but also to make good the expenses of the war on the other side, and also all damages.' Why should a prince do these things ? Because, Francis says, ' A prince who is carrying on a just war is, as it were, his own judge in matters touching the war. . . . Therefore, he can enforce all these claims upon his enemy.'

But even this is not all. The prince in his character of judge may order the destruction of property of the enemy intended for wrongful use, just as the municipal judge may order a building to be torn down which interferes with the enjoyment of our right, in this case to live in peace and quiet ; and he may exact a bond of the enemy to keep the peace in the future which the enemy has disturbed in the past. Lest I may seem to be reading into the text of Francis what it does not expressly contain, I quote :

'Not only are the things just named allowable, but a prince may go even farther in a just war and do whatever is necessary to obtain peace and security from the enemy ; for example, destroy an enemy's fortress and even build on an enemy's soil, if this is necessary in order to avert a dangerous attack of the enemy.'

Why may this be decreed by the prince ? The reason is,

if one citizen does a wrong to a fellow citizen the magistrate may not only compel the wrongdoer to make amends to the injured party, but, if the former is a source of fear to the latter, he is compelled to give bond or quit the city so as to remove the danger of which he is the cause.

The New World was to provide the new remedy and it was to be judicial settlement via arbitration.

Just as the action of individuals within states called into being arbitration to stay self-redress, and arbitration gave birth to judicial procedure, so the people of different states, considered as units, invoked arbitration to stay self-redress, and arbitration between states has given birth in our day to judicial settlement between states and nations.

Why? Because nature, inanimate or human, has a way of repeating itself from day to day and from generation to generation, whether in individuals or in the groups of individuals which we call states or nations. It seems to be characteristic of the human mind that it unconsciously recalls forgotten facts, forgotten experiences, forgotten conceptions, and uses them anew according to time, place, and circumstance. The medieval conception of catholic churchmen of the Old World the protestant politicians of the New did not know; but the human mind projects anew past experience for future progress, and is more likely to do so when it is free to express itself untrammelled by traditions which tend to choke and oppress self-expression and the resort to experiment.

When on 4 July 1776 the representatives of thirteen of the British Colonies in North America declared their independence of the Mother Country, and pronounced themselves free and sovereign States they were, as Francis and his school would say, in a state of nature with one another. There was no superior among them, but there were disputes among them. How and where was this superior to be found?

Unwilling to allow any of the States to pose as a superior even in the redress of wrongs they resorted to arbitration through arbiters of their own choice, a system which excluded self-redress between the States of the New World as between the individuals of an incipient Roman community. The old idea had unconsciously taken possession of them. The States renounced in advance the consequences of arbitration by abandoning a resort to self-redress which, between them, would be war, according to that law of nations to which an appeal had been made in their Declaration of Independence. How was this done? Defensive warfare was not renounced; just as in the case of the individual, State might repel force by force. In the Sixth of the Articles of Confederation, effective on and after 1 March 1781, the thirteen States agreed that none of them should engage in war unless actually invaded, and the danger so imminent as not to admit of delay. War in the sense of private warfare of the individual is thus renounced except in the case of immediate and unavoidable self-defence.

What of public war between the States? It was renounced expressly in the first seven words of the fifth and last paragraph of the sixth of the articles. What is to be done with the controversies of any and all kinds between and among the States? A diplomatic body composed of diplomatic representatives of the thirteen States in which each had an equal vote, although it might have according to its pleasure not less than two nor more than seven members, was declared by them ' to be the last resort on appeal in all disputes and differences now subsisting or that may hereafter arise between two or more States concerning '—what you may ask, everything, or as the opening clause of the second paragraph of the ninth of the articles puts it : ' boundary, jurisdiction, or any other cause whatever.'

How was this appeal to be exercised ? As in the early days of Rome the States might appear before the Congress as the private parties might appear before the Praetor, having agreed in advance upon the arbiter or arbiters who thereupon became seized of the affair. In case the State had not agreed in advance they were to agree in the presence of the Congress just as the private parties before the Praetor. In one case selection was to be made from a temporary panel, in the other from a permanent panel—the *album iudicum* ; the States could challenge by striking names from the panel and in the end resort was had by lot ; the private parties of Rome could challenge names from the panel and upon failure to agree resort was had to lot. The Roman procedure had assuredly no influence upon American statesmen, but human minds work unconsciously toward a like end by means not wholly alike. The *album iudicum Americanum* was thus formed. The Congress named three persons from each of the thirteen States, and these thirty-nine persons formed the panel of prospective arbiters, commissioners, and judges. Beginning with the plaintiff, then continuing with the defendant, each of the parties struck a name until thirteen were left ; from them the names of not less than seven nor more than nine were drawn by lot, and these or any five of them were to act as arbiters. The articles of Confederation called them commissioners or judges—' to hear and finally determine the controversy, so always as a major part of the judges who shall hear the cause shall agree in the determina- tion '. Should either plaintiff or defendant fail to appear on the day appointed for the selection of the judges, or, if present, refuse to strike the names from the panel of judges, the secretary of the Congress should strike in its stead and the court so constituted would be the court of the parties. The sentence of the court thus formed by the co-operation of one or other of the parties, and rendered with the co-operation of both or of one or the other was to be ' final and decisive ', and ' lodged among the acts of Congress for the security of the parties concerned '.

As in the Roman procedure there was no provision for execution, the State was expected to look after its interest in the best way it could.

The method of arbitral settlement by commissioners of the parties' choice has an important decision to its credit in the famous controversy between Connecticut and Pennsylvania, in which the claims of the former to a large tract of territory situated within the chartered grant of the latter, although inconsistent with a previous grant contained in that of Connecticut, was unanimously awarded to Pennsylvania. The decision of the case was calculated to appeal to the imagination. It did. Robert R. Livingston, then the first Secretary of Foreign Affairs of the American Confederation, writing to Lafayette then in Europe, under date of 10 January 1783, felt justified in informing him that 'The great cause between Connecticut and Pennsylvania has been decided in favour of the latter'. The reason why the item would interest his noble correspondent as well as humble believers in peaceful settlement, then and now, Livingston himself stated : ' It is a singular event.'

Should we ask why, Livingston would inform us as he did Lafayette that ' There are few instances of independent states submitting their cause to a court of justice '. True, but what of it? ' The day will come ', Livingston went on to say, and I may add that the sun of that day is already on the horizon, ' when all disputes in the great republic of Europe will be tried in the same way, and America be quoted to exemplify the wisdom of the measure.' The States were, in Livingston's opinion, independent although bound together by the Articles of Confederation. Differing largely in size, in population, in importance, and differing even more in their interests they felt it necessary for their prosperity, if not for their peace, to come more closely together. The Congress was at best but a legislature without power to compel or to persuade the States to comply with its resolutions ; the executive department of a government was lacking and there was no judiciary. Each State had these three branches of government, and the question was as to the possibility, propriety, or expediency of strengthening the Union and providing it, to the extent of the delegated powers of Sovereignty, with a government of the threefold division for the exercise of these powers of a general nature, the States withholding the powers of a local nature not granted and which they meant to exercise by themselves and in their several interests. The States made up their minds to the venture. In the Summer of 1787 the delegates of twelve of the thirteen States met in Convention at Philadelphia— Rhode Island held aloof for the nonce—and agreed upon a draft of a more perfect union. The Convention transmitted the Constitution, for such the instrument of Union and of Government thereunder was called, to the Congress of the Confederation, which in turn sent it to each of the thirteen States with the request that it be laid before a special Convention of each of the States chosen for the express purpose of considering and ratifying it, if the proposed Constitution for the States in their united capacities should appeal to each of the States in their individual capacities. The Constitution was to go into effect when ratified by nine States and for the other States when and as they should do so. Eleven of the thirteen did so in the course of the year following the Convention in Philadelphia ; North Carolina hesitated but made up its mind to join the government organized under the Constitution, and Rhode Island after longer hesitation likewise ratified and entered the Union. In the first two years of Washington's administration there was a union of the thirteen States, and to-day the Union consists of no less than forty-eight.

Each of the forty-eight has, as had each of the thirteen, a government of its own consisting of a legislative and executive department, and a judiciary, and the Government of the Federal Union possesses likewise these three departments. The Government of the United States is supreme within the powers of Sovereignty delegated expressly or by necessary implication by the States, and each State is sovereign in the possession and exercise of the powers withheld from the grant and reserved to the States.

Our immediate interest is in the peaceable settlement of disputes between the States and I pass at once to this phase of the subject. When on 6 August 1787 the first draft of the proposed Constitution was laid before the Federal Convention by the drafting Committee—the delegates of the day called it the Committee of detail—it contained a ninth article which reproduced in its essentials the provisions of the ninth of the Articles of Confederation concerning suits between the States, and it vested the exercise of the jurisdiction in the Senate as the representatives of the States of the proposed Union. John Rutledge, a distinguished statesman and lawyer of South Carolina, at the time Chancellor of the Court of Equity of his State and destined to become Chief Justice of the Supreme Court of the United States, objected to the article as unnecessary, as the States were now to have a supreme court to which appeals might be made from judgements of the State courts involving their general interests which were to be transferred to the Federal Government. He, therefore, proposed that the Supreme Court of the States in their united capacities be vested with the jurisdiction of the controversies between the States in their individual capacities. James Wilson, a delegate from Pennsylvania and destined to become a justice of the Supreme Court, remarked that the judicial was the better remedy. The laymen who took part in the discussion, Mr. Gorham, a delegate from Massachusetts, and Mr. Williamson, a delegate from North Carolina, stood for arbitration by temporary tribunals under the Confederation and the proposed article, and they expressed the opinion that cases might arise in which the older method would be preferable to the newer. The lawyers had their way. The ninth article of the proposed Constitution was rejected, and in the end the whole of the jurisdiction which the Congress could exercise under the ninth of the Articles of Confederation was transferred to the Supreme Court of the United States.

The ' superior ' between the nations lacking in Francis of Vitoria's day had not been found ; it was created by the farsighted men of a later day. The ' superior ' of the new world was not a prince, not a person. It was law and the States of America, unwilling to prostrate themselves before prince or potentate, created the Supreme Court of the United States in the exercise of their sovereignty, to which they consented of their own free will, to submit those controversies which, in other lands of an earlier day without the Court of a Superior, had constantly resulted in war.

Arbitration between the independent States of America had, as in the past, disappeared before a Permanent Court of Justice.

The forcesuit had given place to the lawsuit within a vast space of territory destined to assume the proportions of a continent.

II

*The Role of the Supreme Court of the United States in
the settlement of Inter-State Disputes.*

In the first address I endeavoured to show how the peace
of law has become international by an extension to the
nations of arbitration and judicial settlement which has produced peace within every modern state and nation. I have
indicated in a very general and summary way how the peace-
producing processes have been extended beyond the frontiers
of the State into what is often called the international milieu.
Law within the State and administered in a court of justice
has kept the peace; law between the States and administered
in a court of justice is bound to keep the peace ; for the
application of law to disputes within or without the States
settles the controversy without a recourse to arms. And the
law is the same in each case : the dispute between individuals
about a debt, about a tort, about a crime is the same law to
settle a dispute between States about a debt of a like kind,
a tort of similar nature, and a conscious violation of a law to
the intentional injury of the person and property produces
consequences to be measured by the same standard although
the law may be applied differently, due to the fact that in
the one case the individual acts by and for himself without
reference to the State, whereas in the other he acts by
direction of or in behalf of the State. Justice is universal ;
the rule of law is no respecter of persons, although in one case
it reaches the natural individual directly, the artificial person
indirectly. The standard is identical, the application may
differ. The hope of the future, as I conceive, lies in a frank

recognition of the oneness of law and its application by and through appropriate agencies to the private person and the body politic. In America we have consciously adopted the government of law and rejected the government of men, and we foresee the day when the government of men will, in other parts of the world, be replaced by the government of law as found, tested, and administered in courts international as well as national. The Supreme Court of the United States has applied the justice of the individual to the controversies of States and found the rule of law equally applicable to both. The procedure may differ, the State treated with greater consideration, with a more tender solicitude for its rights and their adequate presentation and argument, with, however, the same justice to the litigant before it whether it be private person or a sovereign State.

It is to the conduct of a suit in the Supreme Court, between State and State, to which I invite your attention.

I would like, however, to premise some observations of an historical nature concerning colonial disputes, and the method of their adjustment.

Each of the thirteen Colonies depended directly upon the Crown and each was foreign to the other. Therefore, the Colonies had a common superior and their controversies could be and actually were submitted to the Superior—the King in Council. The questions could be of two kinds, between individuals of one and the same Colony and between two or more Colonies. If the dispute was between individuals, the Court of the Colony whereof they were residents would assume jurisdiction, an appeal lay to the King in Council and a suit based on the common law could be referred to an English common law court ; if the dispute were of an equitable nature, it could be referred to the Court of Chancery. An example of the first is the famous case of Winthrop against Lechmere ; of the second, Penn against Lord Baltimore. If the controversy were between two or more Colonies, it would likewise go to the King in Council where it could be decided by the Council, or referred to a Committee and the recommendations reported to and adopted by the King in Council. There was here a double precedent : an appeal in legal or equitable causes between private parties to a Court of the Superior ; a reference to the Superior of controversies between the Colonies for their consideration and determination. The States in the Federal Convention of 1787 created a common Superior for themselves, in the form of a Government of the Union, and a Supreme Court of the United States, to which appeals lay in federal matters in causes from the Courts of the States ; to which Supreme Court controversies between the States could be brought directly in first instance, and to the same Supreme Court controversies to which the United States may be a party. The double precedent was thus followed in each case : suits between private parties, whether in law or equity, going on appeal to the Supreme Court of the States ; controversies between States or to which the United States were parties going directly to the Supreme Court. The Superior was not found. It did not exist but it was created by voluntary contract of the States, just as later a ' Superior ' was by treaty to be created by the nations and states of our day in matters judicial. The statesmen of the United States filled the international void which Francis of Vitoria had remarked and the internationalists of to-day have followed the American model.

I may not dwell upon the case of Winthrop and Lechmere

(Connecticut Colonial Records, 571) [1] decided in 1728, in which a statute of descent of Connecticut was set aside by the Privy Council, because it distributed real estate in equal portions to the children of the deceased, contrary to the Common Law of England which vested realty in the eldest male. This is an appeal of individuals from a Colonial Court to the King in Council. There are, however, two cases between the Colonies of Rhode Island and Connecticut and Massachusetts, and one between the heirs of Wm. Penn and Lord Baltimore, proprietors respectively of Pennsylvania and Maryland to which I must do more than refer in passing, by way of introduction to the suits of States against States in the Supreme Court.

The case of Rhode Island against Connecticut (3 Acts of the Privy Council, Colonial Series, 10) [2] was a boundary question depending upon their respective charters. The King in Council decided in 1727 that a controversy between Colonies concerning boundaries between them, as set forth by their respective charters, is a judicial question, to be determined by the King in Council at the request of the Colonies. The western boundary of Rhode Island was, therefore, fixed by judicial decision. Nineteen years later, at the request of Rhode Island, the Privy Council decided the eastern boundary of that Colony against the contention of Massachusetts.[3] The northern boundary of Rhode Island was destined to be fixed exactly 100 years later by a decision of the Supreme Court in a suit brought in that Court by the State of Rhode Island against the State of Massachusetts.

[1] J. B. Scott, *Judicial Settlement of Controversies between States of the American Union*, vol. i, p. 93.   [2] *Op. cit.*, p. 573.

[3] 3 Acts of the Privy Council, Colonial Series, 436 ; *Judicial Settlement*, vol. i, p. 377.

The presence of the Atlantic Ocean and the lack of neighbours on the south doubtless prevented a further suit by the litigant little commonwealth.

The cases of Penn and Lord Baltimore were laid before the Privy Council by the Penns and referred to the High Court of Chancery, as they asked the specific performance of an agreement between the two proprietors of which Chancery had jurisdiction. The agreement concerned boundaries and, if carried into effect, it would determine the boundaries between the two Colonies. In 1750 the Court decreed[1] according to the agreement, and the line between them was drawn by Mason and Dixon, two English land surveyors— a line destined to be famous in American history as the boundary between the free and slave states of the Union.

The cases of Rhode Island, Connecticut, and Massachusetts were thus familiar to New England; the controversy between the Penns and Lord Baltimore and the decree of the Court of Chancery deciding it was familiar to the middle and southern States and it appears to have deeply impressed the colonists as a whole.

It is not, therefore, astonishing that the statesmen of the young Republic should carry into effect colonial practice, but it is to their eternal credit that they did so in such a way as to show how a Court of the Community of Nations could be created in the midst of independent States.

Of the many cases in which the Supreme Court has entertained suits between States of the American Union, I select three for examination. The first is the controversy between Rhode Island and Massachusetts. It began in 1833 and terminated thirteen years later with a judgement in favour of Massachusetts. It had no less than eight separate phases

[1] 1 Vesey Senior, 444; *Judicial Settlement*, vol. i, p. 588.

and is the first case in which a final judgement against a State was rendered by the Supreme Court of the Union.

The second is the controversy of Virginia and West Virginia, beginning in 1907 and ending eleven years later by the first decision of the Supreme Court that the judgement against a State may be executed by appropriate measures. In all there are ten separate phases of this important dispute. The judgement was against West Virginia.

The third is the controversy between the Government of the United States and Texas. It consists of two phases decided in 1892 and 1896. The decision in each was in favour of the United States.

The phases of the suits of State against State in the Supreme Court, anterior to those to which Rhode Island and Massachusetts were parties, dealt with matters of procedure, such as the State officials upon whom process should be served and notice given. The officers were declared to be the Governor and the Attorney-General, and the notice to be given was fixed at sixty days. These were preliminaries, important to be sure, but unimportant when once determined. It might happen that the State officials, having notice of the suit and duly summoned to appear in behalf of their State, at a fixed date, might fail to appear. In suits between individuals, judgement would be entered by default in such circumstances, supposing, of course, that the Court had jurisdiction of the case and of the parties plaintiff and defendant. Should the like procedure be followed as between private parties, or what should be done? The Supreme Court felt that the complaining State should have a right to proceed *ex parte*, that is, to conduct its case in the absence of the defendant State as if it were present, reserving to it, however, the right to appear at any time before judgement and to contest the proceedings. The suit against a State was an extraordinary proceeding and was not to be treated as an ordinary affair. So matters stood when Rhode Island filed its suit in the Supreme Court against Massachusetts in 1833.

The procedure already adopted was that of Chancery as in the case of the Penns against Lord Baltimore, appearing respectively in behalf of Pennsylvania and Maryland ; but the procedure of Chancery, as stated in the Rhode Island case, was to be freed from technicalities ; it was to be freer and more flexible, so that the complaining State could put its entire cause of action and the defendant State its entire defence before the Court. In other words, the procedure of Chancery in the case of individuals was to be remodelled so as to be an aid but not an hindrance to the august litigants. A single example must suffice : A demurrer of the defendant State admits the facts contained in the complaint, but denies their sufficiency in point of law. If the demurrer were over-ruled in a suit between private parties, judgement could be entered for the plaintiff, or if the demurrer was sustained, judgement could be entered for the defendant.

Between States on the other hand, the overruling of a demurrer required the defendant to answer the complaint instead of objecting to it ; and sustaining the demurrer required the State to present a more adequate complaint. The delays of procedure binding upon private litigants were extended, as large bodies, such as States, apparently move more slowly and deliberately than individuals.

The Court was without precedent in these matters and it framed the procedure before it, in such a way, as to enable each litigant to get the facts of the case before the Court in accordance with such modification of Chancery practice as to do substantial instead of technical justice to the parties.

In one of the phases of the Rhode Island cases, Massachusetts stated its intention to withdraw its appearance, that is to say, to withdraw from the case. The Court decided that as appearance was voluntary, it could withdraw, but, if it did so, that Rhode Island could continue its case *ex parte*. This holding had the result of keeping Massachusetts before the Court as an active litigant. It might lose the case if it failed to appear, and, if it appeared and lost, it would be none the worse off; if, on the contrary, it appeared, it might win. It had, therefore, nothing to lose, but everything to gain by appearing. After some delay, Massachusetts appeared and won the case.

The greatest phase of the case is the third, decided in 1838 (12 Peters, 657), and the opinion of Mr. Justice Baldwin on behalf of the Court is, it seems to me, the greatest ever delivered in a controversy between States of the American Union, and of fundamental importance in judicial settlement of disputes between nations in a permanent court of their own creation. I have often thought that Mr. Justice Baldwin's opinion should be printed in pamphlet form and widely circulated. This has not yet been done, but it is in the interest of judicial settlement that it be better known.

I shall, therefore, make a short statement of the controversy, sufficient for present purposes, summarize the opinion, and quote here and there a passage which would lose its point if summarized.

A line drawn east and west from a point three miles below the Charles River was, according to the Charters of each of the two Colonies, to form their common boundary. By mistake of Massachusetts, the line was run some seven miles to the south of the river. There appears to have been doubt on the part of Rhode Island authorities that the point fixed by Massachusetts was correct and commissioners had met and

discussed the matter at various times ; but in 1718 the so-
called Woodward and Saffrey stake, marking the point too
far to the south, was agreed to by the Rhode Island commissioners and ratified by the General Assembly of that
Colony as well as by Massachusetts. It was eventually admitted that the case was free from fraud, although a mistake
had been made by Massachusetts authorities to the disadvantage of Rhode Island. The question was whether Rhode
Island could, after the lapse of more than a century, have the
mistake rectified by the Supreme Court of the United States
and the boundary line drawn in strict conformity with the
colonial charters. The legal question was whether the doctrine of prescription could be invoked in the relations between
States as between private parties. In the final decree of the
Supreme Court in 1846 (4 Howard's Reports, 691) prescription was held to apply.

In the phase of the case before the Court in 1838, prescription was not considered, in Justice Baldwin's opinion, as
Massachusetts deemed it more to its interest to have the case
dismissed for want of jurisdiction in the Court, than to
admit jurisdiction with a chance on the part of Rhode Island
to win its contention. The case, therefore, turned solely on
this point. The Supreme Court is one of limited jurisdiction and as an International Court is also one of limited
jurisdiction, and is likely to be so indefinitely, the views
of the Supreme Court on this question are of international
interest.

As defined by Justice Baldwin :

' Jurisdiction is the power to hear and determine the subject
matter in controversy between parties to a suit, to adjudicate or
exercise any judicial power over them ; the question is, whether
on the case before a court, their action is judicial or extra-judicial ;

with or without the authority of the law, to render a judgement or decree upon the rights of the litigant parties. If the law confers the power to render a judgement or decree, then the court has jurisdiction ; what shall be adjudged or decreed between the parties, and with which is the right of the case, is judicial action, by hearing and determining it.'

That is to say, if the National Court is the creature of Statute, then the Statute is at once the source and extent of its power ; if the International Court is the creature of treaty or convention, the treaty or convention is likewise the source and extent of its power, and the attempt of either Court to go beyond the law of its creation is extra-judicial. The question of jurisdiction is of the essence and exception can be taken at any time, however late. If not raised by the parties, it is deemed to have been considered and decided in favour of the Court by the judges, as otherwise they would not assume jurisdiction which they could not legally exercise.

'Before we can proceed in this cause, we must,' Justice Baldwin next said, ' therefore, inquire whether we can hear and determine the matters in controversy between the parties, who are two states of this Union, sovereign within their respective boundaries, save that portion of power which they have granted to the federal government, and foreign to each other for all but federal purposes.'

The next succeeding portion of Justice Baldwin's opinion is as applicable to sovereign nations forming a more limited Union, indeed a mere judicial union, that is to say, a union for a single purpose, instead of the more perfect Union of the American States. 'Those states, in their highest sovereign capacity, in the convention of the people thereof . . . adopted the constitution, by which they respectively made to the

United States a grant of judicial power over controversies between two or more states. . . . The states waived their exemption from judicial power, as sovereigns by original and inherent right, by their own grant of its exercise over themselves in such cases, but which they would not grant to any inferior tribunal.' This is the judicial ' Superior ' of our friend Francis of Vitoria. ' By this grant ', Justice Baldwin continues, ' this Court has acquired jurisdiction over the parties in this cause, by their own consent and delegated authority ; as their agent for executing the judicial power of the United States', it would be the same in a mere judicial union, ' in the cases specified '. Justice Baldwin next mentioned that there existed boundary disputes between eleven of the States at the time of framing the Constitution, and that if the Supreme Court did not assume jurisdiction, there could be no way of settling them, inasmuch as the States had, by the Constitution, renounced the inherent right of the sovereign to make war. Judicial settlement was consciously adopted as the substitute for war between the States and the Supreme Court represents the bystander, or the praetor who, in Roman days, thrust himself between the contending parties and prescribed arbitration by contract as the substitute for self-redress or private warfare.

A court is to assume jurisdiction of and to decide judicial not political questions, and unless questions political may become judicial, the Court can only decide controversies of a restricted nature—controversies which, it is said, rarely result in war. The jurisdiction of the Court would be limited and its service limited, and while it would be worth while to constitute it between States, its usefulness would necessarily be restricted. But political questions at a given time may become judicial and the Court opened to the dangerous newcomer. How may this happen? Justice Baldwin informs us, and this is the great value of his opinion—by the simple agreement of the parties to submit the dispute to a court of justice. Controversies between sovereign nations are to be settled by the States themselves, through their political departments, as they are political questions. When the Colonies became sovereign States, they became entitled, as of right, ' to settle their controversies with a foreign power, or among themselves, which no state and no power could do for them.' When, however, the States ' surrendered ' by the ninth of the Articles of Confederation—

' to Congress, and its appointed Court, the right and power of settling their mutual controversies ; thus making them judicial questions, whether they arose on " boundary, jurisdiction, or any cause whatever ". . . . None can be settled without war or treaty, which is political power ; but under the old and new confederacy they could and can be settled by a court constituted by themselves, as their own substitutes, authorized to do that for states, which states alone could do before.'

These introductory passages enable us to see the full force and effect of a conclusion which Justice Baldwin draws from them, as judicially true as gravitation is physically true, and the one as important to the human animal as the other is to inanimate nature. The conclusion to which the learned, analytical, and far-sighted judge would have his brethren of the Bench accept, and which the world is unconsciously accepting, is put in a few short but pregnant sentences.

' We are thus pointed to the true boundary line between political and judicial power, and questions. A sovereign decides by his own will, which is the supreme law within his own boundary ; a court, or judge, decides according to the law prescribed by the sovereign power, and that law is the rule for judgement. The submission by the sovereigns, or states, to a court of law or equity, of a controversy between them, without prescribing any rule of decision, gives power to decide according to the appropriate law of the case ; which depends on the subject matter, the source and nature of the claims of the parties, and the law which governs them.'

I would like to break the quotation a moment for a word of comment. The mere submission to a court divests the political sovereign of the power to decide and the question becomes judicial although the law be not determined by the submission. The question, having become judicial, is to be decided in ordinary course by judges supposed to be learned in the principles of justice and capable of stating them in the form of rules of law. This is the necessary implication of Justice Baldwin's statement, but he says so expressly that there may be no doubt as to his meaning. ' From the time of such submission, the question ceases to be a political one to be decided by the *sic volo sic iubeo*, of political power ; it comes to the court to be decided by its judgement, legal discretion, and solemn consideration of the rules of law appropriate to its nature as a judicial question, depending on the exercise of judicial power ; as it is bound to act by known and settled principles of national or municipal', and the learned Justice might have added international, ' jurisprudence, as the case requires.' It was not necessary for Justice Baldwin to discourse of the law of nations, but Chief Justice Fuller was obliged to do so some sixty-four years later, in the case of Kansas and Colorado, and he completed, in his opinion, which was likewise that of the Supreme Court, Justice Baldwin's partial enumeration of settled principles which the Supreme Court was to apply by including expressly the Law of Nations. ' Sitting, as it were, as an international as well as a domestic tribunal, we apply federal law, state law, and international law, as the exigencies or the particular case may demand.'

An illustration from prize courts is such an important step in Justice Baldwin's demonstration that submission to a court converts political into judicial questions that his exact language should be quoted :

' It has never been contended ', he positively avers, ' that prize courts of admiralty jurisdiction, or questions before them, are not strictly judicial ; they decide on questions of war and peace, the law of nations, treaties, and the municipal laws of the capturing nation, by which alone they are constituted ; *a fortiori*, if such courts were constituted by a solemn treaty between the state under whose authority the capture was made, and the state whose citizens or subjects suffer from capture. All nations submit to the jurisdiction of such courts over their subjects, and hold their final decrees conclusive on private property.'

After this careful consideration and painstaking analysis of the actual facts as distinct from intangible theories, Justice Baldwin distinguishes, in behalf of the Supreme Court of the United States, political from judicial questions and defines the process by which facts and conditions previously considered political became admittedly judicial.

' These considerations lead to the definition of political and judicial power and questions ; the former is that which a sovereign or a state exerts by his or its own authority, as reprisal and confiscation ; the latter is that which is granted to a court or judicial tribunal. So of controversies between states ; they are by their nature political, when the sovereign or state reserves to itself the right of deciding on it ; makes it the " subject of a treaty, to be settled as between states independant ", or the foundation of representations from state to state. This is political equity, to be judged by the parties themselves, as contradistinguished from judicial equity, administered by a court of justice, decreeing the *equum et bonum* of the case, let who or what be the parties before them.'

The agreement may be between two nations, many or all, as in the case of a confederation ; it may be for single disputes, a class of differences, or for controversies of whatever kind which may arise between the parties to the agreement.

The American States bound themselves in the ninth of the Articles of Confederation to submit all their controversies, in language which left no doubt as to their intention in entering into the agreement, to settle their disputes by temporary courts and the States of the more perfect union agreed to submit in the third Article of the Constitution controversies of the States without words of limitation. Political questions may be made judicial by a series of agreements until the category of political questions be exhausted, or the agreement to submit all questions ' hitherto considered political, may be but ' a single act as in the Articles of Confederation or Constitution of the United States.

One of the most fertile sources of controversy between nations has been disputes as to their boundaries. They have usually been political in the sense that the nations or their sovereigns have treated directly with one another. The result has too often been war, which could and should have been avoided, if the sovereigns or statesmen in charge had converted them into judicial questions by an agreement to submit them to a court, and followed the agreement to do so by their actual submission. Since the resort to arbitration between nations, disputes concerning boundaries have been common occurrence and it would be a safe guess, without adding up the long list of arbitrations since the Jay treaty of 1794, which brought arbitration again into repute, that one of the most frequent single items is that of boundary disputes.

It is difficult to conceive of a dispute more political than that relating to boundaries, and if controversies under that head can be submitted to a court of justice, it would seem that controversies between nations, involving an assertion on one side and a denial on the other, can be taken out of the category of political questions by the willingness to submit them to a court for their determination by a written agreement to that effect.

Good will is the pre-requisite to peace, and who knows but that the submission of the State, like that of the individual, to a court of justice is the way? In any event, we cannot be too grateful to Justice Baldwin for his opinion in the protracted controversy between Rhode Island and Massachusetts, in which that level-headed man of affairs and learned jurist, speaking for the Supreme Court of the United States, declared, in its behalf, that no dispute between nations can escape judicial settlement on the plea that it is of a political nature, and, therefore, withdrawn from the principles of justice everywhere applying between man and man in every civilized country of the world.

It cannot be admitted that the primitive Romans who through a mere wager brought their disputes before arbiters of their own choice, without law at hand for their solution, or that the American States, which have bound themselves by a general agreement to submit their disputes to a permanent court of their own creation, are cleverer than the people of our day and the nations of the world. Good will produces the necessary and fruitful agreement; ill will the unnecessary and futile war.

I now take up the controversy of the State of Virginia against West Virginia which, arising out of a war between the

States of the American Union, was decided by the Supreme Court in the midst of a war of the United States with European powers.

The facts of the case are many and complicated but they are few and simple for our purpose. A convention of the State of Virginia, held in 1861, voted to ' repeal ' the act of the Convention of 1788 ratifying the Constitution of the United States. We do not need to decide whether the ' repeal ' was wise or foolish, valid or invalid. The Federal Government reduced by force of arms the twelve southern States, including Virginia, which had attempted to secede from the Union. The counties of Virginia to the west of the mountains refused to follow the rest of the State out of the Union. Through their delegates, they met in Convention ; declared their loyalty to the Union and asked to be admitted to the Union as the State of West Virginia. The Congress complied with this request and the new State was admitted on an equality with the other States of the Union.

The State of West Virginia, through its delegates in convention and by a provision in its Constitution, assumed the payment of an equitable portion of the outstanding debt of the State of Virginia, as, before the Civil War, the western counties formed a part of that extensive commonwealth and were, like the other beneficiaries of the revenues raised and expended, within what may be called the original or greater Virginia. It was finally determined that the debt of Virginia should be taken as on 1 January 1861, and that the State of West Virginia should assume one-third of that amount.[1] The part of the debt falling upon West Virginia was fixed by the Supreme Court in 1915 at the sum of $12,393,929·50, which seemed large then, but to us to-day, accustomed as

[1] 238 United States Reports, 202 (1915).

we are to the enormous figures of the world war, seems trifling for a great litigation.

As West Virginia took no steps to comply with this judgement, the State of Virginia sought to have an order of the Supreme Court ' directing the levy of a tax by the legislature of West Virginia to pay such judgement '.

West Virginia, naturally enough, protested against the issue of such an order. This phase of the question—the ninth of the series—was argued at length by Counsel of the litigating States and resulted in a pronouncement of the Supreme Court that judgement implied execution; that the power resided in the United States to be exercised through Congress.[1] This decision of the Supreme Court has given rise to much discussion. Chief Justice White, speaking for his brethren, asserted that the authority to enforce its judgement is of the essence of judicial power. Historically this is not so. The duty of the judge is to declare the law and to apply it to the concrete case before the Court. With the rendering of the judgement, the Court has nothing further to do with the matter. The Executive Department of the Government, separate and distinct from the Judiciary, takes up the judgement and executes it or not as he sees fit. President Jackson refused to execute the judgement of the Supreme Court in Worcester against the State of Georgia,[2] and in point of fact it never was executed. The judgement was not affected by its non-execution and it has not lost its value as a precedent.

If it be admitted that judgement in cases between private parties implies execution, it does not necessarily follow that this issoinc ases between States. But whether the Supreme Court was historically or theoretically wrong or right, it has decided

[1] 246 United States Reports, 565 (1918).
[2] 6 Peters Reports, 515 (1832).

that a judgement against a State in favour of another State of the American Union may be executed. The power, according to the Supreme Court, lies with Congress and it would seem that it is, therefore, political and not judicial. Whether the Congress will exercise it is a question for the future.

In any event, the State of West Virginia did not intend to have the case go farther and on 1 March 1918 Counsel for the two States appeared before the Supreme Court and asked that the case be striken from the calender as West Virginia had made arrangements to satisfy the judgement.

The Supreme Court was organized in 1789. The first final judgement in a suit of State against State was rendered in 1846, some fifty-seven years after its establishment ; in 1918, some seventy-two years later, the first decision of the Supreme Court was rendered to the effect that its judgement against a State in favour of another State could be executed by the Congress of the Union. Therefore, a period of 129 years had elapsed before the Supreme Court carried a case of this kind to its completion by declaring the judgement to be capable of execution.

Here the matter rests.

Another question of great importance was raised and settled in 1896, that the United States could bring a controversy with a State of the Union before the Supreme Court of the States. It is clear that the Court would have jurisdiction of such a case because the judicial power of the United States, that is of the States in their united capacity, is expressly extended ' to controversies to which the United States shall be a party '. The first case of this kind was decided in 1896, when the Court assumed jurisdiction of the

suit of the United States against Texas.[1] This enormous
commonwealth, larger than the German Empire, claimed
as part of its territory a large tract to the south which the
Government of the United States claimed as part of Indian
territory, now the State of Oklahoma. The decision was in
favour of the United States.

There are several aspects of the case which justify a word
of comment. We frequently say that the United States are
sovereign and that the States are sovereign. This is true if
we mean that the United States are sovereign within the
exercise of the powers expressly or impliedly granted to them,
and that the individual States are sovereign in respect to the
powers of sovereignty which they have not granted to the
United States or otherwise renounced. It is better to look
at it from Madison's point of view, as he was really responsible
for the formation of this most perfect of Unions and has
preserved for us and for others the debates of the Federal
Convention. In his conception, the States, in their individual capacities, delegated certain powers to the States in their
united capacities, to be exercised by the three-formed
Government of the Union in behalf of all the States. In this
way the States are and remain sovereign, but the United
States became possessed of the delegated powers of sovereignty within the scope of the delegated powers. The Act of the
Government of the Union is superior to that of the State,
provided it be authorized by law, just as the act of the whole
is greater than the act of any of its parts. The suit of the
United States against Texas was, therefore, the suit of all the
States of the Union against one of the States. It was not the
suit of the Government of the Union except in the sense that
it represented the States in their united capacities. It is

[1] 162 United States Reports, 1.

evident, therefore, that the United States could, through the appropriate agent of their United Government, sue one of the States in its individual capacity. It would also seem to follow that the individual State could, by the express language of the Constitution, sue the United States, inasmuch as the judicial power of the Union extends, without words of restriction, to a controversy to which the United States are parties, whether plaintiffs or defendants. The question, however, is not so important as it would appear because the Congress of the United States, in which the States are represented (in the Lower House according to population, in the Senate according to States as such), can authorize suit against the United States. It has done so for individuals in a limited class of cases ; it may do so for States whenever the Congress of the States in their united capacities shall determine. In the meantime, the Supreme Court admits suit in behalf of, not against the United States.

There are three matters of which I should like to say something before drawing these remarks, already too long, to an end.

The first is that there are no words of limitation in the grant of judicial power to the Supreme Court in respect to controversies between States, so that all disputes capable of being passed on by a court by means of law, derived from or based upon principles of justice, may be laid before the Supreme Court of the American States. Boundary controversies predominate, but also disputes relating to the diversion of waters, an important question in our western States, quarantine, sanitation, taxation, State debts, polution of waters, &c., &c. Matters of health, such as sanitation and quarantine, can be and have been decided by the Supreme

Court ; matters of indebtedness and matters of an economic nature, such as the supply of natural gas conveyed under ground from State to State, and of commerce, have been considered and passed upon. There is, however, a reluctance on the part of the Court to decide questions of a local and economic nature, and from time to time the Judges have suggested from the Bench that the States should resort to their reserved power, in accordance with article 1, section 10, clause 3, to make compacts between and among themselves, with the express approval in advance or afterwards, or by the implied approval of the Congress through acquiescence. The exercise of this power by the States is in their local interests, and the supervision of the Congress, representing the general interests of the other States, prevents an abuse of power. I mention this phase of the question as it is of importance in any union of nations or states.

The second matter to which I would refer is that the controversies of the States in the contemplation of the Federal Constitution are, according to the judgement of the Supreme Court, disputes between States as such, and not in behalf of their respective citizens. It would be impertinent on the part of a simple citizen to question this holding of the Court, and yet it is difficult to see what interest the States can have in a controversy which is not, in some way, connected with the interest of its citizens. The States are, we say, sovereign but that term would require a longer explanation than I can possibly give it, even if I were competent to do so, in a paper such as this. Suffice it to say that in the American conception the State has no power other than that conferred upon it by its people ; that when it acts as a sovereign it acts not in its own inherent right but only in behalf of the citizens whose creation it is, and that the

Government of the States is a mere agent to carry out the orders of the State within the powers with which it has been vested by the citizens. From this point of view there seems to be no sufficient reason against, but every reason for, the State to sue another State of the Union in behalf of its citizens. I am bound to say, however, that the question has been decided adversely to this contention in the leading case of *New Hampshire* v. *Louisiana* in 1883.[1] In this respect, the state of international law differs from and is, I think, superior to that of the American Union.

The last of the matters upon which I would touch is that of advisory opinions, and I do so with full knowledge that I am treading on dangerous ground. The Supreme Court was of the opinion, in the early days of its existence when it had a full Bench and an empty court-room, that its duty was to decide, not to advise. That action may have been wise or unwise, but it does not of necessity follow that an advisory opinion would have been the exercise of non-judicial power. The whole history of English law is against such a conclusion, and English law and English practice are the basis of American law and practice. It cannot be successfully contended, it would seem, that the Supreme Judicial Court of Massachusetts, for such is its official name, is performing a non-judicial function whenever it renders one of its numerous advisory opinions to the duly constituted and authorized officials of that commonwealth. In some other States the practice exists, and does not seem to work badly. I would not advocate the introduction of the system in States where it does not exist, nor criticize the Supreme Court for its refusal to render advisory opinions. I only maintain that an advisory opinion is not a non-judicial function inasmuch as

[1] 108 United States Reports, 76.

it has been exercised by the judges of England for centuries and is exercised by American courts of the highest repute without harm to their admittedly judicial decisions. In a scheme of international organization, where there is no Ministry of Justice to advise and where there is no method of executing judgements, the opinions of a judicial body may, without discourtesy, be considered as advisory in fact if not in theory. We have commissions of inquiry to elucidate disputed facts and report their conclusions, leaving the nations free to accept or reject, or neglect the conclusions of the Commissions. Why could we not have Commissions of inquiry for disputed questions of law, leaving the parties free or not to follow the opinions of these Commissions as in other cases? Finding of facts is in our system a judicial function; the finding of the rule of law applicable to a concrete situation is a judicial function and none the less judicial because judgement is not entered. In international organization the judicial function is not changed merely because it operates on a larger scale, and, indeed, its usefulness is greater for this very reason.

It is a majestic spectacle to see the United States enter the Supreme Court as a litigant asking for the application of law, instead of imposing the law whose benefit it seeks. This is particularly so in the case of suits between the States in which the principles of international law are applied—a system of law which, by the language of the Constitution and indeed by decisions of the States antedating the Constitution, was declared to form an integral part of the law of individual States and, therefore, of the States in their united capacities.

It would be a more wonderful spectacle to see the United

States enter the Court room at the instance of an individual State, and before the bar of the Court ask that justice which the States in their united capacities ask from the Court against the individual State.

It is, in any event, a heartening spectacle to see the smallest State of the Union, for Rhode Island is such, hale one of the larger States of the Union before the Supreme Court, to defend the right whereof it claims to be possessed.

In the American system of law there is no small, there is no large ; there is no weak, there is no powerful State ; just as in any adequate system of law for the individual there is no person because of office, class, or wealth possessed of special rights.

Law is the great leveller of man and state. It is fortunate for us of the United States that this is so ; it will not be less fortunate for the world when independent nations bow before the law of their own making.

In the day of judgement we are, we are told, to stand as equals before the Judge of us all ; and whether we will or not, we must, individuals or states, stand as equals in our Courts of justice which administer His will, whether revealed or made by human hands.

III

*The Permanent Court of International Justice :
its origin and nature.*

The First Peace Conference which opened at The Hague on 18 May 1899, the birthday of the Czar Nicholas the Second, through whose happy initiative the Conference had been assembled, had the benefit of an experience with arbitration, brought again into repute through the Jay Treaty of 19 November 1794, between Great Britain and the United States. Possibly a few of its more enlightened members had heard of proposals for the judicial settlement of disputes between and among the nations though a permanent International Tribunal, somewhat like the Supreme Court of the United States, which in the course of a hundred years had decided controversies between the States of the American Union by the simple process of law and its impartial administration. Probably none of its members knew that arbitration was bound to culminate in judicial settlement, as in the case of Rome and the United States. The Conference was, however, destined to take the first step in this development. In America the transition from arbitration to judicial settlement was accomplished within a decade and in the world at large within less than twenty-five years.

The Conference had been called to reduce, if possible, the heavy load of armament under which Europe was staggering, and to prevent bankruptcy of the larger nations, which a competitive increase of armaments suggested, or the even greater menace to civilization of a war between the nations which considered themselves as the guardians of this civilization which bankruptcy or war inevitably destroys.

The Czar's original invitation to the nations accredited

to St. Petersburg dealt with armament, but there was a feeling, not confined to a single Power, that a conference on this subject was doomed in advance to certain failure. Therefore the Czar, keeping to the front the question of armament, broadened the programme of the prospective conference so as to include a discussion of good offices, mediation, and voluntary arbitration ' with the purpose of preventing armed conflicts between nations '.

To this phase of the subject I invite your attention :

The idea of an International Conference for the general instead of special interests of those who called it was not the least of the contributions by Bolivar, to whom Latin America is largely indebted for its independence. The Congress of Panama, which he suggested, met a hundred years ago at Panama in 1826. It was not only a prophecy of other and better days but a precedent. It had shown that the governments of Christendom, to use William Ladd's measured language, would be ' willing to send delegates to any such Congress, wherever it ' should ' be called *by a respectable state* ', well established in its own government, as Russia seemed to the outer world to be in 1898, ' if called in a time of peace to meet at a proper place '. And while it would perhaps be beyond the purpose in hand to dwell upon Mr. Ladd at length, it is nevertheless proper to remark that his *Essay on a Congress of Nations for the adjustment of International Disputes without resort to arms* was published in 1840, that it was widely circulated, distributed by its author ' to the crowned heads and leading men of Christendom ' His proposals were twofold, a Congress and a Court of Nations ; the first to be composed of Ambassadors of the nations, meeting at a given place upon a plane of equality, with one vote and no more to each nation, to settle ' the

principles of international law ', by compact and agreement,
which when accepted by the nations would become a law
to them and to the Court which the Congress was to establish for the settlement of disputes between the nations, to
be ' composed of the most able civilians in the world, to
arbitrate or judge such cases as should be brought before it
by the mutual consent of two or more contending nations '.

The Congress was to be ' the legislature and the Court the
judiciary in the government of nations ', leaving, as Mr. Ladd
added, ' the functions of the executive with public opinion,
the queen of the world '. Mr. Ladd had never, he said,
seen in any ancient or modern authority the threefold plan
of division as set forth in his project, and he was right, it
is to be hoped, in his opinion that his Essay would ' obviate
all the objections which have been heretofore made to such
a plan '.

Without dwelling further upon Mr. Ladd, I commend the
Essay to your careful consideration ; for the first Peace Conference of 1899 was his Congress of the Nations, and the
Permanent Court of International Justice of 1920 is his Court
of Nations.

The delegation of the United States, acting under instructions from Secretary of State Hay, proposed an International Tribunal which became in the end the Permanent
Court of Arbitration, and the Conference facilitated the
recourse to ' voluntary arbitration ' in a further way by preparing for the participating nations, which adopted it without
exception, a code of arbitral procedure.

The Permanent Court of Arbitration was, according to
the Pacific Settlement Convention of 1899, to be composed
of not more than four persons appointed by each of the
signatory Powers for a period of six years, from whom the

nations in controversy could select the judges for the temporary tribunal which was to decide their difference. The names of the judges were arranged in a list and sent to the signatory Powers. From this list or panel the nations could select the judges, if they had not already agreed upon them, by choosing two of their nationals if they so desired; the fifth or umpire was to be chosen by the judges themselves; if they failed to agree a third Power was to be requested to choose the umpire and, in case of failure to agree on the Power in question, each of the contending Powers was to choose another and the two to name the umpire.

This method had two defects: four of the five judges might be citizens of the nations in controversy, and the two Powers might not directly or indirectly agree upon the umpire. Both of these defects were corrected in the second of the Peace Conferences held likewise at The Hague in 1907.

Thereafter only one of the two judges was to be chosen from the nationals of the contending parties, and with a neutral or rather indifferent umpire the award could be reached by the indifferent members who would thus constitute a majority of the Tribunal. But how was the umpire to be chosen in case of continued disagreement? If the two Powers to which the choice was confined did not agree then each proposed the name of an indifferent person from the list or panel of the Court, and lot decided which of the two was to be the umpire. There was thus a guarantee that the neutral or indifferent members could decide the dispute, and that the umpire could be selected whenever the parties in conflict were themselves unable to agree on this point.

The representatives of the signatory and ratifying Powers accredited to The Hague were to form, under the presidency of the Netherland Minister of Foreign Affairs, an administrative body for the Court, and an International Bureau was created at The Hague to act as ' Registrar ', as the English say, or Clerk of the Permanent Court, as we of America would call him.

The machinery was simple : in case of conflict the parties could resort to the list of the Permanent Court, with a registrar or clerk as their intermediary in the further stages of the controversy.

The Permanent Court of Arbitration has justified its creation : it has a number of important awards to its credit and none to its discredit, such as the affair of Casa Blanca between France and Germany, which might have resulted in something more serious than a rupture of diplomatic relations had it not been submitted to and decided by a temporary tribunal of the Court in 1909 ; the North Atlantic Fisheries controversy in 1910 between Great Britain and the United States, and the more recent case after the World War between Norway and the United States, decided at The Hague in 1924 and involving the compensation to be paid by the United States for the sequestration by that Government of Norwegian ships during the war.

The reporter of the proposed Court of Arbitral Justice stated in his report to the second of the Peace Conferences : ' It may not be known generally that the United States instituted a Court of Arbitration exactly a hundred and thirty years ago.' He then proceeded to outline the ninth of the Articles of Confederation of the United States, and continued : ' Even a superficial examination of these provisions shows a striking likeness between the Court at The Hague and its American predecessor.' He followed this statement with a sentence which has lost neither its interest nor timeliness : ' The life of the American Court of Arbitration was short ; it failed to justify its existence ; lacking the essential elements of a court of justice, it was superseded within ten years of its creation by the present Supreme Court, in which controversies which might lead to war, if between sovereign States, are settled by judicial means.' After which he put the pertinent question : ' Will history repeat itself? ' To which we of to-day can answer : It has.

The attempt was made in the second Conference to follow the experience of a single State, Rome, and of thirteen States in Confederation by creating a permanent Court of Justice between and among the forty-four nations present by their plenipotentiaries at the Conference ' without altering the status ' of the Permanent Court of Arbitration. Mr. Ladd's Court of Nations was to be tried. The initiation was to come from the United States but only when the friends of peace had persuaded the sovereign people, and through them the President and Congress of the United States, to act. ' When the whole country ', Mr. Ladd predicted, ' shall understand the subject as the State of Massachusetts ', then leader in the movement for pacific settlement, the ' Congress of the United States will be as favourable to a Congress of Nations as the General Court (Legislature) of Massachusetts ; and when the American Government shall take up the subject in earnest, it will begin to be studied and understood by the enlightened nations of Europe '.

As in 1899 Secretary of State Hay had instructed the American delegates to the first of the Conferences to propose a Permanent International Tribunal, so in 1907 Secretary of State Root instructed the American delegates to the second to propose to and urge upon the representatives of the forty-four nations there assembled a Permanent Court of International Justice. In these instructions, which are already accepted as classic, Secretary Root stated that the fear of partiality in arbitral awards prevented a more frequent recourse to arbitration, but that nations would, in his opinion, be willing to submit their controversies to a Court of Justice composed of members acting impartially, as is the wont of judges, instead of arbiters in whom the negotiating instinct of the diplomat, with its consequent partiality, is supposed to be present. ' If there could be a tribunal ', he impressively said, ' which would pass upon questions between nations the same impartial and impersonal judgement that the Supreme Court of the United States gives to questions arising between citizens of the different states, or between foreign citizens and the citizens of the United States, there can be no doubt that nations would be much more ready to submit their controversies to its decision than they are now to take the chances of arbitration.' For these reasons Secretary Root concluded his instructions on this point :

' It should be your effort to bring about in the second Conference a development of The Hague Tribunal into a Permanent Tribunal '—here we have arbitration giving birth to judicial procedure—' composed of judges who are judicial officers and nothing else, who are paid adequate salaries, who have no other occupation, who will devote their entire time to the trial and decision of international causes by judicial methods and under a sense of judicial responsibility.' Secretary Root had been in charge of the War Department after the Spanish-American war, and he felt, as no person well could without his practical experience in handling appeals from Spanish Courts in the possessions of Spain which had passed, in consequence of the war, into the possession of the

United States, the difficulty of passing upon questions to be decided under a foreign system of procedure and in a foreign language. Therefore, he added the following suggestion, born of practical wisdom, that,

'These judges should be so selected from the different countries that the different system of law and procedure and the principal languages shall be fairly represented.'

I have quoted Secretary Root's language at some length, as otherwise the attempt to create the Court in 1907 and its constitution in 1920 could not be understood as it should be.

The American representatives followed their instructions in letter and spirit. A proposal to form a permanent Court of Justice was made by the American delegation in which Germany and Great Britain joined, with the result that, after weeks of discussion, a draft convention of some thirty-five articles was adopted by the Conference for the creation of a Court of Arbitral Justice at The Hague. Its main features were: free and easy access to the nations composing it, with judges and deputy judges appointed for a period of twelve years, qualified to hold high judicial posts in their respective countries, chosen as far as possible from the Permanent Court of Arbitration, representing the different juridical systems of the world and thus ' capable of ensuring continuity in arbitral jurisprudence '; at least one session a year beginning on the first Wednesday of June and continuing until the business before it was dispatched, with power on the part of the Special Delegation of the Court to dispense with the meeting, or, if necessary, to summon the Court in extraordinary session ; a special committee called the Special Delegation of three judges elected annually for the speedy determination of differences between the contracting parties.

The jurisdiction of the Court was very broad, as broad as the goodwill of the august litigants, for by article 17 it was declared ' competent to deal with all cases submitted to it, in virtue of a general undertaking to have recourse to arbitration or of a special agreement ' ; some rules of procedure were expressly stated in the draft convention and impliedly by general provision of article 22, that the Court was to follow in other respects the procedure set forth at length in the Pacific Settlement Convention of 1899. The Court itself was authorized by article 22 to draw up its own rules of procedure, which were very properly to be communicated to the Contracting Powers for their general information and specific guidance in the conduct of cases which they might have before it. In the matter of language, which apparently worries small minds to whom a foreign tongue is a reflection upon their parts of speech, and the use of a foreign tongue a confession of the inferiority of their own instead of a means of reaching a general understanding, the draft convention wisely authorized the Court to determine the language which it should itself use, and what languages might be used before it in the trial of cases. The International Bureau of the Court of Arbitration, an existing body, was to be used ; the judgement was to give the reasons upon which it was based, to contain the names of the judges taking part in it and to be signed by the president and registrar for purposes of authentication. Each party in litigation was to pay its own costs and an equal share of the costs of the trial ; whereas the general expenses of the Court were to be borne by the contracting Powers, and to be secured from them by the Administrative Council, also an existing body at The Hague. A report of the doings of the Court was to be drawn up each year by the special delegation and forwarded to the contracting Powers by the International Bureau, and communicated to the judges and deputy judges.

It will be observed that nothing has been said of the method by which the judges were to be appointed. The Convention is silent on this point as, owing to the difficulty of the subject and especially its newness, the creation of a permanent Court was being considered for the first time in an official Conference of the Nations. The large Powers wished to be represented permanently in the Court and the smaller Powers, while willing, no doubt, to elect judges from the larger nations, which would be in effect tantamount to permanent representation, were nevertheless unwilling to concede permanency as of right. The larger Powers, although sure of their superiority, were unwilling to risk an election as they had the uncomfortable feeling that the smaller States, larger in number and assuredly equal in intelligence and notoriously superior in their devotion to justice, might prefer judges from the smaller to the exclusion of the larger nations. The result was that the draft convention was therefore silent on this question. However appointed the judges were to be equal and rank according to the dates of the notification of their appointment ; they were before taking their seats to swear or make a solemn affirmation to ' exercise their functions impartially and conscientiously ' ; they were to enjoy diplomatic immunity in the exercise of their functions outside of their respective countries and they were to receive an annual salary of 6,000 Netherland florins ; the additional sum of 100 florins per diem during the period of actual service, and their travelling expenses to and from their respective countries. There were, of course, provisions to the effect that the judges should not take part in the decision of cases in which they had been professionally interested; and that they should not receive compensation for their services in the Court from their respective countries or from other Powers. While the judges were equal it was necessary that one or other of them should preside over the Court and give direction to its proceedings; the Court was, therefore, to elect a President and Vice-President for the period of three years.

From this hasty outline of the draft convention it is evident that we have before us more than a suggestion of a permanent Court of International Justice. The proposed institution bore the name of Arbitral Justice, which was, however, synonymous in the minds of the Powers with a Court in the strict judicial sense of the term. It is an accurate description of a Tribunal although of a permanent character, whose judges are chosen by the parties to its creation. It would, therefore, be applicable to the permanent Court of International Justice, but the presence of the little word ' justice ' without the adjunction of a qualifying word is calculated to inspire confidence, whereas the use of the term ' arbitral ' might seem to imply negotiation and diplomatic standards. As Mr. Choate, the head of the American delegation, wittily and wisely remarked, ' give us the baby and you may baptize it as you will '. The Conference gave the American delegation the baby and baptized it the ' Court of Arbitral Justice '.

We have in the draft the plan of the Permanent Court of International Justice, excluding the elaborate procedure taken from the Pacific Settlement Convention, which, nevertheless, is included by implication, with the exception of the method of appointing the judges. The Conference, however, meant that the Court should be established. It, therefore, adopted the draft convention and referred it to the nations to determine through diplomatic channels the method of selecting the judges and thus bring the Court into being.

In the course of 1910 an agreement of France, Great Britain, and the United States was reached to establish the Court, and on the eve of the Great War it looked as if a permanent Court of a limited number of Powers would be shortly installed in the Peace Palace of The Hague for the judicial settlement of their differences, with provision for its use by other Powers by the appointment of temporary judges of their nationality, on a footing of equality with the permanent judges.

The draft convention of 1910 presupposed the previous ratification of the convention of the Second Peace Conference for the creation of a Court of Prize whose method of appointing the judges was to be adopted for the Court of Arbitral Justice. The failure of the Prize Convention necessarily blocked for the moment the formation of the Arbitral Court. However, the project of 1910 was not in vain, as one of its articles provided for the appointment of temporary judges, a disposition which has made its way into the statute of the present Permanent Court of International Justice. This provision was likewise found in definite and more detailed form in a proposal for the establishment of the Court of Arbitral Justice by and for Germany, the United States, Austria-Hungary, France, Great Britain, Italy, Japan, the Netherlands, Russia—to arrange the proposed contracting parties in the alphabetical order of their names in French, then and now the favourite language of diplomacy. In such a Court each of the nine contracting Powers would appoint a judge, and a controversy between any two of the nine countries would be decided by judges appointed by the seven disinterested judges. The proposed Court was to be at the disposition of all non-contracting countries which might care to use it ; in which event each of the two litigating parties was to appoint a temporary judge. The result would be that the two non-contracting litigants would, like the contracting parties, be represented on the bench during the trial and disposition of their dispute. The Court would thus be composed of eleven judges and the controversies of contracting and non-contracting parties decided by the other disinterested judges of the tribunal.

The Court of the Draft Convention of 1910, as well as that proposed in 1914 for nine contracting Powers, was to be temporary and provisional in its nature. The representatives of the Powers are made to express themselves in the preamble to each as ' desirous ' of rendering effective the recommendation of the Second Peace Conference, as ' Deeming that, if it be impossible as yet to reach a general agreement for putting into force the draft thus recommended, it is nevertheless useful to establish a Court of Arbitral Justice which may operate pending subsequent permanent rules ' ; as ' Being persuaded that such a measure, essentially provisional, does not in any way prejudice any agreement which may be reached later for the permanent organization of the Court of Arbitral Justice, and that such an agreement is particularly likely at the Third Peace Conference.'

The Court was thus to be established by a limited number of Powers interested in its creation and its successful operation ; it was to be opened to non-contracting Powers on a footing of equality during the trial and determination of all cases which they might wish to submit to its decision with an equality in the matter of Counsel, Judges, and Law to be applied. It was believed by negotiators of the Convention that their respective governments would open the records of their Foreign Offices and start the Court with an ample supply of cases, so that it would have demonstrated both its usefulness and capacity, before the meeting of the Third Peace Conference, to such an extent that the nations at large would be anxious to maintain it and to make the necessary changes in its composition to create it a Court of the world instead of the original nine Powers which had brought it into being. The Government of the Netherlands took, as was to be expected of the country of Grotius and the seat of the Court, a special interest in its establishment, and through its instrumentality it was thought possible that it would be installed in the Peace Palace at The Hague in the fall of 1914, at the same time as The Hague Academy which was to have been formally opened in the month of October of that fatal year. The most that we can say at this time and in this place is that the Gods of War were adverse to the peaceful projects of an Academy of International Law for the study and diffusion of the Law of Nations and the establishment of a Court of Justice in which the Law of Nations, as expounded in the Academy, would be interpreted by the Court and applied to the judicial settlement of the differences, however deep-seated or casual they might be, in the clear light of a penetrating and impartial jurisprudence. Both of these institutions are now established at The Hague and installed appropriately in the Palace of Peace of that city.

The Third Peace Conference, to make the law for the Academy to expound and the Court to interpret and apply, which was to have assembled likewise in The Hague before the war, awaits the action of the Nations, although it is known that the Government of the Netherlands is in favour of its meeting, and I am betraying no secret when I say that the Government of the United States has signified formally its willingness to take part in such a conference whenever invited to do so by the Netherlands.

In the course of 1919 the victorious allied and associated Powers were busy imposing terms upon their defeated enemies, the so-called Central Empires and their allies. The terms of the Peace framed by the victors were handed to Germany, the first of the Powers to be treated this way, and signed by the representatives of that Power on 28 June 1919, at Versailles, although they had not been invited to take part in the Conference to determine the articles of a peace which was to be at once just and permanent. The preamble of the treaty was the Covenant of the League of Nations, and it appears as such in each of the successive treaties made with Germany's allies. The purpose of the preamble, technically called ' The Covenant ', was to maintain the terms of the treaty subscribed to by the contracting parties and also to maintain peace among the world at large. For present purposes it is only necessary to refer to articles 13 and 14 of that famous document. By the first of these the members of the League of Nations, constituted by the Covenant, agree to submit to arbitration their disputes which diplomacy should fail to adjust ; the subjects apt for submission are declared to be the interpretation of treaties, questions of international law, existence of facts involving breaches of international obligations and the reparations to be made for such breaches. The disputes could be submitted to Courts, agreed to by the parties, which bound themselves to execute in good faith the awards which should be rendered. There was, unfortunately, no obligation created and accepted by the parties to the Covenant to submit these categories of disputes to arbitration. The article was a suggestion, at most a recommendation to do so. However, as so often happens in such cases, the article was broader in its moral than its legal import and appears in the Statute of the Permanent Court with a slight addition—the interpretation of a sentence passed by the Court—taken from existing law and practice.

Article 13 did not figure in the earliest draft of the Covenant.

The succeeding article consists of but a single paragraph, but each of its three sentences is, in effect, a separate and important part of an extraordinary whole.

The first sentence directs the Council of the League to formulate ' and submit to the members of the League for adoption plans for the establishment of a Permanent Court of International Justice '. It is to be observed that the plans for the Court were to be adopted not by the Council or the Assembly but by the members of the League. That is to say, the plan of the Court was to be a diplomatic document, to be submitted to nations or states constituting the League for their acceptance, in technical language for ratification. The plan was, in effect, if not in form, to be a treaty, to be submitted, however, only, or, at least in first instance, to those nations and states which were at the time regarded as contracting parties to the Covenant.

The second sentence of article 14 provided that the proposed Court was to be competent to hear and determine any dispute of ' an international character ', which the contracting parties should ' submit ' to it—another way of stating article 17 of the draft Convention of the Court of Arbitral Justice. The meaning of this sentence was curiously misunderstood by many enthusiasts of judicial settlement. It did not create an obligation to submit any dispute, but declared the proposed Court competent to receive and decide if the parties in dispute should agree to submit their controversy to the Court—a Court with competence as broad as international law and the goodwill of the parties.

The third and last sentence of article 14 in question authorized the Court to advise the Council or Assembly 'upon any dispute or question referred to it' by one or other of these bodies. The Court was by the second sentence to decide the difference; in the third it was to render an advisory opinion, not, it would seem, at the request of the parties but at the direction of the administrative or legislative organs of the League. It would appear that we are here in the presence of an obligation because in the law of the English-speaking world 'may' is to be interpreted as mandatory in a public statute. In the absence of a perfected international organization, of the threefold division of sovereign powers, the Court was to perform the functions of a ministry of justice.

Article 14 did not figure in the earliest draft of the Covenant.

The Council, a political body, wisely determined to invite, through the Secretary-General of the League, a group of jurists to draft the plan of the Court and submit it to the Council. Finally, ten jurists accepted the invitation of the League and it happened that five were from the so-called Great Powers—France, Great Britain, Italy, Japan, United States, and five from the nations which, for one reason or another, the Great Powers appear to consider as their inferiors—Belgium, Brazil, the Netherlands, Norway, Spain. The Hague was selected as the meeting-place, and the ten jurists forming the Advisory Committee began its session in the Peace Palace on the morning of 17 June, adjourning on the afternoon of 24 July 1920, with an acceptable method to its credit for appointing the judges of the Permanent Court of International Justice.

What was the condition of things at their opening session? A draft project of the Second Peace Conference, the so-called draft Convention of the Court of Arbitral Justice; the additional Convention of France, Germany, Great Britain, and the United States to put the Court into effect; a project for a Court of Nine Powers, to be opened on equal terms to all the nations of the world, and the articles of the Pacific Settlement Convention relating to arbitral procedure. The only thing of importance lacking was the method of appointing the judges; but a Court without judges is very like an empty throne in a deserted palace. Under these conditions the committee might have proceeded at once to the method of selecting the judges, taking the provision of the three documents as the basis of discussion for the other parts of the Court's anatomy. The proposal to do so was made, only to be rejected, inasmuch as international as well as national bodies apparently like to brush aside the labours of their predecessors in order that they may seem to be ancestors in their own behalf. The result, however, was in the end as if they had started where the three documents left off—as even a casual reading of the completed plan would seem to suggest without a word of comment or discussion—and had inserted in its proper place the method of selecting the judges, thus constituting the old Court of Arbitral Justice with sundry modifications and additions to bring it up to date. I say 'in the end', for the innovations, thought possible by the Advisory Committee because of the newer spirit engendered by the war, were either silently dropped in the Council or openly repudiated by the Assembly, for the old world always goes back to its old ways after the emotions of war have subsided.

I shall first consider the method devised for choosing the judges which made the Court, and then say something of the other articles of the original project of the Advisory Committee and its treatment at the hands of the Council and Assembly of the League.

One of the jurists spoke for the large Powers and proposed a court of eleven judges, five of whom should be chosen from the five large Powers, which would give his own country a judge, and six to be selected from the so-called lesser Powers which would enable these latter to dominate if the question of control should arise. Another member who wanted, of course, a judge from his own country on the bench was too shrewd to accept a plan so obviously intended to secure permanent judges for the Lords of creation. He advocated election by the Council, in which the larger Powers predominated, and could, therefore, be trusted to look after their interests. The jurists from the smaller Powers insisted on choice by the Assembly in which they predominated, which would no doubt vote for judges from the larger States, provided they were not obliged to do so, and it seemed to them consistent with their interests. The result was the controversy of 1907 over again between the large, claiming permanent judges because of their bigness, and the small States claiming a right to vote because they were States irrespective of the extent of their territory and the size of their populations. In passing it may be said that the things of the spirit, which make up that indefinable something which we call civilization, do not seem to grow only in large spaces and in proportion to the number of human animals within a given spot. 'A confined triangle, perhaps fifty miles its greatest

T

length, and thirty its greatest breadth ; two elevated rocky barriers, meeting at an angle, three prominent mountains, commanding the plain—Parnes, Pentelicus, and Hymettus ; an unsatisfactory soil ; some streams, not always full ;—such ', Cardinal Newman informs us, ' is about the report which the agent of a London company would have made of Attica.' And if the agent had spoken of the inhabitants he would have doubted whether they were numerous enough for the merchants of Sheffield or Manchester to send their wares thither, even without competition. But in the things of the spirit there has been but one Attica and, although dead in the worldly sense, it exists in the lives and thoughts of those of our day who live rather than exist, and who think rather than deaden thought through the pursuit of pleasure.

The obvious thing to do Mr. Root of the United States did, proposing that the judges should be elected by the concurrent but separate action of Council and Assembly, a compromise which accepted the contention of large and small and made the Council, in which the large had the preponderance, and the Assembly, in which the small dominated, a check upon the abuse of power by one or the other. Mr. Root was, however, unwilling to leave the matter to depend upon mere reason ; he felt it advisable to cite an instance in which the hitherto irrepressible conflict between the large and small States had been so completely overcome as to be forgotten—an instance from the early days of the great Republic of which he is the most distinguished citizen and elder statesman. He recalled the attempt of the larger States to dominate the smaller, the resistance of the latter and the compromise by which the conflict between the large and small States of the American Union has ceased to exist. The delegates to the Federal Convention of 1787, to frame a more adequate government for the thirteen Confederated States of America, were all in favour of a Legislature of the Union to consist of two branches. The large States wanted representation in each to be based upon population, a plan which, if accepted, would have given them control not only of the House of Representatives, but of the Senate or Upper House as well. The debates over this question were long-drawn out and bitter—the smaller States going so far as to threaten separation and foreign protection rather than submit to the domination of their larger neighbours. The Independent States of America were in danger of splitting on the rock which wrecked the Court of Arbitral Justice in 1907. A compromise was found, set forth in Madison's Debates of the Federal Convention, likewise containing the debates from day to day, by which the large States, to-day fewer in number than the small, would be able, in the House of Representatives, to protect their interests from injury at the hands of the small, and the Senate in which each State, irrespective of size or population, would have two members, thus assuring the small States a majority to protect their interests if threatened by the large, and requiring the concurrent but separate action of both for the enactment of legislation. Madison's Debates, in an international edition, printed rapidly for the use of the Advisory Committee, lay on the large table before each member in the Japanese Room of the Peace Palace at The Hague. Mr. Root then stated that the situation confronting the Committee was similar to that confronting the delegates to the Federal Convention of 1787 ; the large States predominating in the Council of the League as in the House of Representatives, and the small States predominating in the Assembly of the League as in the Senate.

Mr. Root's colleagues were visibly impressed. Instead of insisting upon the American method of satisfying the interests of large and small without denying their existence and making each a check upon the abuse of power by the other, he intimated that some such plan might be worthy of consideration. The members who wished a compromise of opposing points of view, which would recognize the contention of each without sacrificing either to the other, plied Mr. Root with questions. What if the Senate and House should differ? To this he replied from his own experience in the Senate that a conference committee of three members from the Senate and House was appointed to consider the Bill which, passing one body, was unacceptable to the other, and to report a compromise measure to Senate and House. But, it was asked, what would happen if the Conference Committee disagreed, or if the Senate and House should not concur in the report of the Conference Committee? Drawing further on his own experience, Mr. Root replied that the pressure of public opinion compelled both Committee and the House to agree. We have thus three steps in the selection of judges: Election by concurrent and separate action of the Council and Assembly of the League; upon failure to agree, the appointment of a conference committee of three from each body and the acceptance of its report by Council and Assembly. But supposing they should not accept the Report? Mr. Root felt that this was unlikely to happen. His colleagues, however, provided against such a contingency by authorizing and indeed directing the judges already elected to choose the remaining judges. Here we have the method of electing the judges.

How were the names of competent persons to be brought to the attention of the Electoral College, as we should say in

America? This was the first but the easiest step in an apparently complicated, but in fact and in practice a simple process. The desire of the Advisory Committee was to eliminate, as far as possible, political influence in the selection of the judges, and some of its members went so far as to suggest that they be elected without the intervention of the nations. Mr. Root pointed out that the selection of a judge was an exercise of political power and that it was only the State which could authorize the judge to act in its behalf and to bind the State by his action. This view prevailed. Mr. Root was, however, of the opinion that the candidates could be properly proposed without the interference of the State. The result was a unanimous agreement that the judges of the Permanent Court of Arbitration, considered as a group in each of the different nations, might very properly be asked to recommend persons who possessed, in their opinion, the requisite qualities for an international judge. The Pacific Settlement Convention authorized each of the contracting parties to appoint four persons who, taken together, form the permanent panel or list of prospective judges for temporary tribunals of arbitration. It is true that these persons are appointed by the Government of the various nations, but it was felt that they would, it would be better to say might, be free from interference in the recommendation of candidates for the International Bench. It was, therefore, decided that each national group should recommend not more than two persons who might be of ' any nationality ', and send their names to the Secretary-General of the League. All the older nations, that is to say those existing before the world war, were or could easily become parties to the Pacific Settlement Convention and thus be authorized to appoint four judges of the Per-

manent Court of Arbitration. The nations coming into
being because of the war might or might not adhere to the
Convention and, therefore, be without national groups for
the recommendation of candidates. Then too, there were
four self-governing colonies of the British Empire—Aus-
tralia, Canada, New Zealand, South Africa, and, in addition,
India—which could not adhere to the Pacific Settlement
Convention although members of the League. This case
was not considered by the Advisory Committee, but the
Statute of the Court accords to the Governments of the new
nations, members of the League, and the British possessions
also members, the right to appoint persons who shall, thereupon, exercise the functions of the National Groups. Here,
of course, the Government acts directly and may control the
choice of candidates, and given human nature as it is, it is
difficult to conceive that some Governments, at least, do not
directly or indirectly exercise influence under either or any
system.

Be that as it may, the Advisory Committee tried to mini-
mize political influence, if it should be attempted, by recom-
mending that the national groups should, before making
their nominations, ' consult ', in their respective countries,
the highest Courts of Justice, their legal Faculties of Law,
National Academies, and ' national sections of International
Academies devoted to the study of Law '.

The Advisory Committee was anxious to have the different
systems of law represented in the Court of judges trained in
their principles. Hence the provision in the plan that the
electors should choose the judges with reference to ' the
principal legal system of the world '. The observance of this
suggestion was intended to produce an understanding Court,
but the Advisory Committee wanted the judges to represent

something more than legal systems and be familiar with their practice and procedure ; they should in their persons represent ' the main forms of civilization '. A Court thus composed would be worthy of the Community of Nations, and it is admitted on all sides that the method of election has secured judges who meet these exacting requirements in letter and in spirit.

The Court was to consist of fifteen members, of whom eleven were titular judges and four deputy judges, and nine required for a quorum. It was foreseen that the entrance of nations, not at the time members of the League, might render an enlargement of the Court advisable and it was, therefore, provided that the number of judges and deputies might be raised to fifteen and six respectively. There can be no doubt that the admission of Germany to the League will mean the addition of a German judge and that Russia will furnish a member at no distant date. The deputies must possess the same qualifications as the titular judges whom they are called upon to replace in case of absence.

As there are some fifty to sixty nations or states which, taken together, form the world of to-day, it is evident that only a portion of them can have judges in the court at any one time. If parties to a controversy are members of the Court, each is the equal of the other. This would not be the case if there were a judge of the nationality of one but not of the other party. If neither litigant had a judge of its nationality in the Court, they would be equal between themselves, but both would be at a disadvantage compared to those nations and prospective litigants with judges of their nationality on the Bench. There were two ways of introducing equality at the trial and disposition of the case ; one by the withdrawal of the permanent judge, which would be a sacrifice of its judge by one litigant, or by permitting the other party in controversy before the Court to appoint a temporary judge. The latter alternative was the one adopted, for the larger Powers were not prepared to have their judges quit the bench during the trial and decision of cases which they might have with non-represented Powers. I say non-represented Powers advisedly, because the judges do not ' cease ' to be citizens of the countries from which they are chosen—at least not in the opinion of the other countries whose nationals do not happen to adorn the international Bench.

There was another question involved. Many nations may never have a judge in the Court, and they would not relish, it is believed, to have their cases always passed on by judges from the larger States which must be represented, it seems, on the Bench if the Court is to exist. The presence of judges of the nationality of the non-represented Powers present on the Bench not only procures equality at the moment of the trial, but enables the nations to take part in the proceedings of the Court and feel that they contribute, although intermittently, of their mite to the development of what—after all—is the law of all nations. This was pointed out by the Brazilian jurist on the Committee, and the provision of the additional Convention of 1910 was transferred bodily to the draft of the Advisory Committee.

What was to be the jurisdiction of the Permanent Court of International Justice? A suggestion was made that the Court should be open to private litigants who might, therefore, present and conduct in person or by Counsel their claim against contracting nations and States. It was rejected and decided that the Court should be open only to States as such. Should State sue State as in the Supreme Court of the United States without a special agreement? If so, the jurisdiction of the Court would need to be confined, at least at the beginning, within narrow lines. Should the controversy between two litigating States be only submitted to the Court by agreement to that effect by the litigating States? The wording of article 14 of the Covenant was clear on this point, for the Court was to be 'competent' for disputes 'of an international character' which the parties should submit to the Court. After much argument, the view prevailed that the ratification of the Committee's draft, containing a clause permitting State to sue State under certain conditions to be specified in the text, would be an acceptance of the Committee's proposal on this head, even if inconsistent with the Covenant. The conditions were first, a finding of the Court that it had been impossible to settle the dispute in question by diplomatic means ; second, that the limits within which State might sue State without a special agreement should be expressly mentioned in the text of the project, and third, that the law to be applied by the Court should be stated as well as the order in which it should be invoked. The first condition, found in article 33 of the project, was proposed by Mr. Root who properly laid great stress upon it ; the second, included in article 34, was taken from article 13 of the Covenant with a slight addition giving the Court power to interpret its own judgements, and the third in article 35, of the Committee's draft.

The first condition is not to be found in the present statute of the Court, inasmuch as the members of the League in the session of the Assembly held in December 1920 rejected the proposal authorizing State to sue State directly, in favour of a resort to the Court by special agreement, and with it necessarily fell the condition regulating its exercise.

Article 34, regarding the limits within which State might be sued without a special agreement, was through the happy thought and personal effort of Mr. Fernandez, the representative of Brazil in the Assembly, kept as an alternative procedure for such States as were willing to bind themselves in advance to the settlement of their disputes by the principles of law set forth in article 35. No large Power, notwithstanding its peaceful professions, has accepted this alternative method although some twenty-six of the so-called smaller Powers, whose only defence of their rights is justice against the arrogant assertion of self interest by the large nations, have confessed their faith in a world of law instead of force by expressly accepting it.

May the Court express its opinion on a question of law without rendering a formal judgement? Article 14 of the Covenant decides the query in the affirmative, and the Advisory Committee, therefore, included a provision to the effect that a special Committee of five should render an opinion at the request of the Council or Assembly on ' a question of an international nature ' which it does not refer to as an actual dispute, and that the full Court, as such, should render its opinion on an actual dispute under ' the same conditions as if the case had been actually submitted to it for decision '. The members of the Assembly rejected this article in its entirety, although most of the questions which have been so far submitted to the Court were for advisory opinion, not for formal judgements. The submission is, therefore, in each case under the Covenant, not the provisions of the Statute.

These modifications are at most negative contributions on the part of the Assembly, which has at least a positive addition to its credit or discredit, according to the judgement or whim of the commentator. The first to be mentioned is the disposition to be found in the Statute in lieu of the Article dealing with advisory opinions. It is short and difficult to summarize: ' This provision ', it is said, meaning the four rules dealing with the authorities to be invoked and the order of their application, ' shall not prejudice the power of the Court to decide a case *ex aequo et bono*, if the parties agree thereto.' This means in plain English, instead of technical Latin, that the judges of the Court may act as arbiters, and the Court itself act as a Tribunal of Arbitration at the request of the contending parties. That is to say, two parties may change the nature of the Court at their pleasure, and have its judges act as diplomats in the negotiation of a dispute without reference to existing law, instead of having it always act as a Court of Justice, in accordance with law, or refusing to act if law does not exist. The Court of the Committee of Jurists was a Court of Justice; it was not a Court of Arbitration. Nor was it a legislature for the creation of the law which it was to apply. That is the function of an International Conference of The Hague type for the advancement of the Law of Nations.

But these matters are, if blemishes, but spots in an otherwise resplendent sun.

The existence of a Council and Assembly of Nations enabled the publicists of 1920 to apply a method of selecting the judges, which did not occur to the publicists of 1907, and debates of the Federal Convention of 1787, reported by James Madison, one of its members from the large State of Virginia and later President of the United States, furnished the method of recognizing the different interests of great and small, and the way of utilizing them so as to make one group a check upon the abuse of power by the other.

William Ladd's Prize Essay on a *Congress of Nations for the Adjustment of International Disputes without resort to Arms*, published in 1840 and widely circulated in subsequent years, reprinted in 1916 by the Carnegie Endowment and also widely distributed, brought and kept the idea of an International Court of Justice before the nations. Ladd's prophecy that, ' When the American Government shall take up the subject in earnest, it will begin to be studied and understood by the enlightened nations of Europe ' was realized by Secretary Hay, who instructed the American delegation to the First Peace Conference of 1899 to propose to that body an International Tribunal, and by Secretary Root in 1907, when he directed the American Delegation to the Second Peace Conference to urge the formation of a Permanent Court of International Justice.

It is, therefore, of interest to ask what was the Court which Ladd modestly suggested in his Essay ? He set forth his proposal in a series of numbered paragraphs, of which I quote the most essential :

1. ' It is proposed to organize a Court of Nations, composed of as many members as the Congress of Nations shall previously agree upon. . . . The power of the Court to be merely advisory. . . . There is to be no sheriff, or posse, to enforce its commands. It is to take cognizance only of such cases as shall be referred to it, by the free and mutual consent of both parties concerned. . . .

2. ' The members of this Court are to be appointed by the governments represented in the Congress of Nations, and shall hold their places according to the tenure previously agreed on in the Congress—probably during good behaviour. Whether they should be paid by the governments sending them or by the nations represented in Congress conjointly, according to the ratio of their population or wealth, may be agreed on in the Congress. The Court should organize itself by choosing a president and vice-president

from among themselves, and appoint the necessary clerks, secretaries, reporters, &c. ; and they should hear Counsel on both sides
of the questions to be judged. They might meet once a year for
the transaction of business and adjourn to such time and place as
they should think proper. Their meeting should never be in a
country which had a case on trial. These persons should have the
same privileges and immunities as ambassadors.

3. ' Their verdicts, like the verdicts of other great courts, should
be decided by a majority, and need not be, like the decrees of the
Congress, unanimous. . . .

4. ' All cases submitted to the Court should be judged by the
true interpretation of existing treaties, and by the laws enacted by
the Congress and ratified by the nations represented ; and where
these treaties and laws fail of establishing the point at issue, they
should judge the cause by the principles of equity and justice.

8. ' It should be the duty of a Court of Nations, from time to
time, to suggest topics for the consideration of the Congress as new
or unsettled principles, favourable to the peace and welfare of
nations, would present themselves to the Court, in the adjudication
of cases. . . .

9. ' There are many other cases besides those above-mentioned,
in which such a Court would either prevent war or end it. A
nation would not be justified, in the opinion of the world, in going
to war when there was an able and impartial umpire to judge its
case ; and many a dispute would be quashed at the outset if it were
known that the world would require an impartial investigation of it
by able judges.'

In view of the American example, American initiative,
American perseverance, and American ingenuity in the sub-
stitution of judicial settlement for the brutal arbitrament of
war, it is devoutly to be hoped that the United States may
participate at no distant date in a Permanent Court of
International Justice.

What was the result of the labours of the Advisory Committee, the Council, and Assembly of the League of Nations in the preparation and enactment of a plan and statute of a Permanent Court of International Justice? The Advisory Committee laid before the Council a project of an International Court fashioned after the Supreme Court of the American States ; the project as it emerged from the Council and Assembly is in all its essentials the draft Convention for the creation of a Court of Arbitral Justice, with the procedure of the Pacific Settlement Convention set forth at large, instead of general reference, and the important provisions taken from the additional Convention of 1910 and the proposed Court of limited membership, to put the Court of Arbitral Justice into effect.

In terminating his report to the Second Hague Peace Conference, the reporter felt justified in expressing himself as to the draft Convention of 1907 :

' We do not conceal from ourselves the fact that our work still presents gaps and difficulties. It is hardly necessary to call attention to the absence, in the project, of provisions for the constitution of the Court and the selection of the judges. These questions were discussed at great length in the committee, but no solution acceptable to all the States represented could be found. It is to be hoped that an agreement will soon be reached in this respect, and, prompted by this hope, the committee declared itself in favour of the following resolution :

' The Conference recommends to the signatory Powers the adoption of the project it has voted for the creation of a Court of Arbitral Justice, and putting it into force as soon as an agreement has been reached respecting the selection of the judges and the constitution of the Court.'

' Our aim, Gentlemen ', he continued, ' has not been merely to build the beautiful façade for the palace of international justice; we have erected, indeed furnished the structure, so that the judges have only to take their places upon the bench. It is for you to open the door; it is for the Governments to usher them in. There can be no doubt that suitors, filled with a sense of deference and security, will appear before this imposing Areopagus in such numbers as to demonstrate that the judicial settlement of international disputes has ceased to be a formula of the future by becoming a reality of the present.'

Fortunately for the partisans of judicial settlement, Mr. Elihu Root, who had directed the American delegation to the Second Peace Conference of The Hague to propose a permanent Court of Justice, was a member of the Advisory Committee of Jurists and took an active and decisive part in its labours. What the Conference of 1907 had failed to do, he himself did in 1920 : he opened the door of the palace of International justice to the judges in order that the Governments might usher them in.

In the life of nations as in the lives of their citizens and subjects the failure of yesterday is often the triumph of the morrow.

CHAPTER XII

INTERNATIONAL GOVERNMENT AND NATIONAL SOVEREIGNTY

Mr. H. J. LASKI :

I HAVE always believed that the first duty of a lecturer is to announce his own personal defects to his audience. I remember Bernard Shaw once said that every journalist, when writing an article, ought to put at the bottom of it his own name and the price the editor gave him for it ; because that would explain to those who read it exactly what the editor thought about it, which is really much more important than what his public thought about it. I do not want any one here to be under an illusion as to the atmosphere which surrounds my own personal thought. In explaining what I want to explain, I am not striving to be impartial, because I disbelieve in impartiality. The only difference between a *soi-distant* impartial person and what is called a prejudiced or partial speaker is that the latter announces the presuppositions he proposes to make, and the impartial speaker endeavours to conceal them from you.

My presuppositions are quite obvious and definite. I speak as a Socialist, and as a Socialist who belongs in England to the Left Wing of the Socialist Movement, and to whom, accordingly, the triumph in international affairs of the international idea, and accordingly the victory, I do not say of the League of Nations, but of the thing for which the League of Nations stands, is of paramount importance at the present time : of far more importance, in fact, than the problem of the future of England, or even the problem of the future of America—if I may make that remark without blasphemy !

It is even more important than the problem of the future of Europe.

I believe that for a reason which an optimistic people like the Americans is sometimes prone to forget. We who live in Europe are above all convinced of the fragility, and not of the strength, of modern civilization. About its margins, on every side, there are prospects which are instinct with disaster. There is the clash of races, the clash of colour, and the clash, above all, of the economic classes into which Europe is divided. Any one of these conflicts might at any time precipitate a struggle in Europe of which, as I believe, the consequences would be the downfall of European civilization. It is the realization of the tenuity of the bases upon which our civilization has its being that has led me to a passionate belief in that general philosophy of life which is called pacifism, and which takes its texture from the international idea.

I do not need to point out to you how much the world about us has become a unified world ; how the fact of a world market has made the boundaries between nation states instinct with difficulty rather than implicit with meaning. I do not need, either, to those of you who have come from America to Switzerland, to point out the futility in anything except the psychological sense of the political boundaries between states. You are discovering for yourselves the meaning of the moral unity of the world as it is, a moral unity which goes the more deep the more profoundly it is understood by men and women.

The case I want to put before you is that the case of international unity that the facts are forcing on us is hindered and made increasingly difficult by the form taken by modern nationality in the world as we know it, the form of a sovereign

U

state. The argument I want to present is the essentially simple argument that only by the abrogation of the idea of sovereignty in international affairs is there any real prospect of the working of international ideas being placed upon a basis at once successful and sound. ' He who can, does ; he who cannot, teaches,' says Mr. Bernard Shaw ; and I am by profession a University teacher. You will, therefore, forgive me if I yield to the weakness of my profession and begin with some definitions.

I begin first with the word ' sovereignty ', which, unlike Saul, but like King David, is a word that has slain its tens of thousands. I mean by ' sovereignty ' the power to will acts of universal reference without being called to account for them. I am not concerned this evening with the purely legal problem of whether there must be in any state a power of ultimate appeal that cannot be called to account. I am not for a moment concerned to deny that if a lawyer chooses to define law as John Austin defined law one hundred years ago, all the normal consequences of sovereignty will flow therefrom. I am concerned to deny that the legal theory of sovereignty has got any application to life, and I am in especial concerned to deny that the working of the principle of sovereignty in relation to modern nationality is instinct with other than difficulty. I believe it involves ultimate disaster.

May I recall to you the history of the idea of sovereignty ? Learned men write of the idea of the sovereign state as though it were a permanent feature of universal history. That, of course, is entirely false. In between the decline of the Roman Empire and the Reformation, there was no such thing as a sovereign state. Had you told any medieval thinker of any competence that there was in any community a power

entitled to give orders to any one without regard to the substance of the order, and itself receiving orders from no one,
you would certainly have been described as a blasphemer of
what is eternal in the moral life. You would have been told
that that alone is sovereign which reveals the principles of
the Divine Order, and that the principles of the Divine Order
are, as nearly as may be, reflected in natural law, and that
natural law is the effort on the part of man to discover or to
rediscover what he acted upon before he entered into the
state of sin. The whole of medieval life is occupied by the
belief that there are certain fundamental verities without
which no state (though the word ' state ' is itself a misnomer)
can realize its need—the perfect life for each individual.

About the time of Luther, the medieval idea of a unified
Christendom broke down. Luther exalted the state, and
those who shared his or kindred ideas took advantage of the
position in which they found themselves to assert, mainly for
the victory of theological principles, the right of a prince in
his own dominions to determine for himself, and without
hindrance of any kind, the life that was to govern that state.
It is, broadly, out of the conflict between the State and
ecclesiastical community that the idea of sovereignty arose.

It is traditional—and I want to make a comment on the
tradition—to associate the idea of sovereignty with the name
of a great French thinker, Bodin, who, in 1576, published
a book on the Commonwealth which has ever since been the
text-book of writers on sovereignty. Those of you who
occupy yourselves with the problem of research will know
that it is mainly a state of respectful coma in which men
repeat the fallacies of their predecessors. I am unable to find
in *La République* of Bodin that he anywhere promulgated
the theory of sovereignty in its modern form. What he did

in fact say was that there must be a reserve power in any community for occasions of emergency, but that in general the sovereign is bound by two sets of laws : the law of God on the one hand, and the law of nature on the other.

I do not want to trouble you with the theoretical difficulties that sovereignty encounters, but to put it in one sentence : If a state is omnipotent it can create a thing that it cannot destroy. If it can create a thing it cannot destroy, it obviously is not omnipotent since it cannot destroy it ; but if it cannot create a thing it cannot destroy, it obviously is not omnipotent because it cannot create it. Even the sovereign state is subject to the law of contradictions.

I am more interested in the way in which the modern nation, assuming the panoply of the modern state in the world as we know it, lives its life. I would point out to you, first, what is meant by the political consequences of sovereignty. The state is irresponsible. It owes no obligation save that which is made by itself to any other community or group of communities. In the hinterland between states man is to his neighbour what Hobbes says was true of him in the state of nature—nasty, mean, brutish. Politically, in its judgement of what it is entitled to do, a state considers not the interest of humanity as a whole, not the obvious precepts of judgement and right, but the basest considerations of expediency, as it chooses to interpret them. A state becomes, in short, the judge of its own cause, and it is elementary that that is a denial of justice.

Secondly, I want to remind you of the moral consequences of such doctrine—that there should be in any community a power that demands the allegiance of men upon any other consideration except equity. Inherent in that demand, by its substance, seems to me, at any rate, to be a contradiction of all that is worth most in the ethical precepts of 2,000 years. If I am to obey because an order has been issued without regard to the substance of that order I cease to be a moral being for a reason that is essentially simple and straightforward. It was put better than I can put it by Samuel Taylor Coleridge a hundred years ago : ' He who begins by loving Christianity better than truth will continue by loving his sect or church better than Christianity, and will end by loving himself best of all.' If citizenship (which I take to mean the power of contributing one's own instructed judgement to the public good) is the business of the citizen to act on the basis of his public judgement he must as a consequence of having made the judgement be, if necessary, an Athanasius against the whole world. That has been put in a sentence that I would like to write over the entrance to the Congress of the United States : ' In a time of injustice, the only place for a just man is in prison.' If that is true it is a denial of the idea of sovereignty. Government in a state has the power to issue orders, but the consequence of the issue of orders depends upon me, upon my judgement, and there is a contingency surrounding the issuance of authority that only becomes active and operates so long as citizens lend their consent to the demands of the Government of the day.

Thirdly, I want to point out to you the economic consequences of this doctrine. If there is one outstanding fact in the modern world it is that the fact of a world-market has made a world-economy, and that everything that interferes with the movement of that world-economy is so much taken from the prosperity of the world, and by that amount so much taken from the standard of life of the people. Things that are shared in common by one nation and another can only be decided in common by one nation and another.

The politics of power or the politics of prestige are in this connexion fatal to the well-being of the world. The national sovereignty that makes up its mind that its tariff laws or its immigration laws, or what you will, are matters upon which its own unaided and uncontradicted word is the final decision in the making of the ultimate result is thereby a traitor to the unification that we need.

The idea of nationality is a very modern idea. Roughly speaking, though it is easy to trace, even in medieval history, things that are recognizably English—for instance, there is a complaint made in 1489 of the quality of English cooking which is obviously a direct reflex of permanent national habits—it is quite clear that, while something that is recognizably a nationalizing force existed, nationality in the modern sense of the word is not really earlier than the first partition of Poland (about the end of the eighteenth century), and assumed its modern form, the form in which I want particularly to deal with it, as a result of the French Revolution. Those soldiers of the Republic in the years from 1789 to 1793 who poured over the frontiers of France ' lighting their pipes at the altar candles and singing the Marseillaise ' were making the nation-state. They were claiming, that is, that because the nation had come to be it must be strong ; and in order that it may be strong it must assume on its own behalf that panoply of moral independence of all other factors in the civilized universe out of which the war of 1914 eventually came.

It represents, if I may so phrase it, the idea to its citizens, or at least to its protagonists, of ideal right ; and ideal right, so it was said by generations of philosophers, must take ideal might into itself in order that it might cease to be merely ideal.

The argument that I want to make in contradiction of this view has at least the merit of simplicity. It is the argument that things which affect the world in common have got to be decided by the world in common, and that in the making of those decisions, nothing matters except the ultima.e consent, upon the basis of a rational judgement of the facts, of the parties concerned. My argument is that force decides nothing in the long run, and that, therefore, the utilization of sovereignty decides nothing in the long run.

When, in July 1914, Austria presented its demands to Serbia we all agree she could have enforced those demands on Serbia. But that did not make the demands just, nor did the manner of their enforcement make Serbia a model of moral rectitude.

When England entered the war (whether, as we were told, for Belgium or for whatever cause) the main fact that she decided, without reference to the will or purposes of other people, did not give to her effort any inherently superior justice than the effort of any other people. With America, of course, it may have been different ; I will not venture to pronounce on so complex and delicate a question !

All that I am concerned to pronounce on is that if any nation-state is entitled to regard itself as an isolated factor in an inter-connected world, and to use its rights as a sovereign power to enforce the consequences of its isolation, the result is the destruction of the civilization, for which I, at any rate, am deeply concerned to care. I think that is too obvious to require proof.

I want to prove it, however, by turning aside for a moment from the international side of the question, because I realize that passions are involved there that are much more difficult to use as a basis for reasoning than if I take the internal side of the state and urge the necessity of its responsibility. I propose mainly to use some English cases because the English, as the French tell us, are an inherently illogical people, and, accordingly, their actions bring out my point with some adequacy. I also want to use one American case because it is too exquisite to be omitted.

I ask you to picture to yourself a Mr. Albert Baker who was living in the year 1911 in Harley Mansions, just off Nottingham Place, in London. You may be able to identify that place if I say that it is a stone's throw from one of the historic houses of London, No. 221 B, Baker Street, where Mr. Sherlock Holmes used to live. Mr. Albert Baker, in the process of occupying a flat in that apartment-house, met and won the affections of a Miss Amelia Mighell, who lived opposite to him. They exchanged, first of all, greetings, and then more substantial tokens of affection. He proposed, and Miss Mighell found that he represented to her the ultimate ideal of all the ages, and accepted him. Now, Mr. Albert Baker was in fact the Sultan of Johore, and the Sultan of Johore is under the control—it is called for politeness the suzerainty—of the India Office; and the India Office, finding that he was inclined to dally in London and had already a superfluity of wives, ordered him back to Johore, from whence he came. He bade, I do not doubt, a tender farewell to Miss Mighell, and explained that all was over between them. She then sought what Englishwomen are learning from American women it is in these cases desirable to seek: namely, substantial damages for breach of promise. Miss Mighell went to the courts, and was immediately non-suited on the ground that the Sultan of Johore was a sovereign, and a sovereign can do no wrong. He is incapable, even, of thinking wrong—I quote the words of Mr. Justice Darling, the first of English legal humorists : ' In him there is neither sin nor weakness ' ; and Miss Mighell found she had no right to complain at all.

I will take a second case. Suppose you were to walk across Piccadilly Circus in London—a very dangerous and undesirable thing to do—and were run over by a van which bore the three mystic letters ' G. W. R.'—' Great Western Railway '. If the driver was negligent you would then get damages for his negligence. Suppose, on the other hand, you were run over by a van on which the ' W.' was omitted, and which simply bore the letters ' G. R.'—' George Rex', in him is neither sin nor weakness ; he is incapable of doing wrong and even thinking wrong. You can sue the postman, whose wages at the moment are some three pounds a week, but you cannot sue His Majesty's Postmaster-General, because he is, in effect the Crown. Our state is an irresponsible state. It is not suable for its tortous acts ; it is not bound by the errors of its officials.

It is the same in international affairs. To take another case. The State of Massachusetts ran a fair in one of its cities, and at that fair the grand stand collapsed, and having collapsed, those who assisted—if I may so phrase it—in the collapse, sued for damages and found you could not sue an American State in its own courts. The next year—with an ingenuity I find wholly admirable—the city was persuaded to take over the management of the fair. The stand collapsed again. A city is not a state. You could sue a city and make it responsible for its acts, and the inference I draw is the inference of fact—that the stand did not collapse in the third year.

I am similarly concerned to bring home to the modern nation-state the notion that it is not sovereign in the con-

cerns of the world ; that it is not entitled to form its judgement as though other states were not in existence ; that in
each step that it takes, in which the interests of others are
concerned, the judgement that is formed is a judgement that
must be formed in concert with those others, and in addition
to being formed in concert with those others must be formed
also by the aid and assistance of powers more nearly impartial
than the parties to the conflict.

When, in November of 1925, Sir Lee Stack was murdered
in Egypt, and Great Britain addressed a Note of protest with
penal clauses attached to Egypt, I believe Great Britain to
have been profoundly wrong, politically on the one hand,
and morally on the other. I am taking English cases where
I believe my own country was entirely in the wrong,
and I leave you to draw such inferences as you please in
regard to nations with which you have a closer concern. In
this case England was wrong, not because Egypt was right,
but because she sought to be a judge in her own cause, and
to enforce a penalty about which the opinion of no other
power or group of powers had been asked.

Similarly, to go back for a somewhat long period, I believe
Great Britain was entirely wrong in the decision she took in
1899 in relation to the Boer Republic, and that the solution
of the Transvaal problem was one in which all the peoples of
the world with an interest in the maintenance of peace were
entitled to be consulted, and in which our judgement as
a people had no relevance to the problem of right.

Thirdly, I take a problem which has now been happily
settled—that of Irish Home Rule. I do not believe that
Great Britain had any right to present its struggle with Ireland as a matter in which she herself was the sole and ultimate
judge. If she was right, she ought to have been able to prove

herself right at the bar of world opinion. If she was afraid to prove herself right at the bar of world opinion the probability is that she could not have proved herself right, and was in fact wrong.

I should be prepared similarly to take the same view in relation to the Anglo-Indian problem. I should be prepared to have Great Britain state her case in relation to India before the League of Nations with an entire confidence in the result such as, being an Englishman, I do not have when I am told by Englishmen that we are in India for the benefit of India, and by Indians that we are in India for the benefit of Great Britain. I find a certain margin of difference between those statements that leaves me with a sense of moral discomfort.

The plea I am making is not a plea in denial of all that the League of Nations implies, but is a plea for taking the League of Nations very much farther than it has at present gone. I want to analyse what I mean by taking it very much farther by drawing your attention to the meaning of one phrase as I see it, and, on the other hand, by indicating in a very vague and general way the direction in which my own view would naturally seek to move. We are told that a nation cannot submit to the judgement of other nations, because in certain cases its national honour is involved, and where its national honour is involved a dispute is non-justiciable and incapable of solution—given a proud people— by the ordinary methods of the League of Nations.

I remember vividly in 1916 in New York hearing the late Colonel Roosevelt explaining how Mr. Wilson, after the *Lusitania* incident, had betrayed the honour of America. My answer is very simple, and it is the phrase Mr. Wilson himself used in a speech I am always proud to have been privileged to hear : ' There is such a thing as a nation being

so right that it does not need to convince others by force that
it is right.' May I remind you of the normal history of
national honour by a very simple and classical instance?
Two German adventurers named Manesmann went to
Morocco in the early years of this century and obtained con-
cessions from the Sultan of Morocco which, with economy
I admire, he had already sold to the representatives of the
French people. When the Herren Manesmann came to
exploit their possessions they found them already occupied.
They complained to the Foreign Office at Berlin, and it
became a matter in which the prestige of Germany was at
stake, and ultimately—to take a great leap—the youth of
Germany was asked to die on the battlefield in order that the
Manesmann brothers might have their 20 per cent. You will
forgive me for saying that I disbelieve in that kind of national
honour. I believe that if Englishmen choose to go to Kenya
or India, or if Americans choose to go to Mexico, they must
accept the responsibility of their position, and that when
they go there in pursuit of trade—which after all is what that
vague thing called Imperialism really means, because my own
historic discovery is that what is usually called the white
man's burden is generally borne by the black—they are not
entitled to sacrifice the youth of half the world in the pursuit
of their private fortunes.

I believe there is no case in modern history in which what
is called national honour has been put forward as a rational
argument, and in which analysis would not show that it was
in fact the defence of a small group in the nation whose
economic fortunes were unrelated to the national well-being.
If that is in any sense a broad truth my own belief is that,
whether in my own party or even in other parties in the
modern state, the greatest necessity that is incumbent upon

us is the development of that for which the League of Nations stands. I should want greater courage on its part. I should want the ability, above all, to defy the great powers of the world, even if the great powers of the world chose to withdraw from its counsels. I should want the ending of the rule of unanimity, and its replacement by some such proportionate majority as a two-thirds majority. I should want the extension of the International Court so that the individual citizen in any state could sue the sovereign state before that International Court and obtain satisfaction for private wrong quite apart from the problems of public wrong. Above all, from my own point of view, I should want a much more rigorous and far-reaching control of the mandates system than at present exists. I should want, on the spot, an ambassador of the League of Nations with an adequate staff who, year by year, and, if need be, more often, would report on the working of the mandate, and who, in the event of a collision such as that which occurred in German South-West Africa a few years ago, would be able to remedy the defect that arose from the fact that dead natives do not differ from other men in their inability to tell tales.

I do not deny that the kind of atmosphere with which I should seek to invest the League is an atmosphere extraordinarily difficult to force upon a world as eager for its opposite as this world is. But I am reminded of two things by which always I have been impressed. In international politics, as everywhere else, the real crime is a low aim. The higher you aim the more likely you are to call out the latent idealism of the common people, and the latent idealism of the common people is the greatest single factor that makes for peace in the world to-day. (Applause.)

Secondly, I am reminded of a sentence of Spinoza, which,

because it sounds so much more sonorous in Latin than in English, I should like first to quote in Latin and then, for my weakness, to translate : ' Omnia praeclara tam difficilia quam rara sunt '—' All things excellent are as difficult as they are rare.' I do not deny that to urge on the peoples of this world that, if need be, they should resist their governors when their governors urge on them a policy incompatible with the public good is the most arduous and difficult of adventures. It is because it is arduous and because it is difficult that I find in it the highest expression of ultimate human worth. (Prolonged applause.)

Mr. E. J. PHELAN said he very largely agreed with what the lecturer had said. Mr. Laski regarded the traditional theory of national sovereignty as incompatible with any idea of an international society. When the allied statesmen founded the League of Nations in Paris in 1919 they were working in conditions which fortunately did not occur very often ; they were under the shadow of the greatest war humanity had ever experienced, and they were obliged, in the face of public opinion, to work quickly. He believed, however, that there was much in the intention of the Covenant, and still more both in the spirit and letter of Part Thirteen of the Treaty of Versailles, which went in the direction the lecturer had indicated—more, in fact, than was generally realized, or had been evidenced either by the actual practice of the League or of the International Labour Organization. It had not been evidenced in actual practice because the levers in those machines were mainly held by statesmen who must necessarily take account of public opinion in their respective countries. If, however, as Sir Arthur Salter had said, there was a League which included not only the Council and the

Assembly, but every citizen in every country who was interested in the destiny of his fellows, and if that larger League was prepared to make its influence felt, there was no reason why statesmen should not pull those levers which would lead to the exercise of greater authority by the two international institutions in the direction which both he and the lecturer desired.

Mr. Laski had said he would like to see the rule of unanimity abandoned so far as the League was concerned. In the International Labour Organization it had been abandoned, and the Labour Conventions were adopted by a two-thirds majority, and even the governments who were in the minority had been willing to fulfil certain obligations in respect of them.

Mr. Laski had also expressed the desire that individual persons might have the right of appeal to the Permanent Court of International Justice. Some steps in that direction had already been in fact taken. There was no reason under the existing statutes of the Court why, if public opinion demanded it, Mr. Laski should not have satisfaction. The last case the Court heard was a case concerning one of the Labour Conventions where the employers considered the International Labour Conference had exceeded the competence it was entitled to exercise under its own constitution. No one except states could be parties under the statute, but under certain additions to the statute, which the International Labour Organization succeeded in obtaining, cases concerning Labour Conventions could be heard by a special Chamber of the Court, and before that Chamber the International Labour Organization itself, and interested organizations, had the right to present observations. In the particular case in question the International Federation of Employers considered their rights had been infringed, and that the Court should be asked to decide whether the International Labour Conference was competent to adopt a particular provision of the Convention. The Governing Body, out of courtesy to the unanimous opinion of one of its groups, asked the Council of the League of Nations to request the Court for an advisory opinion, which was done. The case was heard a few weeks previously, and a decision given against the employers' thesis. That was an example, however, which showed that two at all events of Mr. Laski's desiderata had been fulfilled in some measure. A great deal could be done through the international institutions at present existing.

He knew the lecturer had a theory that the modern state was in essence a state of a federal character, and would like to ask him if, seeing that that federal character was growing—not a legal federal character, but the existence of autonomous institutions within a state with which, in fact, the state does not interfere—he did not think international contact between those units within the state would, in the long run, produce that international society he desired to create.

Mr. Hopkins asked if the lecturer supported the policy of Locarno by which the forces of Great Britain were in given circumstances pledged to the support of France or Germany. If he did not support the Locarno policy could he logically support the League of Nations, which had given its blessing to that policy? Finally, if he could not support either Locarno or the League of Nations what measures would he suggest for the prevention of war in Europe?

Mr. Laski said he entirely agreed with Mr. Phelan that there were aspects in which the League had taken steps towards the ideal he had indicated. In his view, however, the use of terms like ' public opinion ' was extremely dangerous because, unless it was accompanied by definitions, no one knew when public opinion was public or when it was opinion. Mr. Baldwin claimed he had public opinion on his side in regard to the present dispute in the English coal-mines, but personally he denied that absolutely.

The growth of autonomous groups in the modern community was, of course, a striking phenomenon, but those groups could not, he thought, attain the autonomy that was essential to their proper functioning in the midst of the glaring economic inequalities characteristic of the modern community. Only when there was approximate equality of economic power—using ' approximate ' in a large sense—could one have approximate equality of political power, and it was impossible to get that inter-relationship between those autonomous groups and a League of Nations which both he and Mr. Phelan desired until men were significant in the community by reason of their personality, and not by reason of the property to which they happened to be annexed.

He had been asked whether, since sovereignty and the decisions of sovereignty were based on consent, the world sovereignty of a body like the League of Nations could not also be based on consent. He did not want to be vehement, but he knew nothing quite so futile in political philosophy as the endeavour to base the modern state on consent. Consent could mean anything, from a complete ignorance of what was in fact being done to an ardent support of it. The number of steps in the argument was so vast, and the question of whether the consent was tacit or implied so vital, that he did not really know what consent meant—and perhaps, to cover his ignorance, he might add that no one else did either.

He had also been asked whether he looked forward to the

abolition of the use of force in the affairs of the modern world. For a short period of time—the period which his generation could hope to see—he did look forward to the abolition of aggression by the use of force against the aggressor—meaning by the aggressor that power or group of powers that, in the opinion of the Council or the Assembly of the League of Nations, had been the first to take up arms. He was perfectly prepared to use unlimited force to put down violence that was so defined.

With regard to the Locarno Treaties, on the basis of what he had already said he did agree with the Locarno Pact. It did not represent all he himself desired, but it did represent an indirect evolution of the whole conception of unanimous rule in the Council of the League, and thereby it seemed to him one of the most useful steps forward that had so far been taken.

A member of the audience said he did not understand what was meant by the sovereign state. When he read Machiavelli's *Prince* he understood that what was referred to was a person such as George Rex. When he read Rousseau, however, he found Rousseau understood the prince to be, for example, the City of Geneva, and not the legislature or executive of the city with whom decisions rested.

Mr. Laski said that when Machiavelli talked about the prince he was not talking about some one like George Rex, who was simply a dignified emollient rather than a source of power. He was talking about a person in whom what, personally, he had called the power to will acts of universal reference was concentrated. What Rousseau was talking about only God and Rousseau knew; but he had a very intimate conviction that Rousseau was not certain.

Personally, he thought the phrase 'sovereignty of the state' was largely meaningless, and what was in fact meant was the sovereignty of the Government, which was acting in the name of the people of the state, whether it did what they wanted it to do or the reverse. Sovereignty was the power of a body of men to issue orders to the vast majority of those outside, and to get them obeyed if they could by all the means at their disposal.

A member of the audience raised the question of the function of the Church in the future in strengthening the will of the individual to resist the state, and asked whether it would not be found useful in that connexion.

Mr. Laski said that, philosophically and otherwise, he was a dissenter from all churches, and had no belief whatever that any church or group of churches was likely, as a body, or as a unified aggregation, to work for ideals which he considered to be the ideals of truth and justice. Looking at the Christian churches of Great Britain he saw everything there except the ideals of Christianity, for which personally he had a high regard as undogmatic ideals. If men could be interested in the spiritual forces embodied in an ecclesiastical organization he believed they could be interested also in the spiritual forces embodied in a political organization, and believing, as he did, in the necessity for the growing secularization of the modern world he pinned his faith to the laic and not the cleric.

Professor Rappard said he would not like the meeting to disband in a state of a certain mental confusion of which he saw some symptoms. Every one present had doubtless been greatly impressed both by the lecturer's brilliancy and by his analysis of the present-day world. What the sovereign state was was not quite clear—was it an ideal, or an institution, or a body of governments? What was clear was that the sovereign state was the object of the lecturer's unmitigated antipathy. The lecturer applauded the efforts of the individual to resist the sovereign state from below, but hated the sovereign state so violently as to be also in favour of abolishing the present rule of unanimity in the League, and thus giving a majority of states the right to impose their united will on the individual state. He ventured to submit there was something contradictory in those two proposals. If one applauded the efforts of the individual who resisted the state it would seem that one was a believer in the cause of individual freedom. National freedom was not individual freedom, yet the position of an individual who was in the minority in his own state and had to bow to the will of the majority was certainly comparable to that of a state which was in a minority and had to bow to the will of the majority of other peoples.

Personally, looking to the future, he fully agreed with the lecturer's ideal, and thought the road of progress lay in the direction of the subordination of the national state to the will of a political unity, be it the League of Nations or be it some super-state which would grow out of the League. But he did not think that if one looked forward to progress in that direction one could at the same time consistently hope to see society organized in such a way that individuals might with impunity resist the will of the majority of their fellow citizens, and he would like the lecturer to indicate the way out of what seemed to be a serious dilemma.

Mr. LASKI said Professor Rappard's observations reminded him of what he had always thought the most admirable of all

Mr. Chesterton's observations, namely, that only logic drove man mad. Obviously, in the thesis he had presented that evening there was omnipresent a contingency for anarchy. He wished to support his argument by a quotation from one whose conservatism could not be impugned—Edmund Burke. ' The people ', said Burke in his speech on conciliation with America, ' has no interest in disorder. Where they do wrong, it is their error and not their crime. Popular violence always arises from popular suffering.' He believed that to be profoundly true. One was only tempted into violence against the sovereign state when there was real ground for temptation. The problem of the relationship between the national right and the right of the commonwealth of nations, or of a super-state growing out of it was one which he thought could be met, and should be met, by drawing up a bill of rights, laying down certain fundamentals, as Cromwell called them, which were untouchable save by special means. In that connexion he did not need to remind any Americans present of the difficulty of amending the constitution of a country ! (Applause.)

The CHAIRMAN said he was sure he expressed the feeling of all those present in saying how very interesting and instructive Mr. Laski's lecture had been. (Applause.)

Mr. MANLEY O. HUDSON said he was delighted to be permitted to propose a vote of thanks to Mr. Laski for what he regarded as a most inspiring address. Mr. Laski always affected him in the same way. It was several years since he last heard him, but he found that he had not outgrown his weakness, and when hearing him was always overcome both by the poetry and the erudition of what he had to say. Mr. Laski had convinced him that if one could only achieve the right measure one could say anything, however ridiculous, however confused and however far from what one's hearers might be thinking at the time, yet one could convince one's hearers that one had delivered a very good address.

Personally, he had found himself so overcome by the lecturer's growing erudition that he distrusted his first impressions entirely. He found himself very much in sympathy with the lecturer's insistence on the importance of getting away from the idea of sovereignty in international affairs. Sovereignty had played a large part in international affairs, in the first place as a legal conception. As a lawyer he found it possible to do his work, however, without ever referring to a conception of sovereignty, and for him the legal conception had simply been thrown out of the window; it seemed to serve no useful purpose whatever. He knew some of his colleagues talked about it, but he did not understand what they meant, and he never felt it necessary to deal with such a conception when addressing himself to one of the problems of political life to which law had to be applied.

There was also, however, a popular, as distinct from a legal, conception of sovereignty, and it was that popular conception the lecturer had in mind that evening. Personally, he was sure that popular conception had done a great deal of harm in recent time, and he had been reminded of that recently by reading a book by one of the most celebrated ex-Foreign Ministers of modern times, in which the author spoke of an experience he had some years ago in a Foreign Office, in which the members of that Foreign Office sat waiting all one day to hear that their country—a great country—was at war with another country—also a great country—separated from them only by a few miles of water. In the early 90's that ex-Secretary for Foreign Affairs expected to find that two countries were at war because a commander of a warship in the harbour of Bangkok refused to fire a salute. He said they waited for the telegram, which might mean that millions of people were to be thrown into war, and finally, when the telegram came it was to say that the commander of the gunboat in question had apologized. Personally, it seemed to him that nothing short of the kind of exaggerated idea of popular sovereignty the lecturer was attacking would make such a situation possible, and he knew of no better comment on the effect of that conception than the instance he had just quoted.

When he came, however, to apply what the lecturer said to any of the current practical problems of international life he found himself extremely disappointed. In reading Mr. Laski's *Grammar of Politics*, and particularly that section of it dealing with international affairs, he found himself equally disappointed, and if the Socialists as a group had no greater contributions to make to current world affairs than the kind of suggestions Mr. Laski made, for his part he did not expect very much help from that quarter. Mr. Laski, for example, had spoken of the League defying the Great Powers. He himself could not envisage such a possibility. The League could not defy the Great Powers. It has no existence apart from the states which composed it ; it was a League of states. Those states determined its character, and he could not envisage any early departure from the principle of unanimity. He certainly could not envisage a position in any immediate future where the Great Powers would be defeated by themselves—for that was what it virtually came to. He ventured to think that to talk of the possibility of a two-thirds majority controlling international affairs was not to make a very helpful contribution towards progress.

Nor did he find the slightest assistance in the lecturer's suggestion that an individual should be able to appeal to an International Court against his own or a foreign Government. He could not entertain the possibility of such a proceeding, and he would like to see Mr. Laski develop that idea very much farther than it was developed in his *Grammar of Politics*.

As for the lecturer's remarks about aiming high he did not know whether the lecturer or himself could be said to be aiming higher. That was a difficult thing to determine. He was not going to say that any one who accepted his views was necessarily aiming high, but, on the other hand, he did not want it to be said that he was aiming low because he endeavoured to put his energies into helping a new method of handling international affairs, a method which was actually being used by the peoples of the world to solve their present-day problems.

As always, while his mind had been very much challenged by everything the lecturer said, he had found himself charmed by the manner of its presentation, and he had great pleasure in proposing that a hearty vote of thanks be accorded him. (Applause.)

Mr. LASKI, in reply, said that Mr. Hudson had posed as the practical man as distinct from the amiable theorist like himself, who stood apart from the heat and dust of the strife in which Mr. Hudson was so strenuously engaged. Personally, however, the only difference he had ever observed between the theorist and the practical man was that the practical man did not know that he was acting upon assumptions, and, accordingly, the theorist spent his time in clearing away the difficulties that the practical man accumulated in the course of his work.

The proceedings then terminated.

CHAPTER XIII

PUBLIC OPINION IN RELATION TO WAR AND PEACE

I. *The Work of Non-official Organizations.*

Dr. JAMES BROWN SCOTT:

WE all believe in peace. President Taft, when delivering an address before the American Judicial Settlement Society, started out with that remark, and then said : ' The trouble is that when we begin to talk about the ways of peace each person has his own method of reaching what may be considered the common goal, and they are so interested in their methods, and so sure that their own particular method is the right one, that they fall out with one another, becoming somewhat more oblivious of the goal than they were before they ventured on the discussion.

In that respect I think we could all afford to take a lesson from Molière and his Bourgeois Gentilhomme. When Monsieur Jourdain made a large fortune and retired from the things of the world and took up those of the spirit, he had a music master, a dancing-master, a fencing-master, and a master of philosophy ; and the master of philosophy, in one part of the scene to which I refer, was explaining to him that the great thing in life was moderation ; whereupon the fencing-master, who happened to be present, stood up for his arms, and after a very short discussion, the fencing-master was ejected by the philosopher, who, on returning, began again quietly to speak of the virtues of moderation.

I would like you to understand that in what I intend to say this morning I hope to be pervaded by a spirit of moderation. I look on every contribution to the peace movement as somewhat in the nature of a rivulet reaching the main stream, enlarging it, and ultimately losing itself in the larger body of waters, to be lost in the immensity of the ocean. Simply because it may be that my drop is from a different continent or a different well, or is not quite what your particular standard would have it, let us realize that we should cultivate moderation to this extent: instead of picking out one path or the other path let us hope that these paths will lead to the great goal which we have in common, and which will not be the contribution of any one or of many, but so far as possible the contribution of all directed towards a common end.

I was brought up as a lawyer, and have practised and taught law, so that my outlook has been coloured by my education and environment, and I am inclined to look on the peace movement as the application of the principles of justice to nations as well as to men expressed in rules of law. I see the hope of the peace movement more, perhaps, in the administration of justice between nations in order to overcome a resort to force, just as those who have studied municipal law are inclined to think that the principles of justice expressed in rules of law and applied in the court-room have kept that equilibrium which, between nations, we are inclined to call peace. It is rather to this phase of the subject that I would invite your attention.

Peace, as I conceive it, is really a state of mind. The elements which enter into this state of mind and help to form it are, I think, goodwill, openness of mind, a knowledge of others and their aims and purposes, and so on. Ignorance, in my opinion, is perhaps a greater curse than war, for it is the mother and the breeder of wars. A readiness to believe that others are as good as we, and the conviction that the past is not wholly past ; that it made and lives in the present and is likely to influence the future is also necessary to achieve that state of mind of which I speak. Without these things we shall in large measure lack the spirit of peace which has to pervade the mind and to control the tongue, that most unruly of our members, for, as it seems to me, the outward and visible state is but the inner and invisible state within us. This, of course, is commonplace. Everything is more or less commonplace. This sun which brings us our light and heat, and without which we should cease to exist, rises, to use the ordinary expression, every morning, and continues its course. The seasons of the year follow one another, and the fruits of the earth all come in their appointed time ; they are nothing but repetitions of continual and continuous process. They are the commonplaces of nature.

I am inclined to think that there is a place for the commonplaces of life, and the commonplaces of life as I conceive them are goodwill, an open mind, a knowledge of others, a readiness to believe that they may be as good as we know that we are, and a faith that the past, which is made up of the actions of people just as intent on good things as we ourselves are, is in the present, and is somehow going to influence the history of the present and future.

There is a statement in the Old Testament : ' No doubt ye are the people, and wisdom shall die with you.' That was said some thousands of years ago, and would be applicable, I take it, at any time except now and in any place except here. We should cultivate the moderation advocated by Molière's master of philosophy, and if inclined to lose our temper a little, try to look at the whole and not at parts of the whole, and beyond and above all have toleration for the views of others. If we could only reach those levels, and if we could only incorporate these commonplaces into our thought, and, still better, into our life, this world of ours would be, in my opinion, a very different place.

At school I learned that everything worth doing was of American origin, and that the world began on 4 July 1776, and that the progress which was being made was exclusively confined to the American side of the Atlantic. Small as I was then I was yet big enough to have a large contempt for others. There was in the neighbourhood a grocery store, the person in charge of which was not an American by birth although he was by inclination. He was known generally as Dirty Bill, and honestly and truly I thought, in my little, prejudiced way, that all his people on the other side of the water were Dirty Bills. I judged all by the only one I knew, and in my ignorance I created a world of my own imagination. I remember, years later, when I had grown up and gone through college and was privileged to cross the Atlantic for the first time, and to stand on the soil where the Dirty Bills lived, I was overwhelmed with admiration, and I was confused and chagrined that at any time I should have had such ideas of that man's country and antecedents and of his kin who had remained at home, instead of taking what I conceived to have been the wise step of crossing the Atlantic.

A conference is being held here for the reduction of armaments. The word ' disarmament ' is at present a misnomer, because very few of us go so far as to advocate disarmament without limitation ; but I take it there is a very general feeling in favour of a general reduction of armaments. I am inclined to think, however, that the reduction of armaments must be a rather futile thing unless at the same time we

manage to bring about a reduction of the spirit which leads
to armaments. I think we have got to demobilize the spirit
which leads to the use of the weapon, because the weapon is
a very powerless thing until some one takes it up to use it.
So long as that spirit is rampant to the extent to which it
is at present you may have agreements to limit armaments,
and you may have a so-called disarmament, but if that spirit
be present nations are going to grasp at those things and
use them when they consider such a step to be in their
interest. If you cut down capital ships they will use smaller
ships, and if you withdraw their weapons who knows but
they will fight with their fists?

I am in favour of the limitation of armaments, and, indeed,
of disarmament, but I think the way to reach that consummation is to possess ourselves of the spirit which, when
achieved, will make the limitation of armaments, and disarmament itself, useless. Without the creation of this spirit
I am afraid there is just enough of the old Adam still left in
us to make us forget the promises we have given when a
violation of such a promise seems to be in our interest.

That this may not seem to be wholly negative let me
make this suggestion. There is a legend of the Church Universal concerning St. Christopher, who was a shepherd taken
by the devil into his service. The devil did many wonderful
things, but whenever they came to a cross-road he made a
detour, and when Christopher asked why, he replied that
that was the sign of the Cross, and he could not cross the
roads. St. Christopher, who, though an ignorant person,
had his eye on the main chance, said that if his master was
afraid of some one and admitted it he himself would endeavour to find this other person and follow him, and so
found the Christ. The thing to do, as I humbly conceive

it, is to find out the greatest interest, the one interest in this world—not an interest of Great Britain, of France, or of Germany, or even of the United States, but the interest which is at the bottom of it all : justice. Justice to men, justice to women, justice to children within the state and justice between the states, and in all their relations one with another, because, as I said the other night, there is but one rule and principle of justice, and that is the justice which is right, which applies to all men, to all women, and which applies to all states, be they little or great. If the nations can be persuaded that justice is, as Daniel Webster put it, the supreme concern of all men on the earth, and if they can be brought to square their actions with the principles of justice, applying them equally in all cases where they themselves or others are affected, we have the least common denominator and the greatest common denominator : we have the one great interest common to all, in which there is neither superior nor inferior—the interest which controls without affecting the rights of others.

I happen to come from a large state. I do not flatter myself on that account for I was in no way responsible for it. Large states have large powers, and they look upon the material sources of power as the means of causing their interests, their judgement, or their desires to prevail. Small states, on the contrary, are in favour of justice, and are advocates of justice. If you look at the Protocol of the Permanent Court of International Justice you will find a large number of small states confessing their faith in the Optional Clause. If you look for the large states you will not find them. Why? Simply because in the nature of things as they are to-day the large state has a way of making its will prevail by means of a resort to force, while the little states know that they cannot compete with the large states in that domain on an equality. They know, on the contrary, that they can compete with the large states in the domain of justice, and that they have an equal chance of succeeding in the settlement of all those disputes which arise between and among them. Therefore it seems to me, without labouring it further, that the common interest which we should seek to inculcate day and night, and especially within ourselves, is this principle of justice. If we permeate ourselves with this feeling of justice and insist upon its formulation and its application, saying that every state can gain by it and cannot possibly lose, we then have a chance of substituting for the spirit of force which exists, that spirit of justice which renders force useless.

Now I would like to sum up this phase of what I have said in a very simple experience. I remember years ago a dinner was given in New York to Mr. Elihu Root, when he ceased to be Secretary of State, and he was congratulated on the services he had rendered. Every one at the dinner was beaming and abounding in expressions of goodwill, and Mr. Root himself was smiling. When he rose to speak he said that he was quite sure that if every person in the world was animated by the feeling of goodwill which pervaded him there would be no wars or rumours of wars in the world. I think, therefore, the thing to do is to cultivate an attitude, is to make peace to depend largely on justice, and in our way to contribute as far as possible to its acceptance.

I should like to say a few words on the steps being taken in our country. The peace movement began in the United States in a very quiet and simple way. There was a young man called John Jay, who was a student at King's College, which is now Columbia University. He chose as his theme the blessings of peace, and he began to study law. His preceptor, a man of wide outlook, had him devote his first year of preparation to the reading of the treatise of Grotius on the Rights and Duties of Nations. It is doubtful whether John Jay could ever have dreamed he was to occupy the place in this world which has been his lot. When, in 1785, he was Secretary of Foreign Affairs of the Confederation, and was not getting on very well in his relations with England, he proposed that the dispute should be settled by a Commission, and recommended that to Congress. It was not done. When, for a few months, he was Acting Secretary of State in Washington's administration until Jefferson returned from Paris to accept the post of Secretary of State, he proposed to Washington that his previous report should be sent to the Senate for the settlement of disputes between Great Britain and the United States, and Washington picked up a draft and inserted the phrase ' and with all other nations '. That was the influence of an unofficial person transferred to the official world, and bringing about a change in the thought of the world. It was through John Jay and his Treaty with Great Britain advocating arbitration that arbitration came into our modern practice.

During the war with Great Britain, which began in 1812, another step forward was made. In 1814 there was a man in New York called David Lowe Dodge, who wrote a book called *War Inconsistent with the Religion of Jesus Christ*. It was published two years before Noah Webster's solemn review of the custom of war, which was issued on Christmas Day 1814. Dodge and his friends started, the next year, a Peace Society, and, on the conclusion of the Treaty of Ghent, which was signed on the eve of Christmas Day 1814, Mr. Dodge got some of his friends together and started the

Peace Society in New York. It was the first of its kind. Next year one was started in England, and in 1828 the various societies in America were merged into one—the American Peace Society.

In 1840 the Peace Society offered a series of prizes for the best essay on the Prevention of War. The addresses which did not receive prizes seemed to be so good that William Ladd took the principal points and put them together, and expressed them in an essay of his own called an Essay on a Congress and Court of Nations, in which he outlined in its minutest detail the meeting of a Hague Conference at the call of a respectable Power (that was the expression he used) in order to consider the laws of nations, and especially to reduce to written form the laws of war so that there might be less violation of them and of the rights of neutrals, and at the same time that conference of nations was to create a Court of International Justice—the Supreme Court of the world, as he called it.

His favourite disciple, Elihu Burritt, went through the world in the '40's preaching the establishment of an International Court for settling disputes between nations, just as there was a Supreme Court for all the American States.

In 1852 the Republic was overthrown in France, and the Empire started under Napoleon III with that rather remarkable phrase : ' The Empire means peace.' It in fact meant war, and wars continued until a later date, when William Ladd's Conference met.

In the 1840's there was published a little book by William Jay, a President of the American Peace Society, on *War and Peace : The Disadvantages of the First and the Advantages of the Second*, in which he advocated that, when his country concluded treaties, there should be inserted in the Treaty a clause to the effect that if any dispute should arise as to the meaning of that Treaty the dispute should be submitted to independent impartial arbitration. One day, many years later, when I happened to be solicitor for the Department of State and was talking to Mr. Root, then Secretary of State, he handed me a treaty which I saw was a treaty between France and the United States, by which those two countries agreed to submit their disputes of a specified kind to arbitration. I said to Mr. Root : ' You have got excellent authority for what you have done.' He said he did not know that he had authority for it, but he felt that he had reason. I told him Mr. William Jay had said in his book that in the next treaty concluded with France, our first and only ally, that clause should be included, and it so happened the very first treaty the United States was privileged to make with foreign countries was in pursuance of that simple suggestion of Jay, the President of the American Peace Society, in his little pamphlet.

In America the peace movement started in unofficial circles. From unofficial circles it passed to official circles, largely through the interest of those who had been convinced before they held office. The two great principles of the American Peace Movement have been : arbitration of our disputes with foreign countries, and the judicial settlement of disputes through courts of justice. Both those proposals originated from unofficial persons.

I should like to say that Mr. Carnegie, a few years ago, created the organization which bears his name—the Carnegie Endowment for International Peace. He endowed it with what was a considerable sum of money in those days, but nowadays we think in hundreds of millions, and 10,000,000 dollars as capital is not very large. The income is small, but

fortunately we have found it possible to do some small
things in a small way which may lead to larger things. For
example, a few years ago we were trying to increase the
efficiency of international law and its teaching, and there
was a conference held in Washington of international law
teachers. A second conference of the same kind was held,
and at the present time there is a conference of teachers of
international relations of the United States meeting on this
holy ground. A number of teachers of international relations have been good enough to accept the invitation of the
Carnegie Endowment to visit The Hague, Paris, and Geneva,
to see how the international mind operates when brought
face to face with great difficulties. We are not a peace
society in the ordinary sense of the word. We are called on
to administer a trust, but in the interests of peace. We
believe in conference, we believe in intercourse, and we
believe in the printed page. In conference we have been
able to bring together many people in America and Europe.
Intercourse is in progress here by means of our visiting guests.
By means of the printed page we have reached many who
would not otherwise have heard not our messages but the
messages of the past ; because we are old-fashioned enough
in our country to believe that the past is worth while considering if you are going to have a future which will last.

In 1920 a meeting of the Advisory Committee of Jurists
was held at The Hague, under the auspices of the League of
Nations, to form the Permanent Court of International
Justice and thus give effect to Mr. Ladd's repeated recommendations. The representative of the American jurists
was Mr. Elihu Root, President of the Carnegie Endowment,
and through his efforts an agreement was reached on the
method of composing the Court that was so acceptable to

those present and to the world at large that it was used in the election of the judges for the Court and found adequate. That new institution is now installed in the Peace Palace at The Hague, the gift of Mr. Carnegie.

Early in 1922 a conference was held at Washington for the Limitation of Armaments, and the Secretary of State asked the Carnegie Endowment to publish various things. We issued Mr. MacMurray's two volumes on the Treaties with China, and Mr. Root said in a public address that the bringing together and publication of these volumes and the putting of them in the hands of the Delegates made an agreement on the Pacific question possible ; and he was bold enough to say the money expended in that simple way was in itself sufficient to justify the existence of the Endowment.

Instead of talking of war and the resort to arms, which has always been a menace in the world, let us rather talk of the things that we have in common, of the things that unite us, and together press forward along the path of justice to our great goal, the horizon of peace, which, as we approach, recedes from us, but which, if we do not stand together and act as a unit, we will never be privileged to see. (Applause.)

Professor RAPPARD then took the chair. The Chairman, in introducing Dr. Maxwell Garnett, said there was no necessity for him to say anything by way of introduction, since Dr. Garnett was well known to those whom he would address. He would like, therefore, to mention one interesting personal experience. He had had the privilege, for nearly five years, of being associated with the League of Nations in an administrative capacity, as the Director of the Mandates Section, and since that time had been doing, in a small way, what Dr. Maxwell Garnett was doing with such success in Great Britain—endeavouring to help towards spreading a general enlightenment on international affairs with a view to strengthening the efforts of those who were working for international peace.

Dr. Garnett's position had some obvious advantages over that of those whose duties were of an official nature, the chief advantage being absolute freedom. Men and women who worked for the League of Nations and for peace must be fully informed of the difficulties and of the concrete tasks before them, and if in many cases peace societies had been looked on by men saddled with real responsibilities with a certain disfavour and indifference, it was too often because the unofficial friends of peace were ignorant of the difficulties attendant on it. When one had the advantage of enjoying the complete freedom which characterized Dr. Garnett's position, and combined with that freedom a full knowledge of the intricacies of the problems which faced the League of Nations, one was extremely privileged. There was one privilege which he himself enjoyed, however, which was more enviable than those of Dr. Garnett—namely, the privilege of listening to his remarks. (Applause.)

II. *The Psychology of Patriotism and the Aims of the League of Nations Associations.*

Dr. J. C. Maxwell Garnett :

DR. Scott has told us that peace is a state of mind, and Mr. Zimmern began the work of our Institute with a discussion of the international mind. To-day we complete the circle, and come back once more to the international mind, for the aim of League of Nations Associations is just that— to create the international mind. It is, of course, true that they have the further aim to organize to some extent the public opinion they create, and perhaps that latter function sometimes attracts more attention than the solid work involved in the discharge of the former function. But as a matter of fact, I think you may take it that not more than one-fifth of the effort of the League of Nations Associations is concerned with the organization of public opinion, and all the rest is concerned with the enlightenment, as Professor Rappard put it, of the public mind—the creation of the international mind and the creation of the right kind of public opinion.

I gather from the discussion yesterday evening that Mr. Laski did not like the sovereign state, but that Professor Hudson was not prepared to adopt Mr. Laski's practical suggestion and abolish the rule of unanimity in the Council and the Assembly of the League, and so override the sovereignty of the States which compose the League. There is one point which was not brought out in that discussion, although it is, of course, familiar to all of us. It is that there are certain matters in which unanimity is not required from the nations that compose the League. There are matters of the organization of the League itself—for example, the admission of a new State—which concern every State, but for which a majority of two-thirds in the Assembly and no majority at all in the Council is sufficient. I fancy that, as time goes on, there will be more and more matters in regard to which unanimity will not be required. I am inclined to think the time is already ripe for a change in article 4 of the Covenant. Article 4 says that for a new nation to take its place, whether with a permanent seat or otherwise, on the Council of the League, unanimity in the Council, but only a simple majority in the Assembly, is required. We conclude from the fact that you do not require more than a simple majority from the Assembly, that there is no serious infraction of sovereign rights in admitting a new State to the Council. If, instead of requiring unanimity, you required, say, four-fifths of the Council to be in favour of admission, you would not have had the difficulties which occurred last March, and I cannot see myself that the League would be any worse off. I discussed that with Lord Phillimore and Lord Grey, and found that neither of them discovered any difficulties. They saw, of course, the great difficulty of amending the Covenant, but neither thought the Covenant would be any the worse, and the opinion was expressed that it would be a change for the better. I think, therefore, that it is likely there will be a very great increase in that class of case in which absolute unanimity is not required, in order that effective action may follow from the decisions of the Council and of the Assembly.

The chief difference, as I understand it, between Mr. Laski and Professor Hudson, lies in the matter of time. Mr. Laski wanted to leap into the new world, while Professor Hudson wanted to go slowly. In this particular matter of unanimity, he wanted to go so slowly that, as I understood him, the motion was not to be perceptible perhaps in our lifetime.

I do not think the reconciliation of those two points of view is to be accomplished in the sphere of international law. The changes that are recommended are not primarily changes in international law; they are primarily changes in the public mind. Indeed, if you brought about a change in the law but did not bring about a change in the public mind, the change in the law would not be worth the making. You have to have both changes to get a practical result. A treaty which does not find public favour is no more than a scrap of paper. If you try to make people good by acts of Parliament or Congress, and the people are not in favour of those acts, the laws are not enforceable. The thing you must do if you want to bring about these changes is to bring about a change in the public mind, and thus it is possible to make the necessary change in the law.

We, therefore, come back to the problem of the minds of people in the different countries, and ultimately to the problem of the international mind with which Mr. Zimmern began our discussions this week, and which it is the aim of the League of Nations Societies to create. I propose, then, that in this session we shall examine from the standpoint of psychology the national and international mind. Let us begin with the psychology of patriotism.

Patriotism, says the dictionary, is love of country. But what is ' country ' ? To that question we shall have to return. For the moment, it is enough to say that the meaning of ' country ' includes an organized community throughout which an accepted system of rights and obligations is maintained by a central government. The paramount importance which most men attach to their country lies just here : that, without the reign of law, man's best work is so unsafe as not to be worth while, and human life is cheap and purposeless.

If we ask what are the conditions of effective life and work, we shall come quickly to the heart of our subject. The first condition is to avoid that uncertain habit of mind where perpetual conflict between rival interests and purposes makes consistent and effective conduct impossible. Such a life can never attain any far-reaching objective. The education of every man and woman should therefore aim at linking up the separate interests and purposes that tend to form as life goes on. This organizing of thought and experience should seek to form one all-embracing system, a *single wide interest*. But it is not merely to connect together all feelings, thoughts, and experiences of whatever kind, including one's sentiment for oneself and for all the groups to which one belongs. It is also to marshal them, introducing a simple and effective order among them. Moreover, this single wide interest must be *centred in a dominant purpose* intimately related to deep emotions. The nature of such a single wide interest, the neural dispositions or neuragrams that correspond to it, and how to form it—or, at least, how approximate to it—in practice I have discussed elsewhere.[1] What most concerns us here is that whoever possesses such a single wide interest will see the world single and will see it whole; he will be consistent in thought, in feeling, in conduct; and, if other people leave him free, his life will be effective, and make steady progress towards the goal of his high purpose.

There was no single wide interest in the mind of the child who thought that the answer to the teacher's question ' Who was the wisest man that ever lived ? ' was either ' Solomon ' or ' Solon ' according as the question was asked before or after half-past nine, when religious instruction was supposed

[1] See *Education and World Citizenship*, Cambridge University Press, 1921.

to end. Equally lacking a single wide interest was a certain clergyman who met a little girl carrying a fine fossil. Being interested in geology as well as in theology, he asked the child when she thought her fossil was made. ' About the Creation, I should think,' was the answer. And he replied, ' Nonsense, child, a long time before that.'

But even this perfectly integrated personality is not enough. It is necessary to integrate, not only individual persons, but also fellow workers, neighbours, fellow citizens, and ultimately all mankind. Conflict must be prevented between men and between groups of men, as well as in each individual mind ; for conflict, wherever it appears, is the enemy of progress and consistency, and hinders the attainment of any noble aim.[1] It follows that the central purpose which, as we said, has to dominate one man's mind, must be in harmony with the master purposes of his neighbours. This makes for freedom throughout the community ; for if what I want to do is also what my neighbours want me to do in the interest of us all, then I am free to do what I want to do, and only so am I free. The only way to freedom is through harmony of central purpose. But if my central purpose is in harmony with those of my neighbours, there must be some supreme element common to the purposes of us all. Even between all men and women in all the groups which may possibly come into conflict with one another—and, in the modern world, that means practically all men and women every-

---

[1] The elimination of conflict between the rival purposes, whether of an individual or of different men or groups of men, need not reduce human life to effortless ease and slothful degeneration. There will always remain the strenuous discipline of the struggle to understand the world we live in, as well as to guide and control the forces of Nature both inside and outside our bodies.

where—there needs to be at least a supreme purpose in common. Only so will the world be safe from war that makes consistent and effective life neither possible nor worth while, since war, as we now know it, can destroy in a few days the fruits of many years of labour and research.

So every one, the world over, is to have his or her thought organized in a single wide interest ; and the different single wide interests of different people are all to be alike centred in a common supreme purpose. What ought it to be ? What is this enterprise on which all of us ought to be engaged ? ' To make a perfect world ' is a simple answer and, no doubt, a true one. But it does not carry us very far.

Elsewhere I have discussed the matter at some length,[1] and we need not examine it fully here. But we must pay attention to one or two aspects of it.

In the first place, the single wide interest of which we have been speaking is an interest in the world of experience : the ' real ' world. It will be of little use to achieve harmony between persons and between groups of persons at the cost of truth. It is fatal to live in a world of dreams. We must think of the world substantially as it is, or perish. If I assume a swimming bath to be full when it is empty, and try a high dive on to a hard floor instead of into six feet of water, my mistake may cost me my life. We have to face the question whether the world of experience really is such that a single wide interest, a perfectly integrated mind, may correspond to it. In realms where human action does not interfere, discovery and scientific thought are organizing and integrating the world of our experience, and Professor White-head tells us that the goal is ' a neat, trim, tidy, exact world '. But where human actions resulting from disorderly thought

[1] Loc. cit., ch. xvii.

can produce disorder in the ' real ' world, there the world of experience will only correspond to perfectly integrated minds when all minds are already perfectly integrated. Since, however, thought leads to action, this portion also of the ' real ' world will tend to become integrated and approach Professor Whitehead's goal as single wide interests become common among men. And in these single wide interests, corresponding not, indeed, to the whole world of experience, but to the parts of it with which the several individuals are acquainted, the central elements, which already correspond to the *same* supreme purpose, must also correspond to the *same* central essences of the ' real ' world : the central purposes of men and women must be in close relation to the central facts of the universe.

The central purposes of men and women are also sure to be in close relation to the men and women themselves. For it is true of any of my purposes, that my thought of it is closely linked with thoughts of myself. If, therefore, I possess a single wide interest dominated by a central purpose, my whole thought of myself—my self-regarding sentiment— will be near the centre of my interest in the universe. But it must not be nearer than my interest in my neighbours. This becomes clear if we think of a small company of explorers on their way to discover the South Pole. They are all dominated, let us suppose, by their common purpose to reach the Pole. While they are actually on the march, that purpose does preserve harmony of action between them : they are acting together consistently and effectively. But much of the day is spent, not in marching, not in discovery, but in cooking and washing up ; and, if each explorer thinks of himself as the most important member of the group, there will be frequent conflict over the humdrum duties although there is harmony over the main enterprise. In the end, the success of the expedition may be endangered, unless each explorer thinks of himself as one of a group for the attainment of the common purpose. His self-regarding sentiment will then be merged in his stronger sentiment for the group. He will feel proud if the group prospers ; dejected if it fails ; angry if it is attacked ; anxious if it is in danger. And, instead of thinking of himself more highly than he ought to think, he will tend to think of, and to treat, his companions and himself with equal justice. So, too, will justice as well as freedom prevail in a larger community of men and women with single wide interests centred in a common purpose, provided that the common centre of interest includes consciousness of the community and of oneself as a member of it.

The common centre of interest must, we said, have some close relation to the central facts of the universe ; but the whole world-wide society of mankind (of which every community and every individual forms part) may very well be one of these central facts. There is, of course, nothing new in the suggestion that some essence of man is closely linked to the central essence of the universe ; or that Man is closely linked to God, and, consequently, politics to religion. Thus, Mr. A. E. Zimmern writes :

' The inspiration of all sound and enduring political and social construction is what has been called the principle of the Commonwealth. The principle of the Commonwealth is the application to the field of government and social policy of the law of human brotherhood, of the duty of a man to his neighbour near and far. . . . A Commonwealth is an organization designed with the ruling motive of love and brotherhood. It seeks to embody, not only in phraseology and constitutional doctrine, but in the actual conduct of public affairs, so far as the frailty and imperfection of man admit, the spirit and ideals of religion. *Whosoever will be great among you shall be your minister ; and whosoever of you will be the chiefest shall be the servant of all.'* [1]

We conclude that all men and women would have the best chance of leading effective lives if every one, the world over, possessed a single wide interest centred in a common purpose to serve the world-wide society of mankind as, next to God, the most important thing there is.   In such a community we saw that freedom and justice would both alike prevail ; freedom, because of the common purpose for the good of all; and justice, because truth and fair play are surely present where every one regards himself as only one of many equal members of the beloved community.   Even the cat-hating dog is kind to the *family* cat.   What will be the result when Frenchmen think of their *Europe's* Germans, and Americans of their *world's* Japanese as ' A ' company thinks of their battalion's ' B ' company ?

Now turn from what ought to be and look at what is.   In the communities we know, freedom is only secured by readiness to coerce, if need be, those law-breakers whose share of the common purpose is insufficient to overcome narrow and selfish purposes of their own ; while justice is maintained by employing a third party to decide between two disputants if either fails to judge his own case fairly.   Moreover, the societies which are accustomed to receive devoted service from their members, and of which their members often think as directly linked to the central essence of the universe,[2] are far from being world wide.

[1] *Nationality and Government* (1918), p. 355.
[2] Cf. the Kaiser's ' Old German God', or the British ' For God and the Empire ', instead of (like the bidding prayer) ' For God and the welfare

They do, however, exist. There are groups of men and women whose self-regarding sentiments are, in many cases, merged in their stronger sentiments for the group. In particular, people often do, quite literally, give their lives for their country. Many men are willing, at times, to die for it ; men have even been known to live for it. It is this group sentiment, this love of country, which we have to examine if we would understand the psychology of patriotism.

First of all, then, it *is* a sentiment—not an instinct, not innate ; but the product of education and environment, capable of alteration, helped by some conditions and hindered by others.

A sentiment, according to Mr. Shand's definition, is ' an organized system of emotional tendencies centred about the same object '.[1] (The emotional tendencies, affective parts of instinctive processes, are, of course, innate : what is not inborn is the grouping of these tendencies around a particular object—as when I love a dog or dogs and then, after being bitten by one, come to hate them instead.) And, to quote Professor Pillsbury,

' The individuals who compose a nation suffer real pain when it is in any way injured, when an outsider even speaks disparagingly of it, and are correspondingly elated when it thrives, when it grows in any way. A true Britisher feels a thrill of pride when he hears that the sun never sets on British soil. . . . The American, however humble, is never left unmoved by the statistics of billions of imports and exports, particularly when the balance is in favour of America. Neither may be in any degree better off for the fact . . . [but] he

of mankind and herein especially for the British Empire ' ; or, as Lord Balfour put it (in thanking the Prince of Wales for his Presidential address to the British Association), ' the world and especially that part of it covered by the British Empire.'

[1] Cf. W. McDougall, *Social Psychology*, p. 122.

thrills as he does at his own success. As the ideal source or occasion of emotion, the nation is as real an entity as a person.' [1]

That a sentiment is the product of education and experience has been shown by Dr. McDougall,[2] and this is particularly true, as he points out, of the sentiment of patriotism. 'The cult of patriotism is', he says, 'a field for educational effort of the highest order.' [3]

The educator who sets out to produce the sentiment of patriotism in his pupils tells them fine and noble things about their country. He stirs his pupils with stories of heroes, whom they cannot help admiring and wanting to imitate. As they hear how these great men lived and ventured and suffered and died for the country to which they themselves belong, each of them comes to think of himself as the servant of all his fellow countrymen, to merge his self-regarding sentiment in a stronger sentiment for his country. But example is better than precept. So the teacher of patriotism takes some emblem or symbol of his country—probably a flag—and treats it with the greatest possible respect. Moreover, he tries to link it, in his pupils' minds, with all that matters most in the world : if possible, to God. So Girl Guides are led to bring their Union Jack to church, where the priest takes it reverently from their hands, prays over it, and places it near the altar until they receive it back, with further marks of veneration, at the end of the service.

Of course, the sentiment of patriotism is more easily created in young people or immigrants if it is already strongly developed among the adult citizens. And, apart from direct educational effort, the patriotism of a community is in-

---

[1] *Psychology of Nationality and Internationalism*, p. 215.
[2] Symposium on Instinct and Emotion, *Proc. Aristotelian Society*, p. 30.
[3] *The Group Mind*, p. 180.

creased (as Mr. Ramsay Muir has said) by occupation of
a defined geographical area, such as an island ; by unity of
race ; by unity of language ; by unity of religion ; by common subjection, during a long stretch of time, to a firm and
systematic government ; by community of economic interest ; and, most potent of all, by the possession of a common
tradition, a memory of sufferings endured and victories won
in common, expressed in song and legend, in the dear names
of great personalities that seem to embody in themselves the
character and ideals of the nation, in the names also of sacred
places wherein the national memory is enshrined.[1] Our
English patriotism is certainly greater to-day because Shakespeare could write of—

> This fortress, built by Nature for herself,
> Against infection and the hand of war ;
> This happy breed of men, this little world,
> This precious stone set in the silver sea.

But none of these things—land,[2] race, language, and the
rest—except perhaps a common tradition, is a necessary condition of patriotism. Poland has no clear geographical outline like Britain or Japan or Spain ; the Welsh race shares
British patriotism with the English ; Switzerland has three
languages, not one ; unity of religion no longer marks French
patriots ; and Germany has had a single systematic government for less than a lifetime.

Indeed, patriotism does not chiefly depend on conditions

---

[1] *Nationalism and Internationalism*, Ramsay Muir, London, 1917.
[2] Some may think with Mr. Zimmern that the land is essential. But
certainly not all the people who dwell in the land ! I remember asking
a Polish landowner in the ' Corridor ' if they were much troubled with
mosquitoes—he had nets over his windows. He thought I said ' Musco-
vites ', and replied that they were more troubled with Germans.

outside the individual. It is, as we said, a sentiment, a bit of mental organization. It is psychological, through and through.[1] It includes the self-regarding sentiment as part of a larger whole, and so makes for self-sacrifice. And, among the primary emotional tendencies centred about its object, we can readily distinguish two, which Dr. McDougall has called ' tender emotion ' and ' negative self-feeling '. Their practical effect is friendliness and kindness, and such humility as befits the man or woman whose highest aim is to be the servant of all.

We have kept the hardest problem for the last. What is, and what ought to be, the object of the sentiment of patriotism ? A patriot loves his country, but just what *is* his country ? It is not always a State : patriotic Czechs or Slovaks did not commonly love the Empire of Austria or the Kingdom of Hungary before the war, any more than patriotic Austrians or Magyars in Prague or Pressburg to-day generally love the Republic of Czecho-Slovakia. And after every civil war—in England in 1670 no less than in America 200 years later—there are, for a time, two rival patriotisms in the same State. Moreover, we have seen that patriotism may override differences of language, of religion, and even of race ; an eloquent debater once asked the Cambridge Union Society ' What makes us Englishmen great ? '—and I remember it because the speaker was a dark-skinned native of Ceylon.

What, then, is the object of patriotism ? Nothing else than nationality ; and that is perhaps the best definition of a nation. It must needs be vague, since nations interpenetrate and overlap. Is an Israelite from Warsaw, Jewish or

[1] W. McDougall, *The Group Mind*, p. 99.

Polish? Is an Ulsterman Irish or British? About his state
there may be no doubt, but what about his nation? 'The
only way', says Professor Pillsbury, 'to decide whether an
individual belongs to one nation rather than another is to
ask him.'[1] And, according to Mr. Zimmern, 'Nationality,
like religion, is subjective . . . psychological . . . a condition of
mind . . . a spiritual possession . . . a way of feeling, thinking,
and living.'[2] Mr. Zimmern draws very clearly the distinction between States and Nations. But much confusion
remains in common speech. 'Nationalization' expresses
State-ownership; and when some one cancels his War Bonds
and so makes a present to the State, the Chancellor of the
Exchequer acknowledges a gift to the nation.

The special importance of the nation among human
groups, and the special position of patriotism among group
sentiments, arise in this way. Every group to which a man
consciously belongs, and with the other members of which
he shares experiences, tends to become the object of a sentiment in his mind. This sentiment will be stronger if the
common experiences are intense, if they are peculiar to the
group, and if they include a common purpose.[3] When a great
orator has deeply impressed his audience, they feel the faint
beginnings of a group sentiment as they walk home from the
meeting; and if, instead of walking home, they run off to
act together on some exhortation of the speaker's, their group
sentiment will be notably less faint.

Thus every man tends to have a sentiment for his family,
for his neighbourhood and those who live there, for people

[1] Loc. cit., p. 267.
[2] *Nationality and Government*, p. 51.
[3] For a discussion of the special potency of purposes to influence
thought and conduct, see Garnett, *Education and World Citizenship*, p. 153.

engaged in the same occupation as himself, for his church and especially for his nation, since it often happens that the nation includes all the other groups to which men conceive themselves as belonging. An Englishman may even find all these groups separately represented in the British Parliament. His neighbourhood is represented in the House of Commons through the territorial franchise ; so is his occupation, if he happens to be a University teacher (and there is much to be said for a wider extension of the occupational franchise). His church is represented in the House of Lords if he is a member of the Church of England ; and so is his family if the head of it happens to be a peer. But, whether or not these smaller groups are represented by separate persons in the supreme governing body of the nation (as they very seldom are), it is still true that patriotism, the sentiment for the national group, when that is the lowest common multiple of all the other chief groups to which a man belongs, is strengthened by all the other group sentiments and so tends to be of outstanding importance. It is made stronger still by common land, language, race, and the rest of which we have spoken already. It will tend to be strongest of all when the nation is co-extensive with the State, as in the case of the nation-states of Europe and America.

Dr. McDougall speaks of a Nation-State as ideal.[1] But Lord Acton, writing nearly sixty years ago, took a different view. There is a danger in excessive strength whether of patriotism or of its object, the nation. We began our inquiry by seeking the conditions of effective life and work for individual men and women ; and we must not too readily accept from Imperial Germany or Fascist Italy the view that political institutions and machinery matter more than men,

[1] Loc. cit., p. 175.

or that States rather than persons are made in the likeness of God.

Now a person will have most freedom to lead a useful and effective life if each group to which he belongs is free to manage those of its affairs which substantially concern all the people inside, and none outside, the group. If the group is too large, his freedom will be reduced because he will have less say than if it were smaller. If the group is too small, there is danger of conflict with those who are outside it but whose interests it affects. Thus the group which controls side streets should be smaller than that which manages main roads; and the authority responsible for public elementary schools smaller than for higher education. So, too, a nation-wide control may still suffice for telephones, but wireless needs a world group to manage it.

In so far as these and other similarly ordered groups actually exist, the group sentiments of one who consciously belongs to them all will form a hierarchy of loyalties, each in turn strengthened by all that are below it. But we have already observed that the ordered grouping will tend to follow the ordered thought as well as vice versa : the process is twofold. As single wide interests become common among men, the sentiments of the average man for the groups to which he consciously belongs will tend to form a hierarchy of loyalties, and the groups themselves will consequently tend towards an orderly relationship, the minor groups becoming subordinate to, and incorporated in, larger groups which they strengthen and support. In the end the largest loyalty —the sentiment for the most inclusive group—will be like a river and the lesser loyalties like tributaries that pour their waters into it : the wider and deeper the contributory streams, the greater the resulting river. Already, a good

Cornishman or a good Yorkshireman is a better Englishman on that account; and the best Englishman, or Frenchman, is also a good European.[1]

The immensely strong nation-state fits hardly into such a scheme. Its internal affairs tend to be too centralized; and, in external relations, its national selfishness is not easily subordinated to the good of all. Excessive patriotism [2] is apt to override international justice, instead of allowing allegiance to truth and fair play to override ' allegiance to one's country, even to its crimes'. So Lord Acton preferred diversity to uniformity in a State's internal structure; and added that ' Private rights, which are sacrificed to the unity, are preserved by the union of nations '.[3] There is more individual

---

[1] Cf. W. McDougall: ' Just as the minor group sentiments are not incompatible with, but rather may strengthen, the national sentiment, when subordinated to and incorporated in it, so the national sentiment is not incompatible with still more widely inclusive group sentiments, as, for example, that for a European system of nations, for the ' League of Nations ' or for Western Civilization in general. And, while loyalty to humanity as a whole is a noble ideal, it is one which can only be reached by a further extension of the object of the group sentiment, of which extension patriotism itself is the culmination at present for the great mass of mankind. The attempt to achieve it by any other road is bound to fail because psychologically unsound.'—*The Group Mind*, p. 181.

[2] It is not meant that one's patriotism can be too great, either absolutely or in comparison with the patriotism of other people. But it may be excessive in relation to the patriot's sentiments for other groups to which he also belongs. When the first dispute between Great Britain and France came before the Permanent Court of International Justice on 8 January 1923, and the Court, four weeks later, gave a unanimous decision, the French judge voted with the others against the French claim. He may have been the most patriotic of Frenchmen, but his patriotism was not excessive: it was subordinated to his sense of justice.

[3] Essay on *Nationality*, *Collected Essays* (Macmillan, 1909), p. 289.

freedom to be got from international co-operation than from a single cosmopolitan world state.

In this matter Englishmen are fortunately placed. Their history tells them of the union of other nations with their own. Partnership with the Welsh, and then with the Scots, while preventing conflict between the three nations, has preserved the liberties of each, and enabled them all to work together and achieve results which have been of immense benefit both to themselves and to the world. They are now the nucleus of a union of five or six other self-governing nations. And that British Commonwealth of nations, according to one of its most distinguished sons, himself a Dutch South African,[1] has been in turn the model for the still wider League of Nations. Meanwhile, a new British patriotism (and a British nation) is evolving out of the English, Welsh, and Scots that preceded it; and already the Scotsman travelling abroad gives his nationality as British, and the Englishman is half inclined to do the same. A wider patriotism still, but also called British, astonished the world in 1914, when Canadians and Australians, New Zealanders and South Africans, proved their solidarity with the English, Scots, and Welsh, although they themselves were just achieving separate nationalities of their own.

For the Englishman, for the Britisher, for the citizen of the British Commonwealth of nations, there can be no valid reason why the union of nations and the building of larger loyalties out of present patriotisms should not keep pace with the widening of individual human interests to cover the whole shrinking world. The world is, in effect, many times

[1] General the Rt. Hon. Jan Christian Smuts, in a speech delivered on the occasion of his receiving an honorary degree from Manchester University, one week after he signed the Treaty of Versailles.

smaller since the train and the telephone, the steamship and
the telegraph, the aeroplane and wireless, have multiplied
communications and interdependence between nations. Indeed, the world has changed almost out of recognition in the
century since the first railway was opened in Darlington in
1825. A corresponding change in men's minds is needed, or
their thought and then their conduct will go wrong, will
cease to correspond to the world of experience and so tend to
bring disaster and destruction.

The change in the world consists, as we said, in the growth
of communications and interdependence. The globe itself
is now ' a little world ' on which, as a whole, the Englishman
of to-day depends far more than did Shakespeare's contemporaries on the England of that day, when most of their
wants were supplied by their own immediate neighbourhood.
If the rest of the world had been suddenly blotted out, their
ways of life might not have been greatly affected by the
catastrophe. But to-day, a murder in Sarajevo may result
in the death of 900,000 Englishmen of military age ; as many
as could have been found in all Shakespeare's England. And
a permanent break in our overseas trade would involve the
disappearance of two-thirds of our population and great
changes in the habits of all the rest.

What must be the corresponding change of mind ? These
mechanical and economic consequences of modern physical
science have been followed at long last by the beginnings of
political adaptation. The rule of law—the peace and quiet
and justice and fair play—which are essential to the fulfilment of the purposes of individual human lives, can no longer
be guaranteed by separate governments with no authority
outside small geographical areas : governments, moreover,
accustomed to behave ' like masters who maintain splendid

order and discipline within their workshops and thus feel free to go out and racket in the streets '.[1] The rule of law is becoming a question of all or none. The governments of the separate States, or most of them, have, therefore, combined in the League of Nations to begin the great experiment of organizing peace on a world scale.[2]

All this change in the world has been so sudden that it has escaped general notice. Those who made and applied the discoveries in physical science had other things to think about than their effect upon human life on this planet ; while those who have been personally concerned with the consequent political adjustments are few in number and always have many pressing problems to think and talk about.

But the fact remains ; and now the truth is that the first thing a patriotic statesman has to consider about any measure he proposes is its effect on the world as a whole. Some effect it is almost sure to have ; and, if it be harmful, the public opinion of the world may say so through the Assembly of the League of Nations. Whatever advantages it might seem to have had will then be outweighed. To seek first the interests of the whole world-wide society of mankind—to seek first the Kingdom of God on earth—has come to be the first maxim of practical statesmanship.

The statesmen can only do it if the public opinions of their countries understand and approve. Men's minds, we repeat, must be changed. Μετανοεῖτε is still the beginning of the

[1] Professor R. M. Maciver, *Community* (1917), p. 38.

[2] For a very brief account of how that is being done, see *Organizing Peace* (1926), by Maxwell Garnett (League of Nations Union, 15 Grosvenor Crescent, S.W.1), price 3*d.* Fuller accounts are contained in the *Survey,* published by the League of Nations, price 1*s.* ; in *The League of Nations,* by H. Wilson Harris, price 1*s.* 6*d.* ; and in *Reconstruction,* by Maurice Fanshawe (1925).

gospel of salvation. Patriotism must cease to be the differentiator and become the integrator of nations. It is in this field, as Professor McDougall truly said, that moral and intellectual education may achieve their noblest and most far-reaching effects.

These studies lend themselves in a high degree to creating an architectural consistency of the school curriculum, and so to forming a single wide interest in the mind of the pupil. But much remains to be done. The 100 per cent. American is one who hates the Catholic, hates the Jew, and hates the negro ; and his British counterpart describes the League of Nations as ' A lot of foreign devils, you know ; you can't trust 'em a yard '.

How is the change of mind to be reproduced ? First of all, of course, in the schools with the help of the teachers. In England, and I suspect in America, when we want changes in the schools we go first to the teachers and get their sympathy and support, and only in so far as we have their sympathy and support can any changes be usefully made.

What are the changes in the schools that we desire ? In the first place, there is a real body of knowledge to be taught in the schools. What is it ? It consists of what we have been talking about this week. How foolish it would be to let our boys and girls go out into the world thinking the world is as they read in the history books that do not go beyond 1914.

Although we want a body of knowledge, we do not on that account want the same text-books for all nations. The things that are to be taught are perhaps the same things, but they have to be taught to different minds, and, therefore, it is for each nation, and not for any central body, to produce the books for the teachers, and still more the books for the children.

We must teach history and geography. We must see to
it the schools possess maps which show, not only the old
frontiers, but the new ones. I was shocked some years ago
to go to a school of which I was a governor and find, when
I asked some girls high up in the school about modern Austria
that they did not at all realize the changes which had occurred. We, therefore, had a special map prepared, which is
now possessed by most of the secondary and elementary
schools. I remember talking to the Chairman of an Education Committee about a map which hung in one of his
schools, and I pointed out to him that the Eastern part of
that map was entirely inaccurate. He replied: 'That
Eastern part is shifting sand. We cannot spend the rate-
payers' money on that sort of thing; let us wait until the
frontiers have changed again.' What we look for is unity in
the curriculum, and at present the tendency is to have six or
seven different subjects taught by six or seven different
teachers, each a specialist in his own branch. How is that
to be kept up? All that is being taught in school is part of
our common Western civilization. Let the teacher of
mathematics, when speaking about astronomy, mention
Copernicus, the Pole. We discussed some of these things in
the University of Warsaw last year, and a few steps from
where we were was a statue of Copernicus. Let the children
know where the ideas come from, and then they will see how
our modern knowledge comes from all over the world.

As to the technique of presentation, we have to take
advantage of modern methods, such as films and wireless.
In some country schools there are only two teachers, who
between them take all the children from six to fourteen years
of age. What a splendid thing it is for them to be able to
take senior children to another room, turn on the wireless

and let them hear one of the greatest authorities talking to them about some matter, or giving them one of a series of lectures on some subject which is quite outside the range of their own particular teacher. The teacher herself finds it a great relief to be able to turn on, say, a series of French lessons in that way.

Above all, there is the training of teachers. That is fundamental, and in England the League of Nations Society is forming branches in the training colleges and paying a great deal of attention to that side of the question.

Three weeks ago the League of Nations Committee on Intellectual Co-operation met in this building, and produced a series of recommendations which are contained in a report to be presented to the Assembly when it meets here next month. I would like all of you to read this document.

The churches in England and Scotland work with us. I remember on the day when the bad news reached us from the Assembly here last March, there was a meeting in a church in Glasgow that Wednesday, and they enrolled, in the light of that bad news, more new members for the League of Nations Union than had ever been obtained at any meeting in the West of Scotland before. That is the typical British reaction to bad news. Nearly 2,000 churches co-operate with the Union in the capacity of corporate members, and next winter Dr. Norwood, one of the best-known preachers in our country, will make a tour round Britain and give a series of discourses on the responsibility of the Churches of getting rid of war.

I wonder whether that might not happen in other countries, and I like to picture what might happen in France if Marc Sangnier—some one with no political connexion whatever—were to go round the villages and towns of France.

We work also in conjunction with Labour Organizations, ex-sevicemen, women's organizations—in fact with all the organized groups we can find. More especially we work through our own branches, of which there are 2,000 in England, and through them we arrange something like ten public meetings on every night all through the winter. There are about 560,000 persons who have at one time or another joined the League of Nations Union, and we want those members to talk and talk and talk. We want them to talk in season and out of season, and spread a knowledge of the modern world.

In thirty-six other countries there are also League of Nations Societies. They are to be found in America and in Asia as well as in Europe, and they are just being formed in South Africa. The British Society and many of the others are absolutely free, private, voluntary organizations, having no obligations to government whatever, and free to criticize it. Some of the societies are not in that position ; they are supported by government. The Hungarian Society has two wonderful rooms given them by the Government overlooking the river at Budapest, but of course they may find it more difficult to say plainly what they think of the Hungarian Government than we should to criticize the British Government.

I may be asked : 'Why do you want societies to spread this knowledge? Why cannot it be done through the schools ?' If you look back over history, you will find that it has always been necessary to have a society when it has been desired to make a great and rapid change in human institutions. The Christian Church itself is the best example. Wilberforce found its advisability when he set out to abolish the slave trade, and Cobden in his anti-corn law work.

The British Delegation was often criticized last summer because it was said not to be pursuing so fully a League of Nations policy as some of the smaller nations. The members of the British Delegation were very careful in their attitude. I remember one Committee meeting when the Duchess of Atholl was face to face with Monsieur Albert Thomas, and to every proposal he made she found some objection, until he said : ' They call her the Duchess of Atoll; I call her the Duchess of Not-Atoll.' Lord Cecil replied to this criticism by saying : ' We cannot go farther than public opinion will let us go ' ; and Lord Grey, belonging to a different political party and speaking in England soon afterwards, said he thought Lord Cecil was perfectly right in saying that, but added that that was where the League of Nations Union came in. It is our business to see that the public and the nation do not hold the Government back this year.

John Mott, who came to England from America at the beginning of the war, once said that he would rather be alive for ten years after the war than during any other decade in history. He thought people would then have a greater opportunity of serving their fellows than ever before. That opportunity is ours. The opportunity consists in changing men's minds on the subjects we have been talking about this week. If we do that, we shall have a real share with the League of Nations in getting rid of war in our time. I believe we can get rid of war between sovereign states in our time if we set to work hard enough, and devote all our energies to it. It can and must be done, or the verdict of history on our generation will be that we have failed.

The CHAIRMAN thanked Dr. Garnett for his splendid *exposé*. From Dr. James Brown Scott, whom every one had come to look on as one of the greatest philosophers of peace and as one of the greatest living international lawyers, and who knew how to integrate the steps taken to-day in the general scheme of human evolution, the Institute had had a most practical description of the little devices which could be used to improve relations between nations and men. On the other hand, from Dr. Maxwell Garnett, who was universally regarded as one of the great organizers and leaders of the movement for peace, the Institute had had first a Treatise on the Psychology of Patriotism, which it took some amount of University training fully to appreciate, together with a description of the activity of the League of Nations Societies. He was sure the Institute was very grateful to both those gentlemen. (Applause.)

Sir Eric Drummond here entered the room.

The Chairman said he was sure he expressed the feelings of the whole meeting in telling Sir Eric Drummond how greatly they appreciated the honour of having him amongst them. He was sure the whole Institute appreciated the hospitality generously extended to it during the last week, and even more the privilege of hearing from Sir Eric Drummond that morning.

APPENDIX TO CHAPTER II

The League as an instrument of Political Education.

Professor Rappard being asked to elucidate a point in his lecture referring to the increasing extent to which the League was becoming part of the political life of the States Members, replied that ' the question of League policy is becoming one of the standard subjects of discussion in all the principal parliaments of the world. We see that the different parties in the various States are taking steps with regard to League policy. Broadly speaking the socialist parties on the Continent of Europe are advocating one form of League policy and the conservative parties another. The League as a subject of political discussion is growing in importance in national parliamentary life. It is one of the most interesting, and I think one of the most hopeful developments that the average member of parliament or senator is becoming trained to study international questions because positive problems are being put before him such as that of deciding how to instruct the country's delegates who are attending League meetings, and whether or not to ratify conventions, as well as such problems as that raised by the question of Germany's admission to the Council. The discussions on such subjects which take place in the different parliaments not only afford much enlightenment to the members of those bodies but also to the readers of newspapers, and to the public generally.'

Political v. Justiciable Disputes. Incompatibility of the League and Alliances.

The lecturer was further asked whether the political method of handling disputes did not result in compromises which failed to solve the questions at issue and merely delayed their being the cause of serious international friction.

In his reply the lecturer pointed out that when a political problem is presented to the League it is, of course, susceptible only of a political solution. For instance, the Mosul question—what would be a just frontier between Turkey and Iraq—was not a question that could be settled by any appeal to objective criteria or standards for none such existed. No international court could possibly settle the question unless it was said that the justest frontier was that which conformed most strictly to the wishes of the inhabitants. An attempt to ascertain these wishes would, however, bring out the fact that very contradictory opinions were expressed and that the inhabitants were exceedingly sensitive to means of persuasion, which governments in those cases rarely refrained from using. A lawyer could hardly call the result a legal solution.

When a dispute raises a question where no treaty points the way so that there is no question of interpreting a legal instrument, it is susceptible only of a political solution which must always be a compromise. A compromise is an essential condition of peaceful co-operation. 'You should not compromise on principles, but you must compromise in cases where no principle is involved. The only solution in such a case which could be regarded as just is one which satisfies neither party, because both are half satisfied. Whether a compromise creates peace or delays war is not the question. The delay of war is a removal of the cause of war. If you gain time after an outbreak of discontent you will have retarded, and possibly avoided, war.

'A good compromise is one which leaves the least sting. A political compromise must be arranged by a political authority, namely the Council of the League. But if the Council is to possess the necessary moral authority for making good compromises the practice and tradition of international alliances must obviously be abandoned, for the existence of special ties between Members of the League, one or both of which are on the Council, destroys the moral authority of that body when it comes to deal with a dispute in which such states are involved. The incompatibility of special alliances and the League system was seen very clearly by President Wilson.'

The Political and Legal activities of the League.

In reply to a question as to whether the political or legal activity of the League was more useful in society as now organized, the lecturer said : ' Those are two incommensurable quantities. The legal machinery would not be half as useful as it is if it was not connected with a political authority. The Court at The Hague has, and can have, no initiative. Only a political body can have the initiative to put that legal machinery into motion. A court without any kind of political organization is much less useful than a court which is connected with a political organization. On the other hand, the League of Nations without the Court would be decapitated. Public opinion is attracted towards the idea represented by the Court at least as much as by the political activities of the League. In public estimation in many countries The Hague means more than Geneva. There is a feeling that somewhere there is an absolutely impartial body competent to deal with world affairs, and that that means a greater step forward in the organization of the world than even the creation of the League. I would not, however, like to weigh the two bodies against each other, because they are parts of a whole which would no longer be a whole if it were deprived of one of its two parts.'

The League and the Peace Treaties.

The lecturer was asked whether ' the League for international co-operation and the League to outlaw war ' will not gain in prestige ' when the League to enforce the Treaty has disappeared ' ?

Professor Rappard : ' Yes. I am glad that question has been raised. I believe the League has injured itself in the minds of many people by the duties imposed on it to enforce the Peace Treaties, especially in view of the fact that some of the provisions which have to be enforced do not to-day seem to be absolutely just to the average man. The League has to enforce the Treaty and it is not just to enforce even an unjust Treaty. It is, therefore, saddled with an ungrateful task—the enforcement of a treaty which does not conform to the general sense of justice and humanity. I think that has injured the League in the minds of many people. If you look deeper into the matter, however, you will see that wherever the League has been called upon to co-operate in the execution of the Peace Treaties, its intervention was decided on to avoid a worse injustice. Without the intervention of the League the German colonies would have been annexed, and the minorities in the various new States would have been abandoned to their new masters. Danzig would have become Polish, and the Saar Basin French. In every case the violation of the policy of self-determination had had ill effects which have been minimized by the intervention of the League. Although, however, the League may have injured itself by carrying out these duties, it has contributed thereby to the pacification of Europe at its own expense.'

Relations between the Council and Assembly.

On the relations between the Council and the Assembly the lecturer expressed his view that ' in matters of administration and execution, the Council is practically supreme, because you cannot expect the representatives of fifty-five nations to transact business. On the other hand, I think the Assembly to-day represents a much greater force of public opinion, and, therefore, a much greater power for peace, than was ever anticipated when the Covenant was drafted, for the simple reason that the Covenant calls for a very well-knit machinery. The development has shown that the League cannot run by machinery and must be run through public opinion. The Council is not nearly so much an organ of public opinion as the Assembly, and I think the influence of the Assembly has increased, and will tend still further to increase, especially if it is wisely and courageously used but not overstrained. The Assembly might lose prestige if it became too meddlesome, but if it is wise and courageous I think it can become the determining influence in the movement for peace. That was clearly shown, for example, in the case of Corfu.'

The Personal Element and the Influence of the Great Powers.

In reply to a further question, the lecturer pointed out that the personal element is much more important for a small than for a great power in the League since if a small power is not ably represented it counts for nothing, whereas a great power receives consideration however mediocre its representatives may be. But in any case the personal element is extremely important for both great and small powers.

'Great Britain and France run the League. Is that excessive? Great Britain and France are the most powerful nations in Europe to-day, and, except for the United States, in the world. The idea that the League can be run against the wishes of its most powerful members is a day-dream. The League is what its membership makes it. If, in the case of a club, for instance, two of the members put up all the money for the club, it might be said that they had excessive influence. They would be the people who ran the club, and can it be said that their influence would be excessive? As long as the others cannot make it run without them, they are entitled to have that share of influence which their contribution warrants.

'That is again one of the reasons why I look forward to the inclusion of Germany, and deplore the absence of America. The more bosses you have in an organization, the better it is for those members of it who are not bosses. The League can do nothing against the will of Great Britain, very little against the will of France, and little against the will of Italy.'

The Mandates system.

Finally, in reply to a question on Syria, Professor Rappard said that 'the Syrian question is an exceedingly painful one. The Mandates Commission met and examined it thoroughly in the presence of a representative of France, and published its report. That document is in the hands of newspaper men and of members of the opposition as well as of the Government in the French national parliament. The discussion is being carried out in the periodical press and in parliament. I could give you several quotations from the French Senate, where opponents of the government are attacking it, taking as their basis the report of the Mandates Commission. I do not know whether there will be any repercussions in the Assembly arising out of that report. Members of the Assembly are in a position to be informed of the opinions of the Mandates Commission as to what is going on in Syria, but they are under no obligation to take any steps. There are good reasons why States should hesitate before attacking the policy of France publicly.

The effectiveness of the machinery of the Mandates Commission, however, seems to me to be an important question, because nothing could be more encouraging for a government than to have the praise of an impartial commission, and nothing more terrifying than to receive its strictures. Here, as in so many other directions so far as the work of the League is concerned, you cannot find out by reading the Covenant what happens. The Covenant simply lays down that the Mandates Commission shall report to the Council and the Council advise its members. It is easy to regard that as an absurd procedure, but in reality it has proved effective. During the course of the nineteenth century many governments fell on account of colonial scandals, but when a government is attacked on that ground it could reply that the information used against it was derived from disgruntled officials or from missionaries who were better acquainted with the life hereafter than with conditions here below. To-day, however, an opposition can attack a government on the authority of statements by the Mandates Commission, which is composed of former colonial administrators and whose impartiality is beyond question, and the government is thus deprived of an effective answer to such attacks. That is why—in order to avoid such criticism and if possible to attract praise—governments pay so much attention to the Mandates Commission.'

APPENDIX TO CHAPTER III

MR. ELLISON'S LECTURE

Relations of the League and the Labour Office.

Asked whether the League and the Labour Organization were 'twins' or whether the latter was subordinate to the former, Mr. Ellison replied that the Labour Organization was 'the poor relation of the League of Nations. The more we work, however, the more we find that the subjects with which we deal are linked up with the work of the League, and the more we find that on industrial issues we must have the advice of the League and they must have our advice. As regards our constitutional position under the Treaty of Peace, the International Labour Organization is autonomous. The Conference is empowered to give its instructions irrespective of the Assembly, but the Assembly—or rather the League of Nations—does two things for us : (1) it registers the authentic texts of the international treaties that are adopted by the International Labour Organization, and as the ratifications come through it is the League of Nations and not the Office which informs the countries thereof ; and (2) it performs a splendid and most useful function for us : it collects our money. The League writes round and says : "We want so much money for the League and the Labour Office." As the money comes in from the States, the League automatically hands us over our proportion.'

The System of Voting.

To the question whether employers and workers tended to vote as groups in the Conference and Governing Body of the Labour Organization or whether the four representatives of each country stuck together in the voting, Mr. Ellison replied that the delegates of a country do not as a rule vote together. Each member of the Conference has an entirely independent vote, and cases have even occurred where two Government representatives of the same country have voted in different ways. As a rule workers and employers adopt a 'group' attitude towards a given subject. By degrees discussion brings the 'group' positions closer and closer together until the compromise is finally reached.

The effect on the Organization of changes in Governments.

Asked whether the effect in the Labour Organization was noticeable when governments changed, the lecturer replied that it was difficult to say, since draft conventions discussed by the Conference went through a committee stage when a great deal of compromising and negotiation was done in which it was hard to discern whether Governments tended to go with the employers or with the workers.

The Eight Hours Convention.

Asked to say how many industrial States had ratified the Hours of Work Convention of 1919, Mr. Ellison replied : 'That Convention forms, to a large extent, the corner-stone of our work, and the Office has been much preoccupied by the comparative slowness with which countries are ratifying it. At present nine countries have ratified. The factor of competition arises in no subject more acutely than in that of hours of work ; and the big industrial countries of Europe do not feel they can ratify the Hours of Work Convention without the assurance that their chief competitors will do the same. Two countries—Italy and Latvia—have, indeed, ratified under the express condition that certain other important industrial countries of Europe must ratify before their own ratification comes into effect.

'Great Britain has not yet ratified this Convention. At first it did not ratify because there were technical difficulties in the way in connexion with the railwaymen. The Labour Government came into power and introduced a Bill to enable the Convention to be ratified ; but the Labour Government went out of power and that Bill came to nothing. The present Government began again and has recently held a very interesting and important conference in London, at which were present the Ministers of Labour of Germany, France, Italy, Belgium, and, of course, Great Britain. That meeting of Ministers examined the clauses of the Convention one by one and came to an agreed interpretation of the text. They signed their names to a document at the end of the meeting accepting the common interpretation arrived at.

'The present position is that ten days ago Belgium definitely decided to ratify the Convention. Italy had already ratified it conditionally. France has adopted the Convention in the Chamber and it is now before the Senate, where it will probably be passed without further difficulty. Germany has modified the Factory Bill that was before her Parliament with a view to introducing a special Bill covering the Hours Convention.'

The recent Act establishing eight hours for work in a coal-mine was not regarded by the lecturer as making it impossible for Great Britain to ratify the Eight Hours Convention. It was, it was pointed out, stated by the Minister of Labour to be a temporary emergency measure not changing the main issue of hours of work. As regarded the Italian Government, which had issued a decree establishing a nine-hours day in industry, the lecturer stated that Italy had conditionally ratified the Washington Eight Hours Convention, the ratification to take effect when the Convention had also been ratified by Great Britain, France, Belgium, Germany, and Switzerland. If and when Italy's ratification became effective by the ratifications of these countries, it would appear as though the decree would have to be repealed. In the meantime it had been very definitely stated that the decree was an emergency measure.

Action taken after a Convention is ratified.

In reply to a question, Mr. Ellison stated that ' Under article 408 of the Peace Treaty, countries that ratify a convention are obliged to submit an annual report to the Conference stating exactly what action they have taken to give legislative effect to the convention in question. That means that every year we receive a large quantity of reports from the different countries stating the action they have taken as a result of the ratification of conventions. The difficulty is that we get too many reports. We receive such a detailed mass of information about the action taken in the different countries that the Conference cannot digest it. We have, therefore, now gone a step farther. It was decided at the last Conference that there shall be set up an independent Committee of Experts whose duty it will be each year to take the reports submitted under article 408 and examine them thoroughly. They will furnish a report to the Office, which will in turn report to the Conference. Thus the Conference will have before it, not merely the detailed reports of countries on legislative action arising out of ratification of Conventions, but a reasoned expert opinion on those reports.'

Compulsory Employment of Disabled Men.

In reply to a question as to the action, if any, taken by the International Labour Organization with regard to the employment of war disabled persons and the advisability of universal compulsory legislation on this point, Mr. Ellison replied : ' In 1921 at the request of various organizations of disabled men the Office drew up a preliminary report on the position in the various countries with regard to the compulsory employment of disabled men. In 1923, with the approval of the Governing Body, a special Committee of Disablement Expèrts was also called, consisting of about thirty members, some ten representing Governments and the remainder organizations interested in disablement questions. This Committee passed a resolution which was printed by the Office, together with its preliminary report, under the heading " The Compulsory Employment of Disabled Men ". The resolution, which was adopted unanimously except for the vote of the British Government representative, asked for compulsory State legislation for the employment of the disabled. The matter has, however, never come before the Conference, and thus as far as international legislation is concerned no action has been taken.'

Hours of Labour in Agriculture.

Asked how far it was feasible to regulate the hours of labour in agriculture, Mr. Ellison stated that : ' A decision of the Governing Body placed the question of the regulation of the hours of work in industry on the agenda of the 1921 Conference. The French Government having, however, lodged a formal objection against the consideration of this subject by the Conference, a vote was taken at the beginning of the Session which resulted in its being removed from the agenda. The difficulty of the practical regulation of the hours of work in agriculture was fully recognized by the Office, which in its report suggested that instead of a convention the Conference should adopt a very general Recommendation inviting the Governments to encourage collective agreements between agricultural organizations for the fixing of the maximum hours to be worked in agriculture.'

Night Work for Women.

A member of the audience objected to legislation in which women were grouped with children as regards night work and conditions of labour generally, and suggested that their effect was simply to handicap women in industry as contrasted with men.

To this Mr. Ellison replied that it was a question women must decide for themselves, and that women who came as official representatives to the Labour Organization Conferences took the view that special protection should be afforded. At Washington the Labour Organization adopted a convention limiting night work for women. It also adopted a maternity convention giving special benefits to women before and after childbirth. It seemed to the lecturer essential that there should be some protective legislation of this sort.

APPENDIX TO CHAPTER VIII

GERMANY'S INTERNATIONAL POSITION SINCE LOCARNO

Germany's claims.

Asked what exactly were the claims of Germany that had to be redressed before complete co-operation with her neighbours became possible, the lecturer replied that he did not wish it to be thought that Germany meant to raise innumerable difficulties immediately she was admitted to the League. On the other hand, there were certain problems which would eventually have to be solved. Among them was the occupation of the Rhineland. That, as an act of self-defence on the part of France, would become totally unnecessary if any real meaning was to be attached to Locarno. Secondly, there was the question of disarmament. It was difficult to say what Germany wanted in that respect, but what the Preparatory Commission had so far done had not satisfied the Germans ; it had been a terrible blow to public opinion in Germany because things had been said and proposed which made it look as if the idea was to hide armaments under a mass of formulae, and prevent real disarmament. Thirdly, there was the question of war guilt. Fortunately, most Germans were becoming reasonable enough to realize that that was a matter which could not be treated as a diplomatic affair, and there seemed no reason to believe it was a question Germany intended to raise in the near future. In nationalist quarters, however, it had been made a special point of prestige. Fourthly, there were certain problems in regard to minorities which were, fortunately, being solved more and more by agreement, especially in the case of Czechoslovakia. The question of minorities in Italy could not be raised, because that did not come under the League, but it was to be hoped that there also some agreement would be reached. He did not know if Germany had any programme of action in regard to her Eastern frontiers. The general feeling was that some new solution must be found for the Polish Corridor. He did not think that would come before the League ; it would probably be solved by the two countries concerned resolving to find a friendly solution for their difficulties, which would guarantee Poland an outlet to the sea. The problem of Danzig was a similar one. Fifthly, certain readjustments would have to be made in Upper Silesia. In the sixth and seventh places, there were the Colonial problem and the problem of reparations. The last named had already been settled by the Dawes plan. That plan might come up for discussion, but a wish for its revision had been expressed more strongly in the foreign press than in Germany, because, generally speaking, German economists wished to see how the thing worked before coming to any decision, and thought that the creditor countries would come to see that the reparations were doing them more harm than good. There were, therefore, many points of difference, but not many of them were dangerous the moment France, Germany, and Poland had a real wish and an economic interest to come to some kind of agreement.

Germany and her Eastern neighbours.

In reply to a question as to whether the Locarno Treaty might fail owing to France's relations with Czechoslovakia and Poland, the lecturer said that he had not been able to say much about German relations with Poland and Czechoslovakia, but there were Treaties of Arbitration between Germany and Poland and Germany and Czechoslovakia. Germany had not guaranteed her Eastern boundaries, which simply meant she was not ready to say that they were just. She had given up the right to use violence to change them, but the feeling was that if friendship was established between Germany and France, France would help Germany to come to some agreement with Poland. There was a strong feeling in Germany that both Czechoslovakia and Poland would wish in the long run to come to some new understanding with Germany. It might take time, but there was no longer a desperate feeling that war would be necessary to rectify Germany's Eastern frontiers. It was felt that they might one day be rectified by arbitration, or by some direct agreement with Germany. There was in Germany a strong tendency towards what was called Mittel Europa, and a feeling that Poland and Czechoslovakia, having such great difficulties on all sides, would, when France no longer needed them as military Allies, easily be able to come to an understanding with Germany.

Germany and Mandates.

Asked whether the Locarno Treaty had any bearing on German colonial expansion, the lecturer replied that the Treaty was silent on the point, but that Germany, as a member of the League, would have exactly the same rights to become a mandatory Power as any other member. There were forces in Germany which wanted her one day to ask for a mandate, while there were other people who thought that it was of enormous benefit to Germany not to be a Colonial Power. The fact that Germany was not a Colonial Power had been of benefit to Germans doing business in China and elsewhere. Many people believed the time for European nations to become Colonial Powers had passed.

Germany : International Debts and the U.S.

Asked what he meant by saying that Germany regarded herself as bound to the United States rather than to France under the Dawes plan, Dr. Wolfers said it was a peculiar psychological fact that in Europe to-day, when one spoke of credits and debts, one always thought of the United States of America. The general feeling was that, ultimately, any payments made by Germany would only be sufficient to pay the debts of the Allies to America. There was very little bitterness in Germany against France on the subject of reparations. The feeling was that the European nations were the defeated nations, and a great part of the feeling of solidarity with France resulted from the fact that Germany felt she was simply carrying a part of the Inter-Allied Debt, and that reparations were only a part of that debt. It might be because Germany felt herself, by reason of her indebtedness, to be placed on the same level as Allied debtors that there was so little bitterness towards America.